The Philippine Islands
Vol.-44

by

Ed. Emma Helen Blair and
James Alexander Robertson

The Philippine Islands
Vol.-44
by Ed. Emma Helen Blair and James Alexander Robertson

ISBN: 978-93-59398-94-5

Published by

DOUBLE 9 BOOKS

2/13-B, Ansari Road
Daryaganj, New Delhi – 110002
info@double9books.com
www.double9books.com
Tel. 011-40042856

ABOUT THE EDITOR

Emma Helen Blair (1869-1951) was an American historian and author known for her significant contributions to Philippine history and also scholarship. Born on July 19, 1869, in Ohio, she pursued her education at Ohio Wesleyan University and later at Columbia University. Blair's passion for history and research led her to collaborate with James Alexander Robertson, an esteemed scholar, in editing and compiling "The Philippine Islands, 1493-1898" series. This monumental project spanned fifty-five volumes and covered the colonial history of the Philippines from the 16th to the 19th century. The comprehensive series showcased her expertise in meticulously examining and also presenting historical documents and narratives. Her work significantly contributed to a deeper understanding of the Philippines' complex past and its interactions with various colonial powers. Her commitment to historical accuracy and attention to detail earned her a reputation as a meticulous and reliable historian. Beyond her contributions to Philippine history, and main thing that Emma Helen Blair also authored "The Philippine Policy of Secretary Taft" and co-wrote "A History of the Philippine Islands" with Robertson. Both of these works further demonstrated her dedication to scholarship and the exploration of the Philippines' political and social developments.

James Alexander Robertson was born in Corry, Pennsylvania, in 1873. He was the sixth of eight children born to Canadian parents who became naturalized citizens of the United States after moving to Corry in 1866. His father, John McGregor Robertson, was a builder from Verulam, Ontario, close to Peterborough. His mother, Elizabeth Borrowman Robertson, immigrated to Canada as a child from her native Scotland. When Robertson was seven years old, his mother died. After three years, he and his family relocated to Cleveland, Ohio, where James finished his secondary education. In 1892, he enrolled in Adelbert College at Western Reserve University for graduate study. He studied in Romance languages, majoring in Old French, and received his Bachelor of Philosophy degree from Western Reserve University in 1896.

CONTENTS

PREFACE

The present volume covers the first third of the eighteenth century, besides reviewing the Jesuit missions in Filipinas during that which preceded it. The only occurrence of notable interest in the former period is the murder of Governor Bustamante by a mob (1719), which is even more remarkable for the utterly lawless manner in which the deed was committed, and the successful efforts made to stifle its proper investigation and punishment. The memorial of the religious orders (1701) discloses vividly the tyranny and oppression suffered by the Indians at the hands of their Spanish masters. Especially valuable is Abreu's historical sketch of the commerce between the islands and Nueva España up to 1736, and of the sharp controversy which this aroused between the traders of Manila and those of Cadiz and Sevilla.

An account of Jesuit labors in the islands during the seventeenth century is furnished by Murillo Velarde, historian of that order, in his Historia de Philipinas (Manila, 1749). In 1618 the advent of two comets so terrifies the people that the Jesuits by their preaching win many souls, not only in Manila (the most cosmopolitan city in the Spanish empire), but in its environs. These fathers are eminently successful, both as preachers and as confessors; their manifold duties, and their methods of reaching all classes, are fully recounted. Some of them conduct successful missions in Bondoc (Luzón) and the island of Marinduque; in the latter, many relapsed Christians are reclaimed, and wild Indians are induced to settle in villages. At the desire of the archbishop of Manila, the Jesuits labor for some time in the port of Cavite and at Old Cavite, where they encounter and reform a fearfully corrupt state of morals; they also minister to the Chinese residing near Manila. In 1628 a fatal epidemic causes many deaths in and near that city: in this calamity the Jesuits minister untiringly to the sick and dying, as also do some of the Indian converts. About this time the Jesuit missions are established in Mindanao, and soon afterward in Negros and Mindoro. In 1632 a considerable reënforcement of laborers arrives at Manila: their zealous labors were begun as soon as they embarked at Cadiz, ministering to the people on their ship. The writer narrates the progress of their labors in Mindoro, Maragondong, and Negros; and gives an historical sketch of the early Jesuit labors in Mindanao, and of those carried on after 1642 at Iligan and

Sibuguey. After the conquest of Jolo, Jesuit missionaries labor successfully in that island; their Joloan converts afterward, when the missionaries are obliged to leave them, become exiles from their own land and go to Zamboanga, in order to maintain themselves as Christians. The missions in the Pintados Islands are very flourishing, except for the sufferings of their people from the raids of the southern Moros. All the Philippine missions are greatly hindered and weakened, about 1640, by lack of laborers; but in 1643 large bands of Jesuits and Dominicans arrive at Manila, and give new life to the missions. In 1648–49 Spanish punitive expeditions are sent to Borneo, which do much damage to those piratical natives, carry away many captives, and ransom some Christians held there. These armadas are accompanied by Jesuits as chaplains, who take this opportunity to announce the gospel in Borneo, and baptize seven hundred islanders; this gives them great hopes for a numerous and extensive Christian church to be founded there, "but, lacking the protection of the Spanish military forces, this so beautiful hope faded away almost at its flowering." Our writer expatiates on the dangers and privations, the loneliness and sickness, the difficulties and opposition, that are bravely encountered and patiently endured by the missionaries; and the variety of duties which they must perform, not only ministerial, but those of teacher, umpire, architect, etc. Much is accomplished in Basilan and Mindanao by a few faithful laborers.

The moral and social conditions prevalent in the islands become exceedingly corrupt, and the Spanish colony experiences many calamities and misfortunes, regarded as the Divine chastisement for their transgressions. The remedy sought for this comes as a papal brief authorizing the archbishop of Manila to absolve all the inhabitants of the islands from their transgressions, and from any excommunications incurred by them, and granting plenary indulgence to all who should "worthily prepare to receive it." This grant being duly published (March 1, 1654), great good results from it—within Manila alone, more than 40,000 persons confessing their sins, and a great reformation being made in the morals of the people. Another wave of religious enthusiasm occurs in the following year, under the direction of the Jesuits. In 1654 the cornerstone of the new cathedral building is laid. The spiritual interests of Ternate and Siao are placed in the care of the Jesuits, who gain many souls in both these fields. In 1662 a new mission band arrives at Manila, and some of the Jesuits go out into the ranches and mountain hamlets near Manila; among these, the noted Father Sanvitores baptizes 24,000 heathens in seven days, and prepares many others for baptism. The Pardo controversy leads to so many difficulties between the ecclesiastical authorities and the religious orders that they offer to the king their resignation of the ministries held by them in the islands;

but he refuses to allow the Jesuits to do this, and even restores to them two parishes of which they had been deprived. Our author relates in detail the methods practiced by the Jesuits in administering their parishes, and the devotions and pious exercises that are practiced by the faithful. Finally, the history of the parish of San Matheo, and that of the house of Indian "beatas" in Manila, are presented.

A brief summary of events in the years 1701–15 is presented, condensed from the diffuse account of Concepción. Governor Zabalburú, the successor of Cruzat, constructs various important public works. In the Tournon affair (1704), the governor and archbishop show undue laxity in allowing Tournon to interfere in their jurisdiction and infringe on the royal prerogatives; for this and other causes they are removed from their offices. In 1709 Conde de Lizarraga assumes the office of governor; but little of interest occurs during his term. To this is appended a memorial addressed to Zabalburú (October 7, 1701) by the provincials of the religious orders in the islands, urging him to reform various abuses—the neglect of the military posts and of new conquests of infidels; the sufferings of the natives from the building of galleons; the severity, oppression, and fraud practiced on the Indians in the collection of tributes and in requisitions for personal services; the greed and cruelty of Spanish officials; the prevalence of gambling and vagabondism; laxity in enforcing the laws that prohibit or restrict the immigration of infidels—Moors, Chinese, and others; and neglect of religious affairs. From these abuses result most deplorable effects: the depopulation of the islands, the prevalence of vice, the ruin of many formerly prosperous Indian villages, and the exhaustion and demoralization of the natives. The governor is urged to reform these evils and protect the poor Indians.

In summarized form is presented Concepción's account of the government (ad interim) of the auditor Torralba and (proprietary) of Bustamante, from 1715 to 1719, in which year the latter is attacked and slain by a mob, the people revolting against Bustamante's violent and arbitrary acts. To this are added letters by the Jesuit Otazo and Archbishop Cuesta, the latter of whom is a prominent figure in the history of that time. The court of the Audiencia at Manila had been broken up by the arrest of the auditors, for various charges of official malfeasance, or as a result of hostilities with the governor; and Torralba himself is imprisoned by Bustamante for misconduct. Afterward, desiring the countenance of an audiencia for his proceedings, Bustamante forms one with Torralba and some associates; but the legality of this procedure is questioned by the archbishop and the university professors of law. The governor, as soon as he entered office, had undertaken to collect by force the large amounts due to the treasury from its debtors; he succeeded therein, but of course awakened hatred and resentment in many of the citizens. A controversy arises with the archbishop over a question of ecclesiastical immunity; he excommunicates Torralba, and is afterward arrested by the governor, who also imprisons most of the prominent ecclesiastics. Then arises a tumult among the people, and a conspiracy is formed against Bustamante. The friars sally out from their convents and are joined by the numerous persons who, in fear of the governor's tyrannical acts, have taken refuge in the churches, and by a crowd of the common people. All this throng go to the governor's palace, and attack him; he is terribly wounded, and dies after a few hours, and his son also is slain. At the urgent demand of all, Archbishop Cuesta accepts the post of governor ad interim, and forms an audiencia with the released auditors. Bustamante's children are sent to Mexico. Investigations of the murder are attempted, in both Manila and Mexico, but are practically fruitless. Otazo's letter (November 19, 1719) gives a brief account of the murder and the circumstances connected with it, especially of his own ministrations to the dying Bustamante; he then enlarges on the latter's pious death, and for this reason urges his correspondent to refute the slanders that will doubtless be spread about the dead man. He urges that in the residencia of Bustamante's government action should be taken only in cases which may involve injury to other parties, and that all other matters (including the riot) be "buried in oblivion," for the service of God and the king, the good of souls, and the tranquillity of the colony. In order to prevent the recurrence of such troubles, he advises—his letter being evidently intended to influence those in power, apparently the confessors of the king—that the governor of Filipinas be here-after kept in check by a council composed of prominent ecclesiastics and religious; and that all important appointments to offices in the islands be made by the king instead of the governor. Otazo details this plan quite fully, and calls for more careful selection of governors and other officials for the islands. He closes by praising one of the auditors, Toribio, as an upright official and God-fearing man. The letter of Archbishop Cuesta (June 28, 1720) gives his version of the tragedy lately enacted, and relates how he was forced by the popular will to act as governor until that vacancy should be filled by the crown.

A Spanish officer in Manila, Manuel de Santistevan, writes to a cousin in Spain (January 28, 1730), giving the latter an account of his friendly relations with the new governor of Filipinas, Fernando Valdés Tamón; of various family affairs of his own; and of the troubles which he has experienced at the hands of the members of the Audiencia, who envy his intimacy with the governor and endeavor to undermine it. He has a quarrel with his father-in-law, a passionate, scheming, and selfish man; but it is patched up by the intervention of the governor and archbishop, and they are nominally reconciled. At the same time, Santistevan and his wife, who had had difficulties, are reunited. He asks his correspondent to secure for him several favors from the court: a certain amount of lading-space on the Acapulco galleon; an appointment to a governorship in one of the Spanish colonies; the command of the Acapulco galleon in which he hopes to leave the Philippines; and reimbursement for some property belonging to his wife which was seized by the viceroy of Mexico, on account of the late Governor Bustamante's debts to the crown.

At this point we resume the history of Philippine commerce with Nueva España which is presented in the Extracto historial (Madrid, 1736), the first two "periods" of which appeared in VOL. XXX of this series. On account of its great length and the necessary limitations of the space available to us, we are obliged to condense and abridge much of this work; but "Periods" ii–vi are given in full (save for the text of some long decrees). The third of these gives no information regarding that commerce from 1640 to the end of that century, save that the viceroy of Mexico made remonstrances during 1684–86 as to the difficulties which embarrassed the Mexican government in collecting duties and preventing frauds; and that in 1697 royal decrees command a stricter enforcement in Mexico of the existing laws and regulations for that commerce. This proceeding disturbs the merchants of Manila, who ask for more freedom and the removal of certain restrictions. Along with this, the Spanish government is beset by demands from its American colonies, who desire to profit by the Philippine commerce, and by remonstrances from the Spanish merchants who are being ruined by it. The government thereupon makes new regulations (August 12, 1702) for the Philippine trade, including some concessions to the Manila merchants—who nevertheless raise objections to some of them, as is shown by the governor's report; he makes some temporary concessions to them, which (with one exception) are not sustained by the home government. By its orders, the viceroy of Mexico makes an investigation (in 1712; "Period" iv) of the alleged illegal conduct of the Philippine-Mexican commerce, and finds very serious infractions of the law in many directions. A letter from the viceroy (dated August 4, 1714) to the king shows how these frauds are committed, and how difficult it is to prove them. He does all in his power to check or punish them, but conditions are such as to hamper his efforts and shield the guilty. Linares shows how these things are injuring the commerce of Filipinas and the interests of its native Spanish citizens, and places the whole matter before the home government for action thereon. The fifth "Period" is concerned with the injurious effects of that commerce on the industries and trade of the mother country, and the attempts of the government to remedy these. The merchants of Nueva España ask that the trading-fleets sent thither annually from Spain be discontinued, whereupon the royal Council ask for information on this subject from the commercial houses of Sevilla. The latter remonstrate against allowing the importation of Chinese goods into Nueva España, since this is ruining the commerce of Spain in that country. The Sevillans complain of the abuses in the Filipinas trade, and of the showy and cheap imitations of Spanish goods which the Chinese send by this agency to Acapulco, which have driven out the genuine articles and thus have ruined both the traders and the manufacturers of Spain. Moreover, the wealth of Nueva España is being drained into the heathen land of China. Accordingly, the Sevillans urge that severe restrictions be placed on the Manila-Acapulco trade, and that the Spanish trading fleets be sent regularly and often. As a result of this protest and of the proceedings in the Council, the king decrees (1718) that the trade in Chinese silken goods be henceforth prohibited. In 1719, Viceroy Valero remonstrates ("Period" vi) against this prohibition, in behalf of not only Filipinas but his own subjects in Nueva España, most of whom are too poor to purchase Spanish goods for their garments and depend on the cheap goods from China; he also declares that the Filipinas trade is necessary for enabling the Mexican treasury to meet its obligations. This memorial being submitted to the fiscal at Madrid, he advises that the prohibition of trade in Chinese goods be removed. After much discussion and consultation, the matter is decided thus, a royal decree (dated October 27, 1720) being issued accordingly: the Filipinas commerce with Nueva España must be restricted to 300,000 pesos, and to certain products and manufactured articles, from which are strictly excluded all silken fabrics; the amount of money sent in return is limited to 600,000 pesos; citizens of Nueva España are strictly forbidden to send their own money to Filipinas: and various precautions, restrictions, and penalties are provided.

This decree is received ("Period" vii) at Manila on August 2, 1722. The municipal council address memorials to the governor protesting against the restrictions imposed on the Filipinas trade, and showing that the enforcement of these would ruin them; but the governor refuses to suspend the decree, and the fiscal advises the merchants to appeal to the Madrid court. The citizens send deputies thither, and persuade the Audiencia to second their petitions for more liberal treatment, and for the suspension of the decree of 1720. Letters to this effect from that body inform the home government of the losses previously sustained by the merchants of Filipinas, the dependence of the islands on their commerce with Nueva España, the vital importance to that commerce of the goods from China, and the danger that if these goods are prohibited the conversion of the Chinese will be rendered exceedingly difficult; the Audiencia therefore recommends that the trade in silks be allowed, and the amount of the permission increased to 250,000 pesos. This opinion is supported by one of similar tenor, given by the royal fiscal at Manila; the points which he makes are elaborated at length in a report sent by him to the king, dated November 15, 1722. In the same vein are letters written to support the demands of the citizens, by the royal officials, the archbishop and other prominent ecclesiastics, and the superiors of the religious orders; of these the most forcible is that written by the Jesuit provincial. He urges that the natural resources of the Philippines be more industriously cultivated, and suggests that the Spaniards compel the other inhabitants of the islands (Indians, mestizos, and others) "to weave the cloth goods which are manufactured in other regions." Deputies go from Manila to Madrid, to present the claims of Filipinas, and hand in a printed memorial containing their arguments for the suspension of the decree of 1720. This and similar documents brought forward by both sides show a curious mixture of religious, political, and commercial motives, as well as the jealousy and ill-will aroused in the minds of the Spanish merchants as soon as Manila diverts from Cadiz any notable amount of trade; and interesting revelations are made of the practical workings of the selfish policy pursued by Spain toward her colonies, and the undue paternalism which would keep them forever in leading-strings. It is shown that the strength of Spain as a world-power is being undermined by the heretic nations of Europe—England, France, and Holland—because they display superior energy and ability in manufactures and commerce. From this time (1723) until the year when the Extracto was compiled by order of the Spanish government (1736), there appears a steady and increasingly bitter controversy between the commercial interests of Manila and Cadiz, the former evidently having powerful support in government circles, and the latter becoming alarmed at the precarious condition of both its American trade and the Spanish industry and commerce in silk fabrics. Manila tries to show that its trade in Chinese silks is necessary to the propagation of the Christian faith in China, and to its maintenance in the Philippines; Cadiz laughs this claim to scorn. Manila claims that the decadence of the silk industry in Spain is due to other causes than the importation of Chinese goods into Mexico; and a large part of the raw silk produced in Spain is bought by the industrial nations of Europe and manufactured into fabrics, which are brought back to Spain by these foreigners to supply not only that country but her colonies, the goods being shipped to the Indias in Spanish bottoms. The royal fiscal at Madrid supports the contention of Manila, but would confine its trade strictly to the amount allowed it by the government; and he thinks that the complaints by Cadiz arise from the frauds and abuses in the Manila trade, rather than from the mere fact of its including Chinese goods. Manila proposes for the conduct of the commerce a plan which will obviate the difficulties therein, but this is opposed by the fiscal and other officials. Direct appeal being made to the king, he consents (October, 1726) to test this plan for five years. The remainder of Abreu's work will appear in VOL. XLV.

The Editors

September, 1906.

DOCUMENTS OF 1700-1730

Sources: The first of these documents is compiled from Murillo Velarde's *Historia de Philipinas* (Manila, 1749), using such parts as directly relate to the missionary labors of the Jesuit order in the islands; from a copy of the original in possession of Edward E. Ayer, Chicago. The second is found in the Ventura del Arco MSS., (Ayer library), v, pp. 201–230; and, in the fourth, Otazo's and Cuesta's letters are found in iv, pp. 249–295. The third is summarized from Concepción's *Historia de Philipinas*, viii, pp. 299–391; part of the fourth is from ix, pp. 183–424; and the rest is obtained as stated above. The fifth is translated from a MS. probably the original, in possession of Edward E. Ayer.

Translations: These are all made by Emma Helen Blair.

JESUIT MISSIONS IN THE SEVENTEENTH CENTURY

[In 1618 two unusually brilliant comets were visible in the Philippines; their effects on the minds of the people are thus described (fol. 5):]1 There was great variety and inaccuracy of opinion about the comets; but through that general although confused notion which the majority of people form, that comets presage disastrous events, and that the anger of God threatens men by them, they assisted greatly in awakening contrition in the people, and inciting them to do penance. To this the preachers endeavored to influence them with forcible utterances, for the Society had not been behind [the other orders] in preparing the city for the entire success of the jubilee;2 for there was one occasion when eleven Jesuits were counted, who, distributed at various stations, cried out like Jonah, threatening destruction to impenitent and rebellious souls. God giving power to their words, this preaching was like the seed in the gospel story, scattered on good ground, which not only brought forth its fruit correspondingly, but so promptly that those who heard broke down in tears at hearing the eternal truths; and, like thirsty deer, when the sermon was ended they followed the preacher that he might hear their confessions, already dreading lest some emergency might find them in danger of damnation. This harvest was not confined within the walls of Manila, but extended to its many suburbs, and to the adjacent villages, in which missions had been conducted. Not only was there preaching to the Spaniards, but to the Tagálogs, the Indian natives of the country—who, in token of their fervor, gave from their own scanty supply food in abundance to the jails and prisons, Ours aiding them to carry the food, to the edification of the city. To the Japanese who were living in our village of San Miguel—exiles from their native land, in order to preserve their religion, who had taken refuge in Manila, driven out from that kingdom by the tyrant Taycosama—our fathers preached, in their own language. And it can be said that there was preaching to all the nations, that which occurred to the apostles in Jerusalem on the day of Pentecost being represented in Manila; for I believe that there is no city in the world in which so many nationalities come together as here. For besides the Spaniards (who are the citizens and owners of the country) and the Tagálogs (who are the Indian natives of the land), there are many other Indians from the islands, who speak different tongues—such as the Pampangos, the Camarines [i.e., the Bicols], the Bisayans, the Ilocans, the Pangasinans, and the Cagayans. There are Creoles [Criollos], or Morenos, who are swarthy blacks, natives of the country;3 there are many Cafres, and other negroes from Angola, Congo, and Africa. There are blacks from Asia, Malabars, Coromandels, and Canarins. There are a great many Sangleys, or Chinese—part of them Christians, but the majority heathens. There are Ternatans, and Mardicas (who took refuge here from Ternate); there are some Japanese; there are people from Borney and Timor, and from Bengal; there are Mindanaos, Joloans, and Malays; there are Javanese, Siaos, and Tidorans; there are people from Cambay and Mogol, and from other islands and kingdoms of Asia. There are a considerable number of Armenians, and some Persians; and Tartars, Macedonians, Turks, and Greeks. There are people from all the nations of Europa—French, Germans, and Dutch; Genoese and Venetians; Irísh and Englishmen; Poles and Swedes. There are people from all the kingdoms of España, and from all America; so that he who spends an afternoon on the tuley4 or bridge of Manila will see all these nationalities pass by him, behold their costumes, and hear their languages—something which cannot be done in any other city in the entire Spanish monarchy, and hardly in any other region in all the world.

From this arises the fact that the confessional of Manila is, in my opinion, the most difficult in all the world; for, as it is impossible to confess all these people in their own tongues, it is necessary to confess them in Spanish; and each nationality has made its own vocabulary of the Spanish language, with which those people have intercourse [with us], conduct their affairs, and make themselves understood; and without it Ours can understand them only with great difficulty, and almost by divination. A Sangley, an Armenian, and a Malabar will be heard talking together in Spanish, and our people do not understand them, as they so distort the word and the accent. The Indians have another Spanish language of their own; and the Cafres have one still more peculiar, to which must be added that they eat half of the words. No one save he who has had this experience can state the labors which it costs to confess them; and even when the fault is understood in general, to seek for a specific account of the circumstances is to enter a labyrinth without a clue. For they do not understand our orderly mode of speech, and therefore when they are questioned they say "yes" or "no" as it occurs to them, without rightly understanding what is asked from them—so that in a short time they will utter twenty contradictions. It is therefore necessary to accommodate oneself to their language, and learn their vocabulary. Another of the very serious difficulties is the little capacity of these people to distinguish and explain numbers, incidents, and circumstances; add to this the unbridled licentiousness of some, in accordance with the freedom and opportunities [for vice] in this land, the continual backsliding, and the few indications of fixed purpose. In others, who are capable and explain their meaning well, is found a complication of perplexities—with a thousand reflections, and bargains, and frauds, and oaths all joined together; and faults that are extraordinary and of new kinds, which keep even the most learned man continually studying them. The heat of the country, and the stench or foul odor of the Indians and the negroes, unite in great part to make a hardship of the ministry, which in these islands is the most difficult; and on this account I regard it as being very meritorious. The annual confessions last from the beginning of Lent until Corpus Christi. In our college of Manila the church is open from daylight until eleven o'clock, and from two o'clock until nightfall; and always some fathers are present to hear confessions—for this is done not only by the active ministers, but by the instructors, when their scholastic duties give them opportunity; and I have known some fathers who remain to hear confessions during seven, eight, or more hours a day.

It makes them bear all these annoyances patiently, and even sweetens these, to see how many souls are kept pure by the grace of God, in the midst of so many temptations, like the bramble in the midst of the fire without being burned. There are many who are striving for perfection, who frequent the sacraments, who maintain prayer and spiritual reading, and who give much in alms and perform other works of charity. And it is cause for the greatest consolation to see, at the solemn festivals of the Virgin and other important feasts, the confessional surrounded by Indians, Cafres, and negroes, men and women, great and small, who are awaiting their turns with incredible patience, kept there through the grace of God, against every impulse of their natural dispositions and their slothfulness. And at the season of Lent it is heart-breaking to see the confessor, when he rises from his seat, surrounded by more than a hundred persons of all colors, who go away disconsolate because they have not obtained an opportunity to make their confessions; and in this manner they go and come for eight or ten days, or a fortnight, or even more, with unspeakable patience, but with such eagerness that when the confessor rises they go following him throughout the house, calling to him to hear their confessions. This is done even by boys of seven to twelve years, and hardly with violence can they be made to leave the father, and they continue to call after him; and some remain in the passages, on their knees, asking for confession, so great is the number of the penitents—to which that of the confessors does not correspond by far, nor does their assiduity, even if there were enough of them. The Society is not content with aiding those who come to seek relief in our church, and attending the year round all the sick, of various languages, who summon them to hear confession; but its laborers go forth—as it were, gospel hunters—to search for penitents. They assist almost all who are executed in the city; every week they go to the jails and hospitals; in Lent they hear confessions in all the prisons, and at the foundry, those of the galley-slaves. And in the course of the year they hear confessions in the college of Santa Ysabel—in which there are more than a hundred students, who are receiving the most admirable education—and in the seminary of Santa Potenciana, the students frequenting the sacraments often; and, in fine, they go on a perpetual round in pursuit of the impious.

The confessional is, as it were, the harvesting of the crop; and the pulpit is the sowing, in which the seed of the gospel is scattered in the hearts of men, where with the watering of grace it bears fruit in due time, according to the coöperation [of the Holy Ghost?]. With great constancy and solicitude the Society contributes to the cultivation of these fields of Christianity, with preaching. In Manila the Society has, besides the sermons from the holy men of the order, other endowed feasts, and the set sermons5 in the cathedral and the royal chapel. When necessity requires it, a mission is held, and the attendance is very large, although hardly a fifth of those who hear understand the Spanish language; this to a certain extent discourages the missionaries, as does even much more the fact that they do not encounter those external demonstrations of excitement and tears that they arouse in other places. This originates from the characteristic of a large part of the audience, that these attend with due seriousness only to certain undertakings; and the distractions of their disputes and business affairs, and their indolence and the air of the country, dissipate their attention beyond measure. Their imaginations, overborne with foolish trifles, and accustomed to our voices, become so relaxed that even the most forcible and persuasive discourses make little, if any, impression. Nevertheless, there are many in whom the holy fear of God reigns, and the seed of the gospel takes root—which they embrace with seriousness and simplicity, as the importance of the subject demands. The marvel is, that many Indians and a great many Indian women, only by the sound of [the preaching in] the mission, and without understanding what they hear, are stricken with contrition, confess themselves, and receive communion, in order to gain the indulgences—to their own great advantage, and to the unspeakable consolation of their confessors at seeing the wonderfully loving providence of God for these souls.

This fruit and this consolation are most evident in the Spiritual Exercises of St. Ignatius,6 which are explained through most of the year in our college. The principal citizens make their retreat there, and in the solitude of that retirement God speaks to them within their hearts; and marvelous results have been seen in various persons, in whom has been established a tenor of life so Christian that they may be called the religious of the laymen—in their minds those eternal truths, on which they meditate with seriousness, remaining firm, for the orderly conduct of their lives. The students in the college of San Joseph have their own society, which meets every Sunday, in which they perform their exercises of devotion and have their exhortations, during the course of the year. Every Sunday the Christian doctrine is explained to the boys in the school, and some example [for their imitation] is related to them; and they walk in procession through the streets, chanting the doctrine. The Indian servants of the college have their own assembly, conducted in a very decorous manner, with continual instruction in the doctrine. Every Saturday an address in Tagálog is given to the beatas who attend our church; they have their own society, and exercise themselves in frequent devotions, furnishing an excellent and useful example to the community. Every year they perform the spiritual exercises; and the topics therein are given to them in Tagálog, in our church, by one of Ours. Many devout Indian and mestizo women resort hither on this occasion, to perform these exercises, in various weeks, for which purpose they make retreat in the beaterio during the week required for that; and even Spanish women, including ladies of the most distinguished position, perform their spiritual exercises, and the topics for meditation are assigned to them in our church. This practice is very beneficial for their souls, of great usefulness to the community, and remarkably edifying to all.

The Society also busies itself in the conversion and reconciliation of certain heretics, who are wont to come from the East (as has been observed in recent years), and in catechising and baptizing the Moros or the heathens who sometimes reach the islands—either driven from their route, or called by God in other ways; and He draws them to himself, so that they obtain holy baptism, as has been seen in late years in some persons from the Palaos and Carolina islands, and from Siao. Another of the means of which the Society avails itself for the good of souls is, to print and distribute free many spiritual books in various languages, which are most efficacious although mute preachers. These, removing from men their erroneous ideas by clear exposition [of the truth], and leaving them without the cloak of their own fantastic notions, persuade them, without being wearisome, to abandon vice or error; and then they embrace virtue and the Christian mode of life. In Lent, as being an acceptable time and especially opportune for the harvest, the dikes are opened, in order that the waters of the word of God may flow more abundantly. On Tuesdays there is preaching to the Spaniards, and these sermons usually have the efficacy of a mission, although not given under that name. On Thursdays there is explanation of the doctrine, and preaching, in Tagálog, to the Indians; the attendance is very great, since many come, not only from the numerous suburbs of Manila, but even from the more distant villages. On Saturdays some good example of the Virgin is related, with a moral exhortation; the Spaniards who are members of fraternities attend these, and afterward visit the altars. On Sundays there is preaching to the Cafres, blacks, creoles, and Malabars—who through a sense of propriety are called Morenos, although they are dark-skinned. The sermon is in Spanish, and the greatest difficulty of the preacher is to adapt his language to the understanding of the audience. Various poor Spaniards also attend these sermons, as well as other people, of various shades of color, of both sexes.

Every Sunday certain fathers are sent to preach at the fort or castle, to the soldiers and the other men who live there. The Christian doctrine is chanted through the streets, and in the procession walk the boys of the school; it ends at the royal chapel, where some part of the catechism is explained, and a moral sermon is preached to the soldiers who live in their quarters in order to mount guard. The doctrine is explained at the Puerta Real and at the Puerta del Parián, and there is preaching in the guard-room—where there is a large attendance, not only of soldiers, but of the many people who, on entering or going out from the gates, stop to hear the word of God. Another father goes to the royal foundry, in which the galley-slaves live, where there is such a variety of people—mestizos, Indians of various dialects, Cafres, negroes of different kinds, and Sangleys or Chinese—that exceptional ability and patience are necessary in order to make them understand. Other fathers go to the college of Santa Isabel and the seminary of Santa Potenciana, where they give addresses and exhortations to the students of the former, and the women secluded in the latter. Others go to the prisons of both the ecclesiastical and secular jurisdictions, in order that the prisoners may obtain the spiritual food of the doctrine. On Mondays, Wednesdays, and Fridays there is in our church a Miserere, with the discipline [i.e., scourging]; a spiritual book is read to those who are present, and at least once a week an exhortation is addressed to them.

Such is, in general, the distribution of work for our college at Manila in Lent, and therein are engaged nearly all the men in the college, whether priests or students; and in times when there is a scarcity of workers I have seen some helping at two or three posts, and not only ministers and instructors thus occupied, but even the superiors, and men of seventy years old, to the great edification of the community. At Lent is seen in Manila that which occurred at the destruction of Jericho, where, when the priests sounded around the city the trumpets of the jubilee, the walls immediately gave way and fell to the ground. Thus in Manila do the Jesuits surround the walls, calling to every class of people with the trumpets of the jubilee and offering pardon; and at the sound, through the grace and mercy of the Highest, the lofty walls of lawlessness, vice, and crime, fall in ruins. And even the presence of the ark is not lacking to this marvelous success, for it is not to be doubted that the Blessed Virgin, most merciful mother of sinners, aids us with her intercession. [Our author here relates various instances of miraculous aid from heaven, and other edifying cases.]

[Fol. 13:] Father Juan de Torres, with another priest and a brother, went from the college of Manila to conduct a mission at a place which is called Cabeza de Bondoc,7 about sixty leguas from Manila, in the bishopric of Camarines—the bishop of Nueva Cazeres at that time being his illustrious Lordship Don Fray Diego de Guevara, of the Order of St. Augustine. As soon as that zealous prelate took possession of his see, he began to ask for fathers of the Society, in order that, commencing with the Indians who were already peaceable who reside in Nueva Cazeres, they might establish missions and continue their instructions in other villages which he intended to give them. But the Society, who always have showed due consideration to the other ministers in these islands, not attempting to dispossess them from their ministries—although not always have we found them respond in like spirit—thanked that illustrious prelate for his kindness, without accepting those ministries; and in order that he might see that [the cause of this action] was consideration for the ministers, and not the desire to escape from the labor, Ours consented to conduct a mission in Bondoc, the difficulty of which, and its results, are explained by that prelate in a letter which he wrote to Father Torres, in which he says: "I find that it is true, what was told to me in Manila, when I gave that mission-field to the Society, and I mention it with great consolation to myself; and that is, that it was the Holy Ghost who inspired me to give it—for I see the fruits which are steadily and evidently being gathered therein. For in so many ages it has been impossible to unite those villages, and the Indians in them were regarded as irreclaimable; and now in so short a time those villages have been united, and the Indians, [who were like] wild beasts, appear like gentle lambs. These are the works of God, who operates through the ministers of the Society—who with so much mildness, affection, and zeal are laboring for the welfare of those people." Great hardships were suffered by those of the Society in these missions, and for several years that ministry was cared for by Ours, until it was entrusted to the secular priests.

The mission of Bondoc gained such repute in the island of Marinduque, distant more than forty leguas from Manila, that its minister, who was a zealous cleric, wrote to the father rector at Manila asking him very humbly and urgently to send there a mission, from which he was expecting abundant fruit. So earnest were the entreaties of this fervent minister that a mission was sent to the said island; it had the results which were expected, and afterward the Society was commissioned with its administration. In nearly all the ministries of secular priests the Society was carrying on continual missions, at the petition of the ministers or at the instance of the bishops.... The Society was held in honor not only by the bishop of Camarines, but equally by his illustrious Lordship Don Fray Miguel Garzia Serrano, a son of the great Augustine and most worthy archbishop of Manila. That most zealous father Lorenzo Masonio preached to the negroes who are in this city and outside its walls, according to the custom of this province, which distributes the bread of the gospel doctrine to all classes of people and all nations. And that holy prelate deigned to go to our church, and, taking a wand in his hand, as the Jesuits are accustomed to do, he walked through the aisle of the church, asked questions, and explained the Christian doctrine to the slaves and negroes. The community experienced the greatest edification at seeing their pastor so worthily occupied in instructing his sheep, not heeding the outer color of their bodies, but looking only at their precious souls—for in the presence of God there is no distinction of persons.

[Fol. 22:] The island of Malindig—named thus on account of a high mountain that is in it, and which the Spaniards call Marinduque—is more than forty leguas from Manila, extends north and south, and is in the course which is taken by the galleons on the Nueva España trade-route.8 There Ours carried on a mission with much gain, at the instance of its zealous pastor, who was a cleric; and in the year 1622 this island was transferred to the Society by his illustrious Lordship Don Fray Miguel Garzia Serrano, the archbishop of Manila, who was satisfied by the care with which the Society administers its charges, and desirous that his sheep should have the spiritual nourishment that is necessary for their souls—for it was exceedingly difficult for him always to find a secular priest to station there, on account of the distance from Manila, the difficulty of administering that charge, and the loneliness which one suffers there. The Society gladly overcame these difficulties for the sake of the spiritual fruit which could be gathered among those Indians; and our ministers, applying themselves to the cultivation [of that field], went about among those rugged mountains—from which they brought out some heathens, and others who were Christians, but who were living like heathen, without any spiritual direction. They baptized the heathens and instructed the Christians; and, in order that the results might be permanent, Ours gradually settled them in villages which they formed; there are three of these, Bovac, Santa Cruz, and Gasan, and formerly there was a visita in Mahanguin. The language spoken there is generally the Tagálog, although in various places there is a mixture of Visayan, and of some words peculiar to the island. God chose to prove those people by a sort of epidemic, of which many died; and the fathers not only gave them spiritual assistance, but provided the poor with food, and treated the sick. This trouble obliged them to resort for aid to the Empress of Heaven, to whom they offered a fiesta under the title of the Immaculate Conception, during the week before Christmas, with great devotion; and the Virgin responded to them by aiding them in their troubles and necessities.

[Fol. 27:] In Marinduque Ours labored very fervently to reduce the Christians to a Christian and civilized mode of life; and among them was abolished an abuse which was deeply rooted in that island—which was, that creditors employed their debtors almost as if they were slaves, without the debtor's service ever diminishing his debt. The wild Indians were reduced to settlement; among them were some persons who for thirty years had not received the sacraments of penance and communion. In the Pintados Islands there was now much longing for and attendance upon these holy sacraments, when their necessity and advantage had been explained to the natives.

[Fol. 29:] His illustrious Lordship Don Fray Miguel Garzia Serrano had so much affection for the Society, and so high an opinion of the zeal of its ministers, that he decided to entrust to it the parish of the port of Cavite. This, one may say, is a parish of all the nations, on account of the many peoples who resort to that port from the four quarters of the world; it was especially so then, when its commerce was more opulent, flourishing, and extensive [than now]. It did not seem expedient to the Society to accept this parish; but, in order to show their gratitude for the favor, and to coöperate by their labors with the zeal of that active prelate, they took upon themselves for several months the administration of that port, in which they gathered the fruit corresponding to the necessity—which, with so great a concourse of different peoples there, and the freedom from restraint which exists in this country, was very great. The metropolitan was well satisfied, and very grateful; and he insisted until the Society made itself responsible for the administration of one of the three visitas which the said parish has. This was a village on the shore of the river of Cavite, which on account of being older than the settlement at the port is called Cavite el Viejo [i.e., Old Cavite]; it afterward was located on the shore of the bay, about a legua from the said port—which, in order to distinguish it from this village, is called Cavite la Punta [i.e., Cavite on the Point], because it is on the point of the hook formed by the land; from this is derived the name Cavite, which means "a hook." The ministry [at Old Cavite] was then small, but difficult to administer, on account of the people being scattered, and far more because of the corruption of morals; for, lacking the presence of the pastor, and the wolves of the nations who come here from all parts for trade, being so near, it might better be called a herd of goats than a flock of sheep—this village being, as it were, the public brothel [lupanar] of that port; and there was hardly a house where this sort of commerce was not established. This was a matter which at the beginning gave the ministers much to do, but with invincible firmness they continued to correct this lawless licentiousness; and by explaining the doctrine, preaching, and aiding the people with the sacraments, they made Christians in morals those who before only seemed to be such in outward appearance and name. Ours continued to reclaim these people to the Christian life, and today this village is one of the most Christian and best instructed communities in all the islands; it has a beautiful and very capacious church of stone, dedicated to St. Mary Magdalen, and a handsome house [for the minister]. There are in this village, besides the Tagálogs (who are the natives), some Sangleys and many mestizos, who live in Binacayan, which is a sort of ward of the village.

[Fol. 31 b:] Ardently did the apostle of the Indias desire to go over to China for its conversion; but he died, like another Moses, in sight of the land which his desires promised to him. Since then, without looking for them, thousands of heathen Chinese have settled in these islands. As soon as the Society came to these shores, Ours applied themselves, in the best manner that they could, to the conversion and instruction of those people—and even more in recent times, on account of the Society possessing near Manila some agricultural lands, which the Chinese (or Sangleys, as they are commonly called) began to cultivate. Ours were unwilling to lose the opportunity of converting them to our holy faith, so various persons were actually baptized; and, to render this result more permanent, a minister was stationed there, belonging to this field, who catechised them, preached in their own language, baptized them, and administered the sacraments—with permission from the vice-patron, Don Juan Niño de Tabora, and from the archbishop, Don Fray Miguel Garzia Serrano—and it is called the village of Santa Cruz. Their language is very difficult; the words are all monosyllables, and the same word, according to its various intonations, has many and various significations; on this account not only patience and close study, but a correct ear, are required for learning this language. Don Juan Niño de Tabora was the godfather of the first Sangley who was baptized; the most distinguished persons in the city attended the ceremony; and this very solemn pomp had much influence on the Chinese (who are very material), so that, having formed a high idea of the Catholic religion, many of them embraced it. Some were baptized a little while before they died, leaving behind many tokens of their eternal felicity, through the concurrence of circumstances which were apparently directed by a very special providence.

In Marinduque Father Domingo de Peñalver had just induced some hamlets of wild Indians to settle down; he traveled through the bed of the river, getting his clothing wet, stumbling frequently over the stones, and often falling in the water. He went to take shelter in a hut, where there were so many and so fierce mosquitoes, that he remained awake all night, without being able to rid himself of the insects, notwithstanding all his efforts. He reached a hill so inaccessible that it was necessary that some Indians, going ahead and ascending by grasping the roots [of trees], should draw them all up the ascent with bejucos. There he set up a shed, where, preaching to them morning and afternoon, he prepared them for confession, and persuaded them to go down and settle in one place, as actually they did, to live as Christians. For lack of laborers, the Society resigned the district of Bondoc and several visitas, although Ours went there at various times on missionary trips. The people of Hingoso called upon Father Peñalver to assist them, because many in their village were sick, and the cura was at Manila; the father went there, gave the sacraments to the sick, and preached to the rest twice a day in the church. Three times a week they repaired to the church for the discipline, and he offered for them the act of contrition, and almost all the people in the village confessed. Afterward, at the urgent request of the archbishop of Manila, Father Peñalver went to Mindoro, to see if he could reconcile those Indians and their cura, which the archbishop had not been able to secure by various means; the said father went there, and preached various sermons, with so much earnestness and efficacy (on account of his proficiency in the Tagálog language) that in a short time they were reconciled together, the causes of the dispute bring entirely forgotten. This mission lasted two months; he preached twice every day, and heard some two thousand five hundred confessions; at this the illustrious prelate (who was Don Fray Miguel Garzia Serrano) was greatly pleased, and thoroughly confirmed in the extraordinary esteem which he deigned to show the Society.... One of the greatest hardships and dangers experienced by the ministers of Bisayas (or Pintados), in which are the greater part of our ministries, is that they are journeying on the water all their lives; for, as the villages are many and the ministers few, one father regularly takes care of two villages, and sometimes of three or four; and as these are in different islands, he is continually moving from one to another, for their administration. I have known some fathers who formerly had six or seven visitas, and spent nearly all the year traveling from one to another. Nevertheless, so paternal and benignant is the providence of God that it is not known that any minister in Bisayas has been drowned— which, considering the many hurricanes, tempests, storms, currents, and other dangers in which every year many perish and are drowned, seems a continual miracle. To this it must be added that at various times vessels have capsized in the midst of the sea, and the fathers have fallen into the water; but God succored them by means of the Indians, who are excellent swimmers, or by other special methods of His paternal providence.

[Fol. 38 b:] In this year [1628] Manila and the adjoining villages were grievously afflicted with a sort of epidemic pest, from which many people died—some suddenly, but even he who lingered longest died within twelve hours. Some attributed this pest to the many blacks who had been brought here from India to be sold, and who, sick from ill-usage, communicated their disease to others; and some thought that it arose from an infection in the fish, which is the usual food of the poor. Various corpses were anatomized [se hizo anatomia], and the origin of the disease could not be discovered, although it was considered certain that it arose from a poisonous condition, since the only remedy that was found was theriac.9 In a city where there are so few Spaniards, it is easy to understand the affliction which was felt at seeing the suddenness with which they were dying, since the colony was placed in so great danger of extinction, and the islands of being ruined at one stroke—besides the grief of individual persons at seeing themselves bereft, the wife without a husband, the husband without a wife, the father without children, the children deprived of their parents. All search was made for remedies. Our priests did not cease, day or night, to hear confessions, and to aid the sick and dying; and at the request of the cura they carried with them the consecrated oils, to administer these in case of need. They also carried theriac, after this was discovered to be a remedy, for the relief of the sick; so they exercised their charity at the same time on the souls and on the bodies of men, to the great edification of all.

At San Miguel, one of those attacked by the pest told the father who was hearing his dying confession that he had seen near him two figures in the guise of ministers of justice, who seized people; and that when he had received absolution they went away from him, leaving behind a pestilential odor. The father published this information throughout the village, commanding the people to prepare themselves for confession on the following day, under the patronage of the Blessed Mary and St. Michael. A novenary was offered, and the litanies recited; and in the church the discipline was taken, with other prayers and penances, by which the Lord was moved to have especial mercy on this village—as God showed to a devout soul, in the figure of a ship which sailed through the air, the pilot of which was the common enemy; but he could not enter San Miguel, since there were powers greater than he, who prevented him. Also there were seen in the neighborhood of Manila malign spirits, in the appearance of horrible phantoms, who struck with death those who only looked at them. In the face of a danger so near, many amended their lives, and were converted to God in earnest, making a good confession. Then was seen the charity with which the poor Indians, despising the danger to their own lives, assisted the sick. Among others were two pious married persons, who devoted themselves entirely to aiding the sick, never leaving their bedsides until they either died or recovered; and God most mercifully chose to bring them out unscathed from so continual dangers. With the same kindness He chose to reward Brother Antonio de Miranda, who had charge of the infirmary in our college at Manila, who, on account of his well-known charity and solicitude in caring for the sick, had been commissioned by the father provincial, Juan de Bueras, to devote himself to the care of the sick Indians. But the poison of the pest infected him, so violent being the attack that hardly had he time to receive the sacraments; and he died at Manila on October 15, 1628.... He was a native of Ponferrada, and of a very well known family; he was an exemplary religious, and had been ten years in the Society.

[Fol. 44 b:] In the years 1628 and 1629, at the request of the bishops and of some Indians the Society was placed in charge of various villages of converts. Don Juan Niño de Tabora gave us the chaplaincy of the garrison of Spanish soldiers which is at Iloylo in the island of Panay, and the instruction of the natives and the people from other nations who are gathered there. Also were given to us Ilog in the island of Negros, and Dapitan in Mindanao—of which afterward more special mention will be made.

[Fol. 50:] In this time [about 1630] the Christian faith made great advances in Maragondong, Silang, and Antipolo, bringing many Cimarrons (or wild Indians) from their lurking-places. A very fruitful mission was carried on in Mindoro, and on the northern coast of Mindanao; and Father Pedro Gutierrez went along those rivers, converting the Subanos. In Ilog, in the island of Negros, the fathers labored much in removing an inhuman practice of those barbarians, which was, to abandon entirely the old people, as being useless and only a burden on them; and these poor wretches were going about through the mountains, without knowing where to go, since even their own children drove them away. The fathers gave them shelter, fed them, and instructed them in order to baptize them; and there they converted many heathens.

[Fol. 52:] In the year 1631 the cura of Mindoro, who was a secular priest, gave up that ministry to the Society, and Ours began to minister in that island, making one resilience of this and one of the island of Marinduque, and the superior lived at Nauhan in Mindoro; and they began to preach, and to convert the Manguianes, the heathen Indians of that island.

In the year 1631 was begun the residence of Dapitan, in the great island of Mindanao. The first Jesuit who preached in that island was the apostle of the Indias, St. Francis Xavier, as appears from the bull for his canonization. Ruy Lopez de Villalobos came to these islands with his ships, sent by the viceroy of Nueva España, and gave them the name of Philipinas in honor of Phelipe II; and, driven by storms, he went to Amboyno, where the saint then was, in whose care Villalobos died. At the news of these islands thus obtained by the holy apostle, he came to them. The circumstance that this island was consecrated by the labors of that great apostle has always and very rightly commended it to the Society; and Ours have always and persistently endeavored to occupy themselves in converting the Mindanaos; and Father Valerio de Ledesma and others had begun to form missions on the river of Butuan. In the year 1596 the cabildo of Manila, in sede vacante— in whose charge was then the spiritual government of all the islands, as there was no division into bishoprics—gave possession of Mindanao to the Society in due form; and in 1597 this was confirmed by the vice-patron, Don Francisco Tello, the governor of these islands. Possession of it was taken by Father Juan del Campo, who, going as chaplain of the army, accompanied the adelantado, Estevan Rodriguez de Figueroa, when he set out for the conquest of that kingdom.

The first who began to minister to the Subanos in the coasts of Dapitan was Father Juan Lopez; afterward Father Fabricio Sarsali, and then Father Francisco de Otazo, and various other fathers followed, who made their incursions sometimes from Zebu, sometimes from Bohol. In the year 1629 this ministry was entrusted to the Society by the bishop of Zebu, Don Fray Pedro de Arze. The venerable Father Pedro Gutierrez went through those coasts, carrying the gospel of Christ to the rivers of Quipit, Mucas, Telinga, and others; and in the year 1631 a permanent residence was formed, its rector being Father Pedro Gutierrez. The village of Dapitan is at the foot of a beautiful bay with a good harbor (in which the first conquistadors anchored), on the northern coast of Mindanao; it is south from the island of

Zebu, and to the northeast of Samboangan, which is on the opposite coast [of Mindanao]. It lies at the foot of a hill, at the top of which there is a sort of fortress, so inaccessible that it does not need artillery for its defense. Above it has a parapet, and near the hill is an underground reservoir for collecting water, besides a spring of flowing water. Maize and vegetables can be planted there, in time of siege; and the minister and all the people retire to this place in time of invasions. I was there in the year 1737 [misprinted 1637], and it seemed to me that it might be called the Aorno10 of Philipinas.

[Fol. 60:] In the year 1631 and in part of 1632 this province experienced so great a scarcity of laborers that the father provincial wrote to our father general that he would have been obliged to abandon some of the ministries if the fervor of the few ministers had not supplied the lack of the many, their charity making great exertions. Our affliction was increased by the news that the Dutch had seized Father Francisco Encinas, the procurator of this province, who was going to Europa to bring a mission band here— for which purpose they had sent Father Juan Lopez, who was appointed in the second place11 in the congregation of 1626. But soon God consoled this province, the mission arriving at Cavite on May 26, 1632. On June 18, 1631, they sailed from Cadiz, and on the last day of August arrived at Vera Cruz; they left Acapulco on February 23, 1632, and on May 15 sighted the first land of these islands. Every mission that goes to Indias begins to gather abundant fruit as soon as it sails from España; I will set down the allotment of work in which this band of missionaries was engaged, since from this may be gathered what the others do, since there is very little difference among them all. In the ship a mission was proclaimed which lasted eleven days, closing with general communion on the day of our father St. Ignatius; in this mission, through the sermons, instructions given in addresses, and individual exhortations, the fathers succeeded in obtaining many general confessions, besides the special ones which the men on the ship made, in order to secure the jubilee. Ours assisted the dying, consoled the sick and the afflicted, and established peace between those who were enemies. In Nueva España the priests were distributed in various colleges, in which they continued the exercises of preaching and hearing confessions. They went to Acapulco a month before embarking, by the special providence of God; for there were many diseases at that port, so that they were able to assist the dying. Thirty religious of St. Dominic were there, waiting to come over to these islands; all of them were sick, and five died; and, in order to prevent more deaths, they decided to remove from their house in which they were, on account of its bad condition. It was necessary, on account of their sick condition, to carry them in sedan-chairs; and although many laymen charitably offered their services for this act of piety, Ours did not permit them to do it, but took upon themselves the care of conveying the sick, their charity making this burden very light. In the ship "San Luys" they continued their ministries, preaching, and hearing the confessions of most of the people on the ship—in which the functions of Holy Week were performed, as well as was possible there. Twenty-one Jesuits left Cadiz, and all arrived at Manila except Father Matheo de Aguilar, who died near these islands on May 12, 1632; he was thirty-three years old, and had been in the Society sixteen years—most of which time he spent in Carmona, in the province of Andalusia, where he was an instructor in grammar, minister, and procurator in that college.... The rest who are known to have come in that year with Father Francisco de Encinas, procurator, and Brother Pedro Martinez are: The fathers Hernando Perez (the superior), Rafael de Bonafe, Luys de Aguayo, Magino Sola, and Francisco Perez; and the brothers Ignacio Alcina, Joseph Pimentél, Miguel Ponze, Andres de Ledesma, Antonio de Abarca, Onofre Esbri, Christoval de Lara, Amador Navarro, Bartholome Sanchez; also Brother Juan Gazera, a coadjutor, and Diego Blanco and Pedro Garzia, candidates [for the priesthood].

[Fol. 63 b:] In the islands of Pintados those first laborers made such haste that by this time [1633] there remained no heathens to convert, and they labored perseveringly in ministering to the Christians, with abundant results and consolation.... In the island of Negros and that of Mindanao, which but a short time before had been given up to the Society, the fathers were occupied in catechising and baptizing the heathens and especially in the island of Mindoro, where besides the Christian convents, were the heathen Manguianes, who lived in the mountains, and, according to estimate, numbered more than six thousand souls. These people wandered through the mountains and woods there like wild deer, and went about entirely naked, wearing only a breech-clout [bahaque] for the sake of decency; they had no house, hearth, or fixed habitation; and they slept where night overtook them, in a cave or in the trunk of some tree. They gathered their food on the trees or in the fields, since it was reduced to wild fruits and roots; and as their greatest treat they ate rice boiled in water. Their furnishings were some bows and arrows, or javelins for hunting, and a jar for cooking rice; and he who secured a knife, or any iron instrument, thought that he had a Potosi. They acknowledged no deity, and when they had any good fortune the entire barangay (or family connection) killed and ate a carabao, or buffalo; and what was left they sacrificed to the souls of their ancestors. In order to convert these heathens, a beginning was made by the reformation and instruction of the Christians; and by frequent preaching they gradually established the usage of confession with some frequency, and many received the Eucharist—a matter in which there was more difficulty then than now. Many came down from the mountains, and brought their children to be instructed; various persons were baptized, and even some, who, although they had the name of Christians, had never received the rite of baptism. After the fathers preached to the Christians regarding honesty in their confessions, the result was quickly seen in many general confessions, which were made with such eagerness that the crowds resorting to the church lasted more than two months.

[Fol. 69:] In Maragondong various trips were made into the mountains [by Ours], and although many were reclaimed to a Christian mode of living, yet, as the mountains are so difficult of access and so close by, those people returned to their lurking-places very easily, and it was with difficulty that they were again brought into a village—so that the number of Indians was greatly diminished, not only in Maragondong, but in Looc, which was a visita of the former place, and contained very rugged mountains. In order to encourage the Indians thus settled to make raids on the Cimarrons and wild Indians and punish them, Don Juan Cerezo de Salamanca, the governor ad interim, granted that those wild Indians should for a certain time remain the slaves of him who should bring them out of the hills; and by this means they succeeded in bringing out many from their caverns and hiding-places. Some of these were seventy or eighty years old, of whom many died as soon as they were instructed and baptized. Once the raiders came across an old woman about a hundred years old, near the cave in which those people performed their abominable sacrifices; she was alone, flung down on the ground, naked, and of so horrible aspect that she made it evident, even in external appearance, that she was a slave of the devil. Moved by Christian pity, those who were making the raid carried her to the village, where it was with difficulty that the father could catechise her, on account of her age and her stupidity. He finally catechised and baptized her, and she soon died; so that it seems as if it were a mercy of God that she thus waited for baptism, in order that her soul might not be lost—and the same with the other souls, their lives apparently being preserved in order that they might be saved through the agency of baptism. Blessed be His mercy forever! In Ilog, in the island of Negros, several heathens of those mountains were converted to the faith. An Indian woman was there, so obstinate in her blindness and so open in her hatred to holy baptism that, in order to free herself from the importunities of the minister, she feigned to be deaf and mute. Some of her relatives notified the father to come to baptize her. The father went to her, and began to catechise her, but she, keeping up the deceit, pretended that she did not hear him, and he could not draw a word from her. The father cried out to God for the conversion of that soul, and, at the same time, he continued his efforts to catechise her, suspecting that perhaps she was counterfeiting deafness. God heard his prayers, and, after several days, the first word which that woman uttered was a request for baptism—to the surprise of all who knew what horror of it she had felt. The father catechised and baptized her, and this change was recognized as caused by the right hand of the Highest; for she who formerly was like a wild deer, living alone in the thickets, after this could not go away from the church, and continued to exercise many pious acts until she rested in the Lord.

[Fol. 74 b:] In the year 1596 Father Juan del Campo and Brother Gaspar Gomez went with the adelantado Estevan Rodriguez de Figueroa, who set out for the conquest of this island [Mindanao]. After the death of Father Juan del Campo, Father Juan de San Lucar went to assist that army, performing the functions of its chaplain, and also of vicar for the ecclesiastical judge. Fathers Valerio de Ledesma and Manuel Martinez preached to the Butuans, and afterward they were followed, although with some interruptions, by others, who announced the gospel to the Hadgaguanes—a people untamed and ferocious—to the Manobos, and to other neighboring peoples. Afterward this ministry was abandoned, on account of the lack of laborers for so great a harvest as God was sending us. Secular priests held it for some time, and finally it was given to the discalced Augustinian [i.e., Recollect] religious, who are ministering in that coast, and in Caraga as far as Linao— an inland region, where there is a small fort and a garrison. When Father Francisco Vicente was ministering in Butuan the cazique [meaning the headman] of Linao went to invite him to go to his village; and even the blacks visited him, and gave him hopes for their submission. Thus all those peoples desired the Society, as set aside for the preaching in that island— which work was assigned to the Society by the ecclesiastical judge in the year 1596, and confirmed to them in 1597 by the governor Don Francisco Tello, as vice-patron. And when some controversy afterward occurred over [the region of] Lake Malanao, sentence was given in favor of the Society by Governors Don Juan Niño de Tabora and Don Sebastian Hurtado de Corcuera, as Father Combés states in book iii of his History of Mindanao. These decisions were finally confirmed by Don Fernando Valdès Tamon, in the year 1737.

In the year 1607 Father Pasqual de Acuña, going thither with an armada of the Spaniards, began to preach with great results to the heathens of the hill of Dapitan, where he baptized more than two hundred. He also administered the sacraments to some Christians who were there, who with Pagbuaya, a chief of Bohol, had taken refuge in that place. Afterward, Father Juan Lopez went to supply the Subanos of Dapitan with more regular ministrations. He was succeeded by Father Fabricio Sarsali, and he by Father Francisco Otazo and others, as a dependency of Zebu or of Bohol—until, in the year 1629, his illustrious Lordship the bishop of Zebu, Don Fray Pedro de Arze, governor of the archbishopric of Manila, again assigned this mission to the Society; and in 1631 the residence of Dapitan was founded, its first rector being the venerable Father Pedro Gutierrez; and in those times the Christian faith was already far advanced, and was extending through the region adjoining that place, and making great progress.

[Fol. 92:] The island of Basilan, or Taguima, is three or four leguas south of Samboangan, east from Borney, and almost northeast from Joló. It is a fertile and abounding land, and on this account they call it the storehouse or garden of Samboangan. Its people are Moros and heathens, and almost always they follow the commands received from Joló. The Basilans, who inhabit the principal villages, are of the Lutaya people; those who dwell in the mountains are called Sameacas. Three chiefs had made themselves lords of the island, Ondol, Boto, and Quindinga; and they formed the greatest hindrance to the reduction of that people, who, as barbarians, have for an inviolable law the will of their headmen, [which they follow] heedlessly— that being most just, therefore, which has most following. Nevertheless, the brave constancy of Father Francisco Angel was not dismayed at such difficulties, or at the many perils of death which continually threatened him; and his zeal enabled him to secure the baptism of several persons, and to rescue from the captivity of Mahoma more than three hundred Christians, whom he quickly sent to Samboangan. Moreover, the fervor of the father being aided by the blessing of God, he saw, with unspeakable consolation to his soul, the three chiefs who were lords of the island baptized, with almost all the inhabitants of the villages in it; and in the course of time the Sameacas, or mountain-dwellers, were reduced—in this way mocking the strong opposition which was made by the panditas, who are their priests and doctors. [Here follows an account of the conquest of Joló in 1638, and of affairs there and in Mindanao, in which the Jesuits (especially Alexandro Lopez) took a prominent part; these matters have already been sufficiently recounted in VOLS. XXVIII and XXIX].

[Fol. 111:] [After the Spanish expeditions to Lake Lanao, in 1639–40, the fort built there was abandoned, and soon afterward burned by the natives. On May 7, 1642, the Moros of that region killed a Spanish officer, Captain Andres de Rueda, with three men and a Jesuit, Father Francisco de Mendoza, who accompanied him.] Much were the hopes of the gospel ministers cast down at seeing our military forces abandon that country, since they were expecting that with that protection the Christian church would increase. Notwithstanding, his faith thereby planted more firmly on God, Father Diego Patiño began to catechise the Iligan people—with so good effect that in a few months the larger (and the best) part of the residents in that village were brought under the yoke of Christ; this work was greatly aided by the kindness of the commandant of the garrison, Pedro Duran de Monforte. At this good news various persons of the Malanaos came down [from the mountains], and in the shelter of the fort they formed several small villages or hamlets, and heard the gospel with pleasure. The conversions increasing, it was necessary to station there another minister; this was Father Antonio de Abarca. They founded the village of Nagua, and others, which steadily and continually increased with the people who came down from the lake [i.e., Lanao], where the villages were being broken up.12 This angered a brother of Molobolo, and he tried to avert his own ruin by the murder of the father; and for this purpose his treacherous mind [led him to] pretend that he would come down to the new villages, in order to become a Christian, intending to carry out then his treason at his leisure. But the father, warned by another Malanao, who was less impious, escaped death. The traitor did not desist from his purpose, and, when Father Abarca was in one of those villages toward Layavan, attacked the village; but he was discovered by the blacks of the hill-country, and they rained so many arrows upon the Moros that the latter abandoned their attempt. Another effort was a failure—the preparation of three joangas which the traitor had upon the sea, in order to capture and kill the father when he should return to Iligan; but in all was displayed the special protection with which God defends His ministers. However great the efforts made by the zeal of the gospel laborers, the result did not correspond to their desires, on account of the obstinacy of the Mahometans—although in the heathens they encountered greater docility for the acceptance of our religion. The life of the ministers was very toilsome, since to the task of preaching must be added the vigils and weariness, the heat and winds and rains, the dangers of [travel by] the sea, and the scarcity of food. In a country so poor, and at that time so uncultivated, it was considered a treat to find a few sardines or other fish, some beans, and a little rice; and many times they hardly could get boiled rice, and sometimes they must get along with sweet potatoes, gabes,13 or [other] roots. But God made amends for these privations and toils with various inner pleasures; for they succeeded in obtaining some conversions that they had not expected, and even among the blacks, from whom they feared death, they found help and sustenance. [The author here relates a vision which appeared to an Indian chief, of the spirit of Father Marcelo Mastrilli as the director and patron of Father Abarca; and the renunciation of a mission to Europe which was vowed by Father Patiño in order to regain his health—which accomplished, he returns to his missionary labors at Iligan.]

He returned to the ministry, where he encountered much cause for suffering and tears; because the [military] officers [cabos] who then were governing that jurisdiction, actuated by arrogance and greed of gain, had committed such acts of violence that they had depopulated those little villages, many fleeing to the hills, where among the Moros they found treatment more endurable. The only ones who can oppose the injustice of such men are the gospel ministers. These fathers undertook to defend the Indians, and took it upon themselves to endure the anger of those men—who, raised from a low condition to places of authority, made their mean origin evident in their coarse natures and lawless passions; and the license of some of them went to such extremes that it was necessary for the soldiers to seize them as intolerable; and, to revenge themselves for the outrageous conduct of the officials, they accused the latter as traitors. Not even the Malanao chief Molobolo, who always had been firm on the side of the Spaniards, could endure their acts of violence, and, to avoid these, went back to the lake. This tempest lasted for some time, but afterward some peace was secured, when those officers were succeeded by others who were more compliant. The venerable Father Pedro Gutierrez went to Iligan, and with his amiable and gentle disposition induced a chief to leave the lake, who, with many people, became a resident of Dapitan; and another chief, still more powerful, was added to Iligan with his people. These results were mainly seemed by the virtue of the father, the high opinion which all had of his holy character, and the helpful and forcible effects of his oratory. The land was scorched by a drouth, which was general throughout the islands, from which ensued great losses. The father offered the Indians rain, if they would put a roof on the church; they accepted the proposal, and immediately God fulfilled what His servant had promised—sending them a copious rain on his saying the first mass of a novenary, which he offered to this end. With this the Indians were somewhat awakened from their natural sloth, and the church was finished, so that the fathers could exercise in it their ministries. The drouth was followed by a plague of locusts, which destroyed the grain-fields; the father exorcised them, and, to the wonder of all, the locusts thrust their heads into the ground, and the plague came to an end. This increased the esteem of the natives for our religion, and many heathens and Moros were brought into its bosom; and Father Combés says that when he ministered there he found more than fifty old persons of eighty to a hundred years, and baptized them all, with some three hundred boys this being now one of the largest Christian communities in the islands. The village is upon the shore, at the foot of the great Panguil,14 between Butuan and Dapitan, to the south of Bohol, and north from Malanao, at the mouth of a river with a dangerous bar. The fort is of good stone, dedicated to St. Francis Xavier, in the shape of a star; the wall is two varas high, and half a vara thick, and it has a garrison, with artillery and weapons. The Moros have several times surrounded it, but they could not gain it by assault.

[Fol. 116 b:] In Sibuguey Father Francisco Luzon was preaching, a truly apostolic man, who spent his life coming and going in the most arduous ministries of the islands. The Sibugueys are heathens, of a gentler disposition and more docile to the reception of the gospel than are the Mahometans; therefore this mission aroused great hopes. One Ash Wednesday Father Luzon went to the fort, and he was received by a Lutao of gigantic stature who gave him his hand. The father shook hands with him, supposing that that was all for which he stopped him; but the Lutao trickily let himself be carried on, and with his weight dragged the father into the water, with the assurance that he could not be in danger, on account of his dexterity in swimming. The father went under, because he could not swim, and the captain and the soldiers hastened from the fort to his aid—but so late that there was quite enough time for him to be drowned, on account of having sunk so deep in the water; they pulled him out, half dead, and the first thing that he did was to secure pardon for the Lutao. He gained a little strength and went to the fort; he gave ashes to the Spaniards, and preached with as much fervor as if that hardship had not befallen him. The principal of Sibuguey was Datan, and, to make sure of him, the Spaniards had carried away as a hostage his daughter Paloma; and love for her caused her parents to leave Sibuguey and go to Samboangan to live, to have the company of their daughter. Father Alexandro Lopez went to minister at Sibuguey, and he saw that without the authority of Datan he could do almost nothing among the Sibugueys; this obliged him to go to Samboangan to get him, and he succeeded [in persuading them] to give him the girl. The father went up toward the source of the river, and found several hamlets of peaceable people, and a lake with five hundred people residing about it; and their chief, Sumogog, received him as a friend, and all listened readily to the things of God. He went so far that he could see the mountains of Dapitan, which are so near that place that a messenger went [to Dapitan] and returned in three days. These fair hopes were frustrated by the absence of Datan, who went with all his family to Mindanao; and on Ascension day in 1644 that new church disappeared, no one being left save a boy named Marcelo. Afterward the Moros put the fort in such danger, having killed some men, that it was necessary to dismantle it and withdraw the garrison.

[Fol. 121 (sc. 120):] The Joloans having been subjected by the bravery of Don Pedro de Almonte, they began to listen to the gospel, and they went to fix their abodes in the shelter of our fort. But, [divine] grace accommodating itself to their nature, as the sect of Mahoma have always been so obstinate, it was necessary that God should display His power, in order that their eyes might be opened to the light. The fervent father Alexandro Lopez was preaching in that island, to whose labors efficacy was given by the hand of God with many prodigies. The cures which the ministers made were frequent, now with benedictions, now with St. Paul's earth,15 in many cases of bites from poisonous serpents, or of persons to whom poison was administered. Among other cures, one was famous, that of a woman already given up as beyond hope; having given her some of St. Paul's earth, she came back from the gates of death to entire health. With this they showed more readiness to accept the [Christian] doctrine, which was increased by a singular triumph which the holy cross obtained over hell in all these islands; for, having planted this royal standard of our redemption in an island greatly infested by demons, who were continually frightening the islanders with howls and cries, it imposed upon them perpetual silence, and freed all the other [neighboring] islands from an extraordinary tyranny. For the demons were crossing from island to island, in the sea, in the shape of serpents of enormous size, and did not allow vessels to pass without first compelling their crews to render adoration to the demon in iniquitous sacrifices; but this ceased, the demon taking flight at sight of the cross. [Several incidents of miraculous events are here related.] With these occurrences God opened their eyes, in order that they might see the light and embrace baptism, and in those islands a very notable Christian church was formed; and almost all was due to the miraculous resurrection of Maria Ligo [which our author relates at length]. Many believed, and thus began a flourishing Christian community; and as ministers afterward could not be kept in Joló on account of the wars, [these converts] exiled themselves from their native land, and went to live at Samboangan, in order that they might be able to live as Christians. [This prosperous beginning is spoiled by the lawless conduct of the commandant Gaspar de Morales, which brings on hostilities with the natives, and finally his own death in a fight with them.] Father Alexandro Lopez went to announce the gospel at Pangutaran, (an island distant six leguas east from Joló), and as the people were a simple folk they received the law of Christ with readiness ... The Moros of Tuptup captured a discalced religious of St. Augustine, who, to escape from the pains of captivity, took to flight with a negro. Father Juan Contreras (who was in Joló) went out with some Lutaos in boats to rescue him, calling to him in various places from the shore; but the poor religious was so overcome with fear that, although he heard the voices and was near the beach, he did not dare to go out to our vessels, despite the encouragement of the negro; and on the following day the Joloans, encountering him, carried him back to his captivity, with blows. He wrote a letter from that place, telling the misfortunes that he was suffering; all the soldiers, and even the Lutaos, called upon the governor [of Joló], to ransom that religious at the cost of their wages, but without effect. Then Father Contreras, moved by fervent charity, went to Patical, where the fair16 was held, and offered himself to remain as a captive among the

Moros, in order that they might set free the poor religious, who was feeble and sick. Some Moros agreed to this; but the Orancaya Suil, who was the head chief of the Guimbanos, said that no one should have anything to do with that plan—at which the hopes of that afflicted religious for ransom were cut off. Seeing that he must again endure his hardships, from which death would soon result, he asked Father Contreras to confess him; the latter undertook to set out by water to furnish him that spiritual consolation, but the Lutaos would not allow him to leave the boat, even using some violence, in order not to endanger his person. All admired a charity so ardent, and, having renewed his efforts, he so urgently persuaded the governor, Juan Ruiz Maroto, to ransom him that the latter gave a thousand pesos in order to rescue the religious from captivity. Twice Father Contreras went to the fair, but the Moros did not carry the captive there with them. Afterward he was ransomed for three hundred pesos by Father Alexandro Lopez, the soldiers aiding with part of their pay a work of so great charity.

[Fol. 123:] [The Society of Jesus throughout the world celebrates the centennial anniversary of its foundation; the official order for this does not reach Manila in time, so the Jesuits there observe the proper anniversary (September 27, 1640) with solemn religious functions, besides spending a week in practicing the "spiritual exercises" and various works of charity. "On one day of the octave all the members of the Society went to the prisons, and carried to the prisoners an abundant and delicious repast. The same was done in the hospitals, to which they carried many sweetmeats to regale the sick; they made the beds, swept the halls, and carried the chamber-vessels to the river to clean them; and afterward they sprinkled the halls with scented water. Throughout the octave abundance of food was furnished at the porter's lodge to the beggars; and a free table was set for the poor Spaniards, who were served with food in abundance and neatness. It was a duty, and a very proper manner of celebrating the [virtues of the] men who have rendered the Society illustrious, to imitate them in humility, devotion, and charity."]

[Fol. 123 b:] In the Pintados Islands and other ministries Ours labored fervently in ministering to the Christians and converting the infidels. Nor was the zeal of the Society content with laboring in its own harvest-field; it had the courage to go to the ministers of the secular priests to conduct missions. Two fathers went on a mission to Mindoro and Luban, and when they were near the village their caracoa was attacked by three joangas of Borneans and Camucones. The caracoa, in order to escape from the enemies, ran ashore; and the fathers, leaving there all that they possessed—books, missal, and the clothing that they were carrying to distribute as alms to the poor Indians—took to the woods, through which they made their way to Naujan. On the road it frequently rained, and they had no change of clothing, nor any food save some buds of the wild palm-tree; they suffered weariness, hunger, and thirst, and to slake this last they drank the water which they found in the pools there. After twenty days of this so toilsome journeying they reached the chief town [of the island], their feet covered with wounds, themselves faint and worn out with hunger, and half dead from fatigue; but they were joyful and contented, because God was giving them this opportunity to suffer for love of Him. One of the fathers went back to Marinduque, where he found other troubles, no less grievous than those which had gone before; for the Camucones had robbed the church, ravaged the grain-fields, captured some Indians, and caused the rest to flee to the hills. The father felt deep compassion for them, and at the cost of much toil he again assembled the Indians and brought them back to their villages.

[Fol. 134:] In the fifth provincial congregation, which was held in the year 1635, Father Diego de Bobadilla was chosen procurator to Roma and Madrid. He embarked in the year 1637, and while he was in España the disturbances in Portugal and Cataluña occurred. The news of these events was very afflicting to this province, considering the difficulty in its securing aid. Besides the usual fields of Tagalos and Bisayas, the province occupied the new missions of Buhayen, Iligan, Basilan, and Jolo; and there were several years when it found itself with only forty priests, who with the utmost difficulty provided as best they could for needs so great. Phelipe IV—whom we may call "the Great," on account of his unconquerable, signal, and unusual patience, which God chose to prove by great and repeated misfortunes—was so zealous for the Catholic religion, its maintenance, and its progress that even in times so hard he did not grudge the grant of forty-seven missionaries for this province. He also gave orders that they should be supplied at Sevilla with a thousand and forty ducados, and at Mexico with thirteen thousand pesos—a contribution of the greatest value in those circumstances, and which could only be dictated by a heart so Catholic as that of this prince, who every day renewed the vow that he had taken that he would not make friends with the infidels, to the detriment of religion, even though it should cost him his crown and his life. On Holy Tuesday, March 31, in 1643, forty-seven Jesuits embarked at Acapulco; and on the second of April mass was sung, and communion was celebrated—not only by the missionaries, but by almost all the laymen who came in the almiranta, where was established a distribution [of their labors] as well planned as in an Observant college. For at daybreak17 a bell was rung tor rising; there was a season of prayer; mass was said, once on working-days and twice on feast-days; the priests who did not say mass received communion every day, and the lay-brothers, students, and coadjutors two or three times a week; there was reading at meal-times; and at the approach of night the litanies were recited and the Salve sung. Every night a father went to the forecastle to explain the Christian doctrine, and ended with some brief address. When night began, the father procurator rang a little bell, in order that they might pray to God for the souls in purgatory and for those who are in mortal sin, imitating the example of St. Francis Xavier. Before the hour for retiring, the bell was rung for the examination of conscience. Every Sunday, feast-day, and Saturday, addresses were made to all the [people of the] ship.

Soon after they had embarked, a sort of wind blew which made nearly all those who were coming in the ship fall ill; and from this sickness died five Jesuits, and thirty-three laymen; and in the flagship six religious of St. Dominic and seventy [other] persons. These sick persons gave sufficient occasion for the charity of Ours, who assisted them by administering the sacraments and caring for their souls; and they even busied themselves in relieving the sick, so far as was possible, with delicacies and personal attentions. This occupation was an excellent preparation in order that the sermons and exhortations that the ministers uttered might produce the desired result—that a great reform in morals and much attendance on the sacraments might be secured. [After perils and hardships by sea, and in the overland passage from Lampon to Manila, they reach that city. "It was a very numerous mission band, who accomplished much work; and there were some of them who spent fifty and even more than sixty years in Philipinas, which is a very extraordinary thing." Five of them had died on the voyage: fathers Francisco Casela, a native of Naples, aged thirty years; Francois Boursin, a native of Arras, aged thirty-four; Georg Kocart, from Neuburg, aged twenty-eight; Gonzalo Cisneros, an Aragonese (?), aged twenty-eight; and Dominic Vaybel (probably for Waibl), a native of Constance, of the same age.] In the college of Zebu the Society labored with apostolic zeal; for, although regularly there was no one in it besides the father rector and another priest, they maintained preaching and confession, and attended to the spiritual welfare of the Spaniards, Indians, mestizos, and other people who gathered there; and God gave His blessing to our pious desires and labors. Many Indians attended the sermons that were preached in that church, even when the sermons were in Spanish.

[Fol. 152 b:] Our military forces, being set free from the nearer enemies, were employed against those more distant. Accordingly, the commander of our armada, Pedro Duran de Monforte, directed his course to the great island of Borney, where he burned many villages on that coast, and carried away forty captives; and he succeeded in making this voyage known [to navigators], and in observing the shoals, monsoons, and other difficulties. With this experience he again set out, on January 11, 1649, with fourteen vessels, his people being partly Indian adventurers from Pintados, partly Lutaos; and Father Francisco Lado accompanied him. He touched at Lacaylacay; went on to Onsan, the limit of the former expedition; and went to the island of Bangui. Everywhere he found abundance of rice, swine, and goats. He plundered and destroyed several villages; burned more than three hundred vessels, among them the armed fleet which they held ready that year to infest these islands—which on account of this exploit remained for the time free from their fury and barbarity. He brought back more than two hundred captives, and ransomed some Christians. All this was done in a short time and with ease, because these affairs were undertaken with proper seriousness. As a result of this, when the governor of Samboangan, Rafael Omen, died, Pedro Duran de Monforte was appointed in his place; and the latter imitated his predecessor in his zeal for religion, in his Christian mode of life, in disinterestedness, and in an affable and mild bearing, for which he was beloved by all, while his government was peaceful and prosperous. With the opportunity afforded by these armadas, the Jesuits (who went as chaplains) began to announce the gospel in the great island of Borney, than which there is no larger island in the world. So prosperous were those beginnings that they succeeded in having seven hundred islanders baptized. Two chiefs of the neighboring islands offered vassalage to the king of Spain, and asked for gospel ministers, as Father Colin testifies; and this mission finally gave hopes that a numerous and extensive Christian church would be founded which would compensate for the losses in Japon and the Orient; but, lacking the protection of the Spanish military forces, this so beautiful hope faded away almost at its flowering. Deplorable and repeated experiences persuade us that in these latter times the Christian missions are maintained and increased only when in the shelter of Catholic arms; sad witnesses to this are Japon, India, and now China. If in these islands and America our kings did not protect religion, I believe that those regions would now be as heathen as in their former times. Experience teaches this, and the rest I regard as speculation—although the powerful arm of the Highest easily overcomes the greatest impossibilities.

[Fol. 155 b:] The testimony of the venerable Father Mastrili, and the voluntary choice of so many distinguished Jesuits and martyrs who embraced these missions with the greatest eagerness, are sufficient recommendation for them. With just reason they can be esteemed, as being among the most laborious and difficult which the Society maintains anywhere in the world. This title is deserved by the missions of Philipinas, and among them those to Mindanao and the Subanos are some of the most difficult. No one accuses this statement of being exaggerated, and still less of being arrogant, before he has examined it minutely; and then he cannot find more moderate terms [than the above] in order not to fall short of the truth. Whatever dangers, inconveniences, and privations are experienced on land are also experienced on the sea, with an [additional] sort of circumstances which renders them more grievous, and besides this there are the hardships natural and peculiar to that element; and even that which on land is chosen for convenience and relief costs on the sea inconvenience and trouble—as, for instance, sleeping, eating, and taking exercise. Every boat is a prison without chains, but more closely shut than the narrowest jail; it is a broad coffin, in which the living suffer the discomforts of death. Whoever sets foot in a boat resolutely confronts all the elements, which conspire in arms to terrify and destroy him. The water upon which he journeys, the air by which he sails, the fire by which he lives, the land which he so anxiously seeks—all are declared enemies of the traveler. The sea is, by antonomasia, the theater for [all] perils; and no one who has not been tossed upon its foaming waves can speak with justice of its dangers, just as the blind man cannot dispute about colors. A heart of steel or of diamond, say the ancients, he must have had who first boldly launched himself upon the [waters of the] gulfs, so many perils did they conceive of an element which has as many treacheries as waves. Therefore, as nearly all the missions of this province are established along the seas, on which our missionaries go about, continually on the move, these are the (or among the) most difficult, arduous and perilous that exist on the whole round globe. To this sacrifice charity gladly constrained us. Let to all this be added the nature of the country, in which earthquakes, baguios, hurricanes, storms of thunder and lightning, and tempests often occur. The winds are violent and hurtful, the season hot; the rainy season gloomy, dark and persistent; the wet soil producing many disgusting insects that are troublesome and vexatious. The care for the temporal welfare of the people—seeing that they pay their tributes to the king, and that they plant their fields in time—is an employment that is troublesome, tedious, and necessary. Nor is it a less task to take care for the provisioning of the [missionary's] own house, without having in this respect the aid which the apostles had; because the minister must rather care for his own house and for that of others, a charge which charity lays upon us. Charitas omnia sustinet [i.e., "Charity endures all things"].

Each missionary in Bisayas (or Pintados) has the care of two to five thousand souls, and even more. These commonly are divided among two or three villages, quite far apart; and throughout the year the minister is sailing from one to another, to preach to them and aid them. Among the Subanos there are not so many people [in each mission], but their little villages are more numerous. Formerly each minister had ten or twelve villages of Subanos, [each] divided on as many rivers, in the form of hamlets. There were houses round about the church or pavilion [camarin], and the rest [of the people] lived scattered in the hills, forests, and thickets. I have seen some native huts [buhios] on the peaks of the mountains, [so far away] that they could hardly be reached in half an hour from the river. Others I saw placed among the branches of the trees, in the same manner as nests. Their houses regularly are very high, with a bamboo for a ladder, which they remove at night. All this they do in order to hide themselves and be free from the frequent invasions of the Moros; and from the stratagems and treacheries of their own countrymen, who are inclined to vengeance and perfidy. Among these people we live. The rivers are full of ferocious and blood-thirsty crocodiles, which kill many persons. When I was in Dapitan there was one of these beasts in the river of Iraya, so sanguinary and fierce that no one dared to pass that river by night, on account of the ravages that it committed—leaping into the boats, and taking people out of them. In the books of those villages, I read with horror and pity: "On such a day was buried the head of N., which was all that was found, because the crocodile had torn him to pieces." The bars of the rivers are dangerous, and with the freshets and the waves some channels are easily closed and others opened, to the great risk of those who are sailing. The seas are rough, and so restless that the continual lashing of the waves on the shores, rocks, and reefs makes a sound which causes fear even in those who live inland. On that coast are headlands so difficult to double that sometimes the caracoas spend twenty or thirty days in voyages which in favorable weather require half an hour. As a result, the ministers live in great loneliness, without being able to communicate with one another—save that, when the monsoons blow, in order to make one's confession a voyage is necessary; and therefore this consolation is attained by some but few times in the year. If a fatal accident occurs to one, it is not possible to assist him with the holy sacraments— which is the greatest affliction that can be endured in the hour of death; and their only recourse is to place themselves in the hands of that Lord for whom they expose themselves to these sufferings. Even greater are the fatigues endured by the soul in the frequent occasions which disturb its patience. The feeling of indifference which is native to the country tends to undermine gradually the wall of poverty, weaken the spirit of obedience, and cool the most fervent spiritual ardor and strictness of observance. Even the blood which animates us and gives us life is mutinous, and stirs up the passions against their own master; and, aided by the noxious air of the country, the extreme solitude, and the common enemy, wages a war that is cruel, obstinate, bloody, and so pertinacious that it does not yield until the last breath of life....

The soil is very poor, and the greater part of the provisions and clothing must be carried from Manila; and consequently a thousand miseries are suffered during the year without recourse. The feeling of loneliness is very great; we are in this world, which, besides being a vale of tears, for us is as it were, a limbo,18 separated by thousands of leguas from the rest of the world; it is exceedingly seldom that the missionary meets any person through whom he can obtain any alleviation of his troubles, or any assistance or consolation. Few Spaniards traverse those regions, and those who do pass through are usually of such character that merely the knowledge that they are going about through the country causes grief, anxiety, and vigilance to the minister. During the entire week the Indians are on the sea, in the mountains, or in their grain-fields, and on Sundays they come together in the village—but usually little to the comfort of the missionary. Rather, they increase his annoyances, in [having to] settle their lawsuits, quarrels, misunderstandings, and accounts; in defending them from the alcaldes and petty officials, and from one another; and in the minister's defending himself from all—for there are a thousand entanglements, snares, and deceits. Hardly do they set foot in the missionary's house, except when they go to ask for something; they are like the cat, and only look the father in the face when they are expecting some scrap of meat; and when this is seized, friendship, homage, and gratitude are at an end. Would to God that these qualities were left in the Indians! But it cannot be said that all are of this sort, but that there are enough of them for exercising the patience of the minister, although others serve for his comfort and consolation. If the minister is sick, he has no physician or apothecary to resort to; and his only resource is an Indian medicaster who applies some herbs, and whose prescriptions are quickly exhausted. If the sickness be a distressing one, it is necessary to go to Zebu, to which place [Ours] make a voyage of thirty or forty leguas, with the risk of not finding [there] a blood-letter. If radical treatment is needed, there is no other remedy than to sail a hundred or two hundred leguas to Manila, where there is not an over-supply of Galens. Fortunate is he who, without failing in his obligations, can preserve his health unimpaired; for in this land certain diseases quickly take root [in one's system] which are a slow and most grievous martyrdom through life. And there is, almost peculiar to these countries, a sort of profound melancholy, which, like a corrupt root, renders all that he can do either insipid or repulsive. Sometimes it disorders the mind,19 and even life itself becomes abhorrent. It persistently oppresses the mind, which needs great courage, and aid from above, in order that one may not faint in the ministry. All this is the effect of solitude, and of one's nature becoming suffocated under the continual annoyances and troubles which administration [of these missions] involves. Nor is it easy to explain, without actual eyewitness, the various modes of suffering which here present themselves, so unusual, extraordinary, and acute. In these workshops patience is wrought, purified, and assayed until it becomes heroic, with the heavy hammer of mortifications, troubles, and petty details, which chance each day arranges and disarranges.

To this must be added the continual dread of invasions by the Moros, of whose barbarous and inhuman cruelty alone the missionaries are assured, fleeing to the mountains amid thorns, woods, miry places, and precipices. On the coast from Yligan to Samboangan, I saw with great sorrow various churches and villages that had been burned. The ministers saw themselves in the greatest danger of being captured or slain, and in their flight they suffered unspeakable hardships. Nor are dangers wanting among even the Indians themselves; they were very near putting to death by treachery Father Joseph Lamberti at Hagna, and Father Gaspar de Morales at Ynabangan, in the year 1746. For others they have laid ambushes, others have been wounded, and even some have been injured by witchcraft—so that in all directions there is danger.

Finally, let him who wishes to survey the missions which the Society has in these islands, open the map of Asia; and in the western part, in the Ægean archipelago, he will see the Apostle of the Gentiles journeying from Jerusalem to Tarsus, to Ephesus, to Jerusalem, to Seleucia, to Cyprus, to Pergamos in Pamphylia, to Antioch in Pisidia, to Iconium, to Macedonia, and to other cities, islands, and provinces, in continual movement from one place to another. Let him now look at the Eastern part of the same Asia, and he will see in the Philippine archipelago the Jesuits, journeying [in like manner] in Tagalos, in Bisayas, in Mindanao, in Jolo, in Marianas, in Palaos, in Borney, in Ternate, in Siao, in Macazar, in Japon, in China, and in other islands, kingdoms, and provinces of the Orient, preaching the gospel to these nations. To these laborers it is a fitting command: Euntes in mundum universum, prædicate Evangelium omni creaturæ.20 I do not know whether in any other region there is a concourse of so many peoples as in Philipinas, or where this mandate of Christ to His apostles is so literally carried out. There is not in the entire universe a journey more extensive or dangerous, by land or by sea. There is preaching and ministration in the Spanish tongue and in the Tagal; and in those of Samar and Bohol, and of Marianas; of the Lutaos, of Mindanao, and of the Subanos; and in that of the Sangleys or Chinese. The study of the language is difficult, dry, and insipid, but it is necessary; it is a thorn causing many scruples, a bitterness for many years, and a labor for one's whole life.

In Tagalos there are not so many navigations or journeys, although these are not wanting; but this advantage is strictly compensated by other difficulties, for on the ministers falls the entire burden of sermons, missions, Lenten services, novenaries, and other functions, and usually the professorships [in the college] of Manila. In the villages, the solitude and the lack of various conveniences are almost the same [as in Bisayas]; and although the Indians are as simple as the rest they are not so artless, but are cunning and deceitful. They do not use lances or daggers against the ministers, but they employ gossip, misrepresentations, and calumnies. In almost all the villages there are some Indians who have been clerks to the Spaniards in Manila, and accustomed to petitions and lawsuits, they influence the Indians to innumerable quarrels; for through frequent communication with the Spaniards stamped paper has become a favorite with them. And if the father calls them to account [les va á los alcanzes], a crowd of them get together, and draw up a writing against the minister, which is quickly filled with signatures and crosses. Often that happens which is told by the lord bishop of Montenegro: how a visitor, considering as impossible a complaint that was presented to him by some Indians against their cura, began to examine one of those who had signed it; and, seeing that the Indian said "Amen" to everything, without stopping for reflection, the visitor suspected that the complaint was a calumny. He then said, very sagaciously: "Man, in this petition it is stated that one Sunday, after prayers, your cura killed King David." "Yes, sir," said the Indian, "I saw that done;" and thus the prudent judge recognized the falsity of the charges. When the Indians wish to accuse the minister, they resort to the clerk, who has certain bundles and old papers, carefully kept, of accusations and complaints; and according to the amount they pay him the accusation amplifies—as when one prepares a good purgative medicine, and augments the dose in order to secure its operation. A number of the Indians affix their signatures, without knowing what they are signing; for the heat of wine takes the place of all these formalities of law. They carry this document, full of sprawling signatures and cross-marks [letrones y cruzes], to those who, as they know, have least good-will to the minister—and in this [sort of knowledge] the Indians are eminent, nor is there a pilot who follows more closely the winds by which he must navigate; and just so these Indians know where their complaint will be received with approval. If he to whom the accusation is presented be credulous, innocence suffers much until the truth is made clear. Great strength of mind is required to endure these calumnies, and it is one of the kinds of martyrdom (and not the least cruel) in Indias. In the other matters of administration there are hardships, on account of the great number of people [for whom the father must care], and their scattered mode of life, since they are distant from the church sometimes three or four leguas. The roads are wretched, the heat of the sun burning, and the rainstorms very heavy, with innumerable other inclemencies and annoyances, which have disabled many, and killed others. The variety of duties which the minister has to exercise is very great, for he has to be preacher, teacher of the doctrine, and confessor; adjuster and umpire of their petty quarrels; physician and apothecary, to treat them in their sicknesses; schoolmaster, and teacher of music; architect and builder, and competent for everything [un todo para todo]; for if the minister does not take care of everything, all will soon be lost. Enough of [this] parenthetical explanation;21 although it is long, a knowledge of it is very necessary for the completeness of history, in order that it may be known what the gospel ministers are doing and suffering, which is more than what superficial persons suppose.

[Fol. 183 b:] In the conversion of Basilan, fervent were the labors of Father Francisco Angel and Father Nicolas Deñe; and both suffered great dangers to their lives and liberty. They were succeeded by Father Francisco Lado, who by his persistence in enduring innumerable fatigues subdued the entire island; went through all of it, on foot, alone, and without escort; made his way through its thickets, forests, mountains, and hamlets; and did this in such peace that he could build a very neat church and substantial house—for he was much loved by the Lutaos; and he had, with the aid of the governors of Samboangan, cleared the island from all the panditas, and from mischievous and suspicious persons, who might disturb the people with evil doctrines or with immoral practices. Only one remained there, who by his malice was disturbing even the peaceful natives; this was Tabaco, who had incited to rebellion the Sameacas, who are the natives of the island. [This man is finally slain by a daring young Spanish officer, Alonso Tenorio; see our Vol. XXXVIII, pp. 134–136.]

With similar success the religion of Jesus Christ was published along the coast which extends toward the kingdom of Mindanao. Father Pedro Tellez zealously traveled through those shores, where he formed several villages, erected more than sixteen churches, and established Christian living; and he made his abode in Tungavan. Notable aid was given to this enterprise by Don Antonio Ampi, the lord of the river, who always promoted the Christian religion with extraordinary constancy—although he had in Jolo a brother named Libot, a renegade and a cruel pirate—and he gave to the college at Samboangan some fertile and productive lands. At the cost of toils and privations, Father Tellez reduced the barbarous Subanos to rational and Christian customs, drawing them out of their caves and huts, and from under the cruel tyrannical yoke of the demon—who made apparent the great resentment that was roused in him by the loss of those his long-time slaves; for at various times the horrible howls that he uttered were heard at Curuan. For ministration on the coast of La Caldera and Siocon, which was left deserted by the death of Father Juan del Campo, the father provincial Francisco de Roa assigned Father Francisco Combés, who gladly went to instruct the Subanos. Most earnestly he applied himself to bringing those wild and timid creatures into closer social relations, and in doing this he was able to forward their instruction in the mysteries of the faith; and gradually they became accustomed to a more rational and Christian mode of life. On the river of Sibuco there was an Indian named Ondol; this man and his brother, worse than Moors, were married to several wives; and Ondol was so cruel that he slew whomsoever he chose, without further cause than his own whim. He tried to kill Father Adolfo de Pedrosa, greatly applauded the killing of Father Juan del Campo, and threatened that he would kill Father Combés; but the latter pretended to take no notice of it, and was cautious, and concealed his intentions; and Ondol went on confidently, so that, when he least thought of such a thing, he found himself a prisoner, and was sent to Samboangan where he was received by the Spaniards and by the fathers with great pleasure at seeing removed from the midst [of the mission] so great an obstacle to the Christian faith. His brothel continued to stir up the people, and an armed fleet was sent against him, but without any result; for the noise [of their coming] warned him so that he could avoid the blow, among woods, hills, miry places, and thickets. The escort of the father [i.e., Combés] continued to make arrests, with cunning devices, until they seized fifteen of this man's relatives; and the father sent them to Samboangan. Love for his kindred brought that wild man to the church, to ask mercy from the father. He was admitted to favor, and all the past forgotten, with one condition: that he and all his people, since they were Lutaos, must live under the artillery of the fort, and serve in the [Spanish] armada. With this arrangement that coast remained peaceable, for the insurgents of Siocon had also been seized by craft. Father Combés went to that place, and encountered very heavy seas, not only at entering but on leaving that village; and arguing [from this] that God was not allowing them to go until they interred the bones of the companions of Father Campo, they all lauded on the shore, and searched for the bodies among the thorny thickets. Having interred all of them together, and said a mass for them, the Spaniards placed a cross over the sepulcher; and immediately the weather became calm, so that the caracoas were able to set out. At that time Father Combés carried away a hermit, who, clothed as a woman, strictly observed the law of nature, and professed celibacy. He was called "the Labia of Malandi;" and he was converted to the religion of Christ, in which he lived as a faithful servant.

In La Caldera was introduced the devotion to the blessed souls in purgatory, and suffrages for the deceased, which never had been publicly performed among any Subanos. To render this service more solemn, the musicians were carried thither from Samboangan; and this, joined with the father's exhortations, introduced in their hearts pious solicitude for their dead—so well begun that, in the midst of their native poverty and the dulness of their minds, they carried with them many candles, with rice and other offerings. From that place this holy devotion was gradually communicated through all those villages, following the example of La Caldera—which then was the principal village, in which the minister resided; and to it were annexed Bocot, Malandi, and Baldasan. Besides the above-mentioned cases, others occurred with which the Lord consoled the ministers, in recompense for the misery, hardships, and forlorn condition of those arduous and remote missions.

[Fol. 229 b:] About this time dissoluteness was reigning in these islands, with as unrestrained and despotic dominion as if there were no law superior to it, which could repress it. Fraud in trade and commerce, hatred, falsehood, and malice prevailed everywhere, and without restraint. Above all, sensuality was, so to speak, the prince and master vice; and so general that, unrestricted in time, sex, rank, or age, it kept these regions aflame with an infernal and inextinguishable fire. These crimes were aggravated by the scandalous publicity with which they were committed, almost without punishment; and they had so filled the country with iniquity and abomination that they had to a certain extent corrupted the land itself, filling it with malediction, as Scripture tells us of the time of Noe: Corrupta est autem terra coram Deo, & repleta est iniquitate.22 This provoked the wrath of God so much that in those times were experienced such calamities, wars, misfortunes, earthquakes, deaths, factions, shipwrecks, imprisonments, and so great disturbances, that the citizens themselves, obliged to begin to reflect on these things, believed that the sword of divine indignation was unsheathed among them; and those who with prosperity seemed to be losing their senses came to themselves, as did the prodigal son with his coming to want. They had recourse to the holy Pope, the vicar of Christ on earth; and at his feet, submitting themselves with humble repentances, they explained to him the cause of their affliction. He who then presided over the Church of God was his Holiness Innocent X, who as a benign father despatched an apostolic brief to the archbishop of Manila directing him to absolve all the inhabitants and citizens of these islands from whatever crime or transgression they might have committed, or excommunication that they might have incurred. He sent them his apostolic benediction, and granted a plenary indulgence to those who should worthily prepare to receive it.

On the first day of March, 1654, the archbishop made publication of these favors conferred by the pontiff; and all the people prepared with great fervor to obtain them—so universally that the many confessors of the clergy and the religious orders were hardly sufficient for the numbers who resorted to them; and it was estimated that within the city more than forty thousand persons made their confessions. The result was very excellent, for many confessions were made anew that had been for many years faultily made—either to conceal sins, or for lack of sorrow for them—and of their own accord. Many general confessions were made, and the grace of God was made apparent in the excellent results which were experienced. Restitution was made of honors and property, inveterate hatreds were uprooted, immoral associations of many years' standing were broken up, and occasions for continual stumbling were removed. On the twenty-second day a solemn mass was sung in the cathedral, the blessed sacrament was exposed, and the archbishop preached with the fervor that the case demanded. At twelve o'clock the bells began to ring for prayers in all the churches, the sound of the bells being a fresh awakener of consciences. In the afternoon the archbishop went to the main plaza, where a stage had been erected, of sufficient size, almost, for a court from above; on it was an altar, with a crucifix for devotion, under a canopy. On this stage sat the archbishop, with the ecclesiastical cabildo; and the royal Audiencia were there with their president, the governor and captain-general, also the regidors and the holy religious orders; while there was an innumerable assembly from every sort of nation and people, for whom there was not room in the plaza or in the streets, or on the roofs. The archbishop put on his pontifical robes, and, when the psalms were sung and the usual prayers offered, he publicly uttered the blessing on the land and all its inhabitants in the name of the supreme pontiff; and afterward the Te Deum was intoned, and the chimes were rung by all the bells.

[Our author here relates the beginning of the rebuilding of the cathedral (which had been destroyed in the earthquakes of 1645), and the solemn religious functions which accompany the laying of its cornerstone in 1654; and the formal adoption of St. Francis Xavier as the patron saint of the islands (1653), by action of the secular cabildo of Manila, who bind themselves "to attend the vespers and the feasts of that saint's day in a body, as the municipal council, and to furnish the wax necessary for the feast." He is also chosen as patron saint of all the voyages made to, from, or among the islands. This action is followed by that of the ecclesiastical cabildo (1654) and the archbishop. That saint is chosen because he had preached in Ternate and Mindanao, which belonged to the jurisdiction of the Philippines; in imitation of India, where also he was the patron saint, and where his favor had been experienced by navigators; and "because the glorious saint had shown himself, especially in recent years in this region, very propitious to the voyages of our ships," of which various examples are cited.]

[Fol. 231 b:] The archbishop had seen in the publication of the jubilee the persistence with which the Jesuits labored in the confessional; and desiring to finish gathering in the harvest which the broad field of these environs promised him, if the proper cultivation were applied, in the year 1655 he asked Father Miguel Solana, the provincial of this province, that the "jubilee of the missions" might be published. This was done in the following Lenten season, with so felicitous results that more than twenty thousand certificates of confession were counted which had been issued in our college at Manila. The zeal of the archbishop aided greatly [in this result], for he took part in the procession in which the mission was published, and preached one day in our church.... Extraordinary was the fruit which he gathered that Lent; and confessions were made [for a period] of sixty or eighty years. [Here are related various cases of conversion and edification, in some of which demons appear to the faithful. Governor Diego Faxardo sends workmen to Camboja to build a galleon there, and asks for Jesuits to go with them as chaplains, and to labor for the introduction of the Christian faith into that kingdom; two are sent, one of whom is Father Francisco Mesina, who was then ministering to the Chinese at Santa Cruz. These men build a fine galleon, but it is lost in a storm on the way to Manila; moreover, the galleon "Nuestra Señora del Rosario," in which they had sailed to Camboja, "one of the strongest which had been built in these islands," was wrecked on the shoals of the Me-Khong (or Cambodia) River, before the Spaniards could establish themselves on its shores. These accidents cause the idea of building ships in Camboja to be abandoned.] Although the temporal government of Ternate belonged to the crown of Castilla, and to this government of Philipinas, its spiritual affairs were cared for by the bishop of Malaca; and when that city was conquered by the Dutch, Ternate remained in the care of only one Jesuit and one secular priest for many years. Don Sabiniano Manrique brought to Manila the father and the Portuguese priest, and in their place two fathers from this province were sent, whom the archbishop of Manila constituted his provisors and vicars-general. These fathers preached with great fervor and corresponding results; for many Christians improved their mode of life, and some Moors and heretics of that country, giving up their errors, embraced the true religion. Among all these the ones who excelled in fervor were two young girls, about fourteen years old, who, abandoning their parents (who professed the Moorish faith), came to Ours to be made Christians—with so dauntless resolution that, although their parents followed them in order to take them back to their own village, they could not persuade them to return; and God bestowed such efficacy upon the utterances of these girls that even their parents, illumined by the light of the Highest, determined to follow the same religious faith. Various results of the mercy of God were seen in some persons who, a short time after receiving grace in baptism, ascended to enjoy their reward in glory.

In Siao the king was Don Bentura Pinto de Morales, who, grieving that his island should lack gospel ministers, despatched an embassy to Don Sabiniano Manrique, laying before him the extreme necessity of that island and kingdom, and entreating that he would send thither religious to preach the holy gospel; the zealous governor [accordingly] asked the father provincial, Miguel de Solana, to send two fathers to relieve that need. They were immediately sent, and began their work on so good a footing that in a short time they commenced to gather the fruit that they desired; and, not content to labor with the old Christians, they added to the flock of Christ a great multitude of souls, so that in a few months nearly all the islanders were asking for baptism. The city of Macan had sent to Manila a nobleman named Don Diego Furtado de Mendoza, to regulate the commerce [between the two cities]; and Don Diego Faxardo, perhaps for [well-grounded] suspicions, ordered that he be arrested. But afterward Don Sabiniano sent this envoy back to Macan; and in November of the year 1653 he sent a vessel, and in it Father Magino Sola with the title of ambassador, to establish friendly relations between this and that city, and with other commissions; and they arrived at Macan about March, 1654.

In these times [of which we are writing] many Subanos had come down to Dapitan from some neighboring mountains, and were brought into the fold of Christ. Afterward a chief from Dicayo came down with his people, and was followed by others, from other hamlets; the ministers were greatly consoled at seeing the fruit that was gathered in that district of heathens. At the same time some Moros from the lake of Malanao settled at Yligan, in order to be instructed and to live as Christians in that village; and God deigned to work some marvels, so that they might properly appreciate the Catholic religion. [Some of these are related; then follows a long account of the schemes and perfidious acts of Corralat, and of the murder (December 13, 1655) by his nephew Balatamay of the Jesuits Alexandro Lopez and Juan de Montiel, and the Spanish officer Claudio de Ribera, who were going to Corralat as envoys from Governor Manrique de Lara. All these occurrences have received due attention in previous volumes.]

[Fol. 277:] The archbishop of Manila, Don Miguel Poblete, a pastor zealous for the good of souls, asked the father provincial of the Society to employ some of his men, now that this succor had arrived,23 in a ministry so proper for our Institute as is that of the missions; and some of them accordingly went out to look after the ranches [estancias], where usually live many vagabonds, who, as a result of their idleness and lack of any restraint, commit innumerable sinful and evil acts, and are a people greatly in need of religious instruction. In those places are found some Spaniards, various [sorts of] mestizos, negroes, Cafres, and Indians from all the islands. At the cost of many inconveniences, the ministers gathered a large harvest in the numerous confessions that were made to them, and in many licentious unions which were broken up; and, above all, light was given to those people on what they ought to believe and do in order to secure the eternal salvation of their souls. An old man eighty years of age, whose confessions were almost sacrilegious, was reached by the mission, and, wounded by his conscience, said: "Oh, if Father San Vitores" (whom perhaps he knew by reputation) "were one of the missionaries, how I could get out of this wretched condition in which I am!" And afterward, learning that Father San Vitores was going to that place, this old man cast himself at his feet, and with more tears than words made a general confession, and [thus] was set free from that abominable condition in which he found himself. Afterward the archbishop entreated that the mission should go to the mountain of Maralaya, near the lake of Bay, where a colony of highwaymen and vagrants had been gathered by the desire for freedom and the fear of punishment, secure in their lawless mode of life in the ruggedness of the mountain. The missionaries reached that place, and on the slope of the mountain established their camp, where they remained in the inclemencies of weather until a pavilion was built in which they could say mass, and a wretched hut for their shelter. There, with affection, prayer, and exercises of penance, they were able to persuade those people to come down to hear the word of God; and so efficacious was this that many were induced to return to their own villages, in order to live as Christians. Several women whom those men kept there, who had been separated from their husbands, were restored [to their families]; and among the rest the missionaries employed instruction and teaching. One man had lived in that barbarous community worse than if he were a heathen; and the only indication of his Christian faith that remained to him in so demoralized a condition was his constant devotion to the blessed Virgin—to whom he fasted every Saturday, and whom he urgently entreated that he might not die without the sacraments. That most merciful Lady heard him, for, although he had been ten times in danger of death, she had always set him free with special favor. Now he made his confession with many tears, with the firm resolve to do whatever might be necessary for his eternal salvation.

A mission was conducted in the mountains of Santa Inez of Lanating, a visita of Antipolo. One of the missionaries was the same Father Diego Luis de San Vitores, and in seven days he gathered a very abundant harvest; for in that short time twenty-four thousand heathens, Aetas or Cimarrons, were baptized, and many others were prepared for the rite, who received baptism afterward. [The author describes several of these conversions; he also cites various entries of especial interest from "the books of the old mission of Santa Ines, which I have before me;" many of these are of baptisms made by Father San Vitores. "This mission was cared for by a devout Indian named Don Juan Estevan, who afterward was a donado, and in the absence of the minister instructed and baptized them—as did the Canacopoles, whom St. Xavier chose in India."]

In the year 1669 there was a church and visita in Bosoboso; in 1672 there was a church in Paynaan; and in 1678 was established the church of San Isidro. These two [latter] villages lasted until recent years, when they were included in Bosoboso. Excursions were made into the mountains, and many Aetas, Christian and heathen, were brought out from their hamlets; and with charity and kindness efforts were made to settle them in the said visitas, wherein, in due time, a permanent minister was stationed. It appears from the books of the said visitas and villages that many adults were baptized— of twenty, thirty, forty, and fifty years, and even more; this was a task of the utmost difficulty for the ministers, in drawing those people out of their lairs, and even more in maintaining them in a social and Christian mode of life, on account of their natural inclination to go wandering through the woods and mountains. In the year 1699 the zealous archbishop Don Diego Camacho came to this mission, and baptized several of them—among others, four heathen adults—as appears from the books of Paynaan.

In the year 1665, on the nineteenth of July, there was a violent earthquake in Manila, in which nine persons died; and it inflicted considerable damage in the wing of our college. At this the zealous archbishop arranged that a mission should be held in Manila and Cavite; and through the preaching and example of those engaged therein great results were obtained. In October of the same year, Father Diego Luis de San Vitores and some companions went to the island of Mindoro, then in charge of secular priests. On sea and on land they suffered great fatigues and hunger, heat and storms, toils and dangers; but all this they regarded as [time and strength] well spent, when they saw how the liberal hand of God was rewarding them with the consolation of beholding with their own eyes the fruit of their labors— not only in the old Christians, who had reformed their morals; but in the infidel Manguianes, many of whom were converted to [our] religion. They experienced a thousand tokens of the providence and kindness of God. Although there were several languages in the island, they easily gained a knowledge of what was necessary for instructing the natives, preaching to them, hearing their confessions, and settling their affairs. Sometimes a contrary wind obliged them to put back, directed by the hand of God, in order to relieve the necessity which demanded their coöperation in those hamlets. Sometimes the rivers overflowed their banks, and they found it necessary to travel to places in which they found sufficient occasion for the exercise of their charity. Many conversions of special interest were obtained, of both Christians and heathens; and remarkable among all of them was that of a Manguian woman, a heathen, married to a Christian man. She was baptized, and named Maria; and afterward they called her "the Samaritan," on account of the many persons whom she brought to the knowledge of Christ, the ministers availing themselves of her aid for the conversion of many persons, not only heathens but Christians, with most happy results. Her husband was a Christian by baptism, but worse than a heathen in his life; he would not even accept the rosary of the blessed Virgin, and it was necessary for his wife to put it about his neck by force; and it had so much efficacy that from that time he undertook to be a Christian in his acts, as he was one by name. The fathers erected three churches for the converted Manguianes: the church of our Lady, near Bongabon; that of San Ignacio, near Pola; and that of San Xavier, on the coast of Naojan. Another was built, named for the holy Christ of Burgos, for the old Christians who were roaming about through the mountains.

[The rest of Murillo Velarde's Historia is mainly occupied with the history of the Spanish conquest of the Marianas Islands, and the missions of the Jesuit order therein; also with the Pardo controversy and various other matters which have been already treated in this series, besides the lives of Jesuits in the Philippines—which here, as throughout our series, we have presented only in very brief and condensed form; but which in these religious histories are often exceedingly detailed and prolix. We present a few more extracts from our writer, showing the distinctive occupations, methods, and achievements of the Jesuit missionaries there, and events affecting those missions.]

[Fol. 346 b:] These and other acts of violence [i.e., connected with the Pardo controversy] which in that time were suffered by this province of Philipinas are evident from the printed memorial which was presented to the king by Father Antonio Xaramillo, procurator of this province in Madrid, and a witness of most of the things which are contained in the said memorial. He concludes this document by offering, at the order of our general, the reverend Father Tyrso Gonzalez, our resignation of all the ministries which the Society possesses in these islands, in order thus to remove the cause of disturbances, jealousies, and controversies. But so far was the king from accepting this resignation that instead he issued his royal decrees that the doctrinas of Cainta and Jesus de la Peña (or Mariquina), of which the Society had been despoiled, should be restored to it. In the year 1696, not only did the very reverend Augustinian fathers surrender these posts, with politeness and courtesy, but in token of mutual affection and friendly relations an exchange was made of the ministry of San Matheo (which is near Mariquina), the fathers of St. Augustine ceding it to us for that of Binangonan (which is called "de los Perros" [i.e., "of the dogs"]), on the lake of Bay, which belonged to the Society; [this was done] by another exchange, made with the religious of St. Francis, to whom we gave the ministry of Baras on the same lake. The sentences of examination and review given by the royal and supreme Council of the Indias; the royal executory decree, which in consequence of these was issued in regard to Jesus de la Peña, on March 31, 1694; and the decrees which on the same day were despatched, as regards Cainta, to the governor and the archbishop of these islands: all these are in the archives of our college at Manila.... I have seen the original of a report made to the king about that time, by a person of great ability, in which he endeavored, with acrimonious expressions, to influence the royal mind against the Society; but the exaggerative and fierce asperity of the report was itself the most efficacious argument in favor of this province, and was entirely rejected by the king and his Council, as prejudiced (a just and deserved punishment). The king not only insisted that this province should continue in its ministries without any change, but restored to it the two of which it had been despoiled by animosity allied with violence. Thus this apostolic province went its way, following the apostle among thorns and roses, among persecutions and favors, per infamiam, & bonam famam.24

In order to justify the manner in which the Society administers its functions in these islands, I will give a brief account of the allotment [distribuçión; i.e., of the minister's duties] which is followed in the villages, in order that the impartial reader, reflecting thereon prudently and carefully, may recognize the incessant and laborious toil with which this field, entrusted to the Society by the confidence of that prince, is cultivated. Every day the boys and girls (with little difference [in number]) up to the age of fourteen years hear mass; these call themselves "schools" and "companies of the rosary." Then they sing all the prayers that belong to the mass, and go to their school. At ten o'clock the signal is given by the bell, and they go to the church to pray before the blessed sacrament, and to the Virgin they recite the Salve and the Alabado hymn; and they go out in procession, singing the prayers, as far as some cross in the village. At two o'clock in the afternoon they return to the school; and at four or five o'clock they go again to the church, where they recite the rosary, and go out in procession singing the prayers. On Saturdays, not only the children recite the prayers, but the baguntaos and dalagas25—who are the older youths and girls, who do not yet pay tribute—and also the acolytes, the treble singers, and the barbatecas. In the afternoon the people recite the rosary, and the singers and musicians sing the mysteries and the litany. On Sundays, the boys go out with a banner around the village, singing the prayers, to call together the people. The minister says mass, which the musicians accompany with voices and instruments; and afterward all the people together recite the prayers, and [answer] a brief questioning on the principal mysteries of the Christian doctrine, and [listen to] an instruction on the mode of baptism, which is called tocsohan. With this there are many of them who are well instructed, so that they can aid one to die well, and in case of necessity confer baptism, like the Canacapoles of St. Xavier. The minister preaches a moral sermon, and usually calls the roll [suele leer el padron], in order to see whether the Indians fail to attend mass. In the afternoon all come together—schools, companies of the rosary, acolytes, singing children, barbatecas, and dalagas and baguntaos—and they offer prayers. Afterward the father goes down to the church, and catechises, explains the Christian doctrine, and confers baptism. On Thursdays there is no school, that being a vacation day. Every Saturday there is a mass sung in honor of the Virgin; and in the afternoon the minister chants the Salve for the occasion, with the image uncovered, which is then locked up. During the nine days preceding Christmas, mass is sung very early in the morning, with great solemnity, before a large assembly of people, and accompanied by an indulgence [granted] for the preservation of the Christian religion in these islands; and these are called "masses for Christmas" [misas de Aguinaldo].26 Always, when the host is elevated at mass the signal is given with a bell, so that all the people may adore it; and the Indiana, even the little children who cannot speak, clasp their hands and raise them toward heaven as a token of adoration, while in the church a motet is sung for the same purpose, after the custom of the primitive Church—which this body of Christians resembles in many ways; and St. John in his Apocalypse even represents it to us in those mysterious creatures who day and night were praising God, dicentia: Sanctus, Sanctus, Sanctus, Dominus Deus Omnipotens, qui erat, qui est, & qui venturus est.27 The Indians in general have the highest respect and esteem for the priests. As soon as they see the fathers, they rise to their feet, take off their hats,28 kiss the father's hand, and often fall on their knees to speak to him, especially if they are going to ask forgiveness for some offense that they have committed; they patiently endure the penances that the ministers appoint for them, and promptly obey whatever the fathers command them. Even the little children who cannot speak run when they see the father in the street, fall on their knees, and kiss his hand; and then go back greatly pleased at this. At every function which pertains to the church, all the people, from the greatest to the least, work with gladness in building altars and adorning the temples. The house-servants offer their prayers in the morning; and they write, read, and perform their duties after they have heard mass. At night they read a spiritual lesson, recite the rosary, and before retiring pray before the blessed sacrament and sing the Salve to the Virgin; and during the year they frequent the sacraments.

In each of our villages there is a "Congregation of the Blessed Virgin," which enjoys many indulgences and favors; its members display great fervor, attend regularly, and perform many exercises of devotion and charity, especially on Saturdays. The women of the congregation sweep the church very early, adorn the images, place roses and other flowers on the altars, and carry about pans of coals with perfumes. The minister recites the litany before the image, and the members of the congregation say the responses; and afterwards he makes an address to them; or a book of devotion, or the rules, or the indulgences, are read aloud; or the list of saints for the month is announced, according to their proper place on the calendar. There are some persons who frequent the sacraments during the year, confessing and receiving communion on the most solemn days of the year, especially on the feast-days of the Virgin, and before a marriage is solemnized; and it is a custom often practiced among the Indians to confess and receive communion on one's saint's day. In the afternoon those who have received communion go to the church for a short season of prayer. When the women approach the time of childbirth, they confess and receive communion, and remain in the village. Thus an Indian hardly ever dies without the sacraments, except by some sudden fatal accident; for at the instance of the ministers the people are instructed to summon the father as soon as any one becomes dangerously ill. Many Indians hear mass every day; recite the rosary in concert in their houses, on the streets, and while they are sailing; say the litanies, and sing with most delightful harmony the Salve, the praises of God and of His mother resounding in every direction. They offer to the Church the first-fruits of their products; and carry the images, the shrouds, and other things to bless the seed-sowing. After childbirth, they offer the infants to the Virgin on Saturday, and receive the benediction. They order masses to be said for the souls in purgatory, and present candles and other offerings to the Virgin and the saints. They furnish light at mass with lighted tapers, give food to the poor on Holy Thursday, and make other contributions according to their means. They make pilgrimages to the most notable sanctuaries, and offer their vows there; they read spiritual books, and practice other devotions. When they bring the little angels [i.e., their infants] for burial, they dress and adorn the bodies neatly with birds' wings, palm-leaves, wreaths, flowers, and lights, even when the parents are very poor; for the rest of the people aid them, so that they may bring the dead with the decency and solemnity which the ritual requires. The burials of adults are attended by all the people, all clothed in mourning from the headman to the constable; and even though the dead person be from some other village, or some wretched unknown creature who died there, the body is escorted by the people of the village and the singers, in very charitable and edifying fashion. Those who are most eminent in all this are the members of the congregation, by whose zeal and pious customs the Christian religion is preserved and promoted in these islands. They are the select of the select, like the soldiers of Gideon; and may be called the religious among the Indians. The functions of Holy Week, the principal feast-days, and the processions are carried out with great solemnity and pomp. In their houses the people erect little altars, which they adorn with various prints and images; on their arms they depict crosses, and almost all wear rosaries about their necks; when the blessed sacrament is exposed, they escort it, and take their turn in assisting in the church with many lights. In the processions of Holy Week there are many bloody flagellations [disciplinas de sangre], and other most severe penances. In Lent there are, on three days, the Miserere and scourging; but this has fallen into disuse, and in various places is little more than a ceremony. In every village there is a musical choir, of both instruments and voices, by means of which the festival and solemn days, and divine worship, are at least decently celebrated; and in some places there are excellent instruments and voices. Moreover, all these singers understand harmony [solfa], a thing which has not its like in all Christendom. Every Saturday and Sunday, prime is sung in the choir. The Lenten stations and services, those for the dead, and others during the year, cause devotion and tender feelings through the skill and good order with which they are conducted. The Indians use holy water in their houses, and show great devotion to the holy cross, which they set up in their houses, on the roads, and in their grain-fields. The adornment of the churches— reredos, images, furnishings of silver, lamps, ornaments—the multitude of lights, and the magnificence of the edifices, are so extraordinary that no one would believe that in this remote corner of the world religion could exist with such splendor, or Christianity be so well established,29 or divine worship conducted with such magnificence. The zeal of the ministers has secured these results, by their activity, piety, and kind treatment of the natives; but no little is accomplished by the sharp spur,30 managed with discretion, qui parcit virgæ, odit filium. The harvest in this field is like that which the parable represents; there is the greatest and the least, just as it is throughout the universe. There is fertile ground and sterile; there are untilled and stony tracts; some land is productive, and some is full of bramble-patches. But what soil is free from darnel and tares?31 Where are lilies found without having nettles near them? In what garden do the roses, magnificent and fragrant, surpass [the other flowers], without the thorns that surround them? He who is always declaiming, in either a gloomy or a careless spirit, against the faith and Christian spirit of the Indians, shows great ignorance of the world, if not levity or malice. If he would but reflect that not many years ago this was a land overgrown with the thorns and brambles of ignorance, unbelief, and barbarism, he would give a thousand thanks to the Lord at the sight of so much fruit obtained for heaven; and still more [thankful would he be] if he cast his glance on Japon, India, and Africa, and on Grecia, Inglaterra, Dinamarca, and other kingdoms where the Christian religion was [once] so flourishing, but which today are an abyss of follies and errors—the cause, alas! being their ignorance or their perverseness.... Whoever will read the Instructions of St. Francis Xavier for the missionaries of India and also this account of their allotted tasks [esta distribución], will plainly see that their labors are the punctual execution of those instructions. What greater praise [than this] can be given them? To this should be added the standing of the ministers. Those who are ministering in the native villages are the men who have been masters of theology, and famous preachers, and officials of the order, and even provincials; and other members who, on account of their abilities, have merited repeated applause. The same is true in the other religious orders; as a result, there is not in all the Indias a field of Christian labor that is better cultivated; and I may add that there is no Christian church in the world that has ministers with higher qualifications, or more who have received academic degrees. And some of them there are who, rejecting the comforts of Europe, remain contented in the poverty here.

[Fol. 350 b:] In the year 1696 the very religious province of St. Augustine surrendered the village of San Matheo to the Society, in virtue of a certain exchange; we gladly accepted it, in order to bring in the Aetas who are in the mountains of that region, to live as a Christian community in the village; for, Christians and heathens being mingled in those woods and little hamlets, there was little difference between them in their customs. Here I will bring together the facts pertaining to this ministry, since it is matter belonging to this history for the connection of events. In the year 1699, the convent of San Agustin in Manila made claim to a ranch in this district, on the ground that Governor Santiago de Vera had granted to the said convent two limekilns for the erection of its building. The Indians, on account of the crude notions which they form of things, began to call the limekilns "the ranch;" and this blunder was so prevalent that in some grants which the governors made afterward in that territory they say that the lands "border upon the ranch of San Agustin." In the said year an investigation was made, and all that could be drawn from the declarations of the Indians was this confused notion of a "ranch," which they had heard from their elders, without being able to specify boundaries, or locations, or landmarks. And as there was no other title or grant than this very uncertain information, the judge of land [claims], Don Juan de Ozaeta, auditor of the royal Audiencia, rejecting their claim for lack of authentic documents, was unable to grant to that convent the ranch which it demanded.

In the year 1713 the minister of that village was Father Juan Echazabal, whose scrupulous conscience, added to his natural disposition, made him so inexorable a guardian of the injunction to hear mass that in this point he very seldom excused [an offender] from penance. So active was his zeal that he spared neither labor nor diligence to secure the attendance of the Indians at the holy sacrifice of the mass, at the sermons, and at the other church functions; and he cheerfully endured the inconvenience of waiting for them a long time, in order that their natural slothfulness might not have this excuse. His persistence secured considerable results, notwithstanding that wild grapevines were not lacking even in the midst of so much cultivation. But what assiduity does not the obstinate perversity of men frustrate? An insolent Indian, Captain Pambila, at various times provoked the forbearance of the minister by his shameless conduct; for, purposely staying away from mass, and glorying in this wrong-doing, he boasted among his friends that the father would not dare to rebuke him. The minister endeavored by various means to bring him to reason, but all his efforts proved unsuccessful; and the audacity of this Indian kept continually increasing, continually launching him into new transgressions on top of the old ones—and scandal arising, because some persons were following in his footsteps and others were inclined to do so. In order to check the evil consequences of this, Father Echazabal gave information of the whole matter to the governor, Conde de Lizarraga, who sent thither Captain Don Lorenzo de Yturriaga with twelve soldiers. But Pambila was by this time so bold that when they went to arrest him he went out to meet them with his cutlass, and dealt a blow at the captain; the latter parried the blow, and firing a pistol, killed the bold man. At this occurrence the malcontents were greatly disquieted, and had recourse to the vice-patron, asking that he remove Father Echazabal from that ministry; and they even made the further demand that it be restored to the Augustinian fathers. In order to push their claim, they revived the old [one of the] "ranch"—this time in clearer language, for they indicated locations and boundaries. But, as all these were arbitrary, the measures [of distance] did not correspond [to the facts]; for while it was one site for a ranch that they claimed, there were three or four such sites that were included in the places that they had arbitrarily marked out. Nevertheless, this claim was promoted, so that the convent of San Agustin obtained a favorable decision from the royal Audiencia. But Father Echazabal opposed this, together with the greater part of the people of the village, as did also Father Agustin

Soler, procurator of the college of San Ignacio at Manila, on account of the damage that would ensue to them respectively. The Audiencia, having examined their arguments, reversed its decision—although, through shame at so speedy a reversal, the auditors set down in the decree that possession should be given to the convent of San Pablo [of that] in which there was no dispute. This sentence on review ended the controversy, and matters remained as they were before. To pacify the Indians, the superiors removed Father Echazabal from that place, and everything was quiet for the time— although after many years the old [question of the] "ranch" was revived, with greater energy, as we shall see in due time. Let us proceed to more pleasing matters.

In the year 1705, Father Juan Echazabal began to promote, in the village of San Matheo, the devotion to our Lady of Aranzazu; and the devotion to and adoration of that Lady steadily increased, with the encouragement of the Vizcayans, and especially of Don Juan Antonio Cortes. This incited the minister to undertake the building of a stone church, in order to provide a more suitable abode for the blessed sacrament and for the sovereign Queen. Through the persistence and energy of the father and the contributions of the faithful, a beautiful, substantial, and spacious church was completed, with its transept and handsome gilded reredos. The new church was dedicated in the year 1716, the minister being Father Juan Pedro Confalonier. There was a very large concourse of people, and the devotees of the blessed Virgin of Aranzazu made extraordinary demonstrations of joy and devotion in celebrating her feast; and great was the satisfaction of those who with their contributions had aided [to provide] the costly building and adorn it with ornaments and rich furnishings of silver—especially the illustrious benefactor of that church and village, General Don Juan Antonio Cortes. And the Society, with the pleasure of dedicating to God and to His blessed mother this new temple, forgot the great sorrows that they suffered at that time from various defamatory libels, in which malignity repeated what had so many times been condemned, and was anew condemned, as calumny— their author being, most deservedly but impiously, his own executioner, at seeing that the arrows discharged by audacity against the Society were changed into crowns of triumph.

[Fol. 358 b:] [Our author relates the history of the beaterio connected with the Jesuit college at Manila. It began in 1684, with the decision of a mestiza woman of Binondoc to live the religious life; her name was Ignacia del Espiritu Santo, and she began under the direction of Father Paul Clain. Her fame for piety and devout penances grew apace, and attracted to her many Indian girls and mestiza women, until they numbered thirty-three. For some time they lived in the utmost poverty, which, with their severe penances and lack of sleep, "made almost all of the beatas fall ill." Soon, however, charitable offerings were made to them, enough to support them when added to what they earned with their needles. Their spiritual directors are Jesuits, whose church they attend, and who form them into a religious community ("commonly known as 'the beatas of the Society'"), with rules and employment prescribed for their living. At the time of Murillo Velarde's writing (1749), "there are, besides the beatas, some Spanish girls who are being trained there as their wards, and are learning sewing and other accomplishments, besides a Christian manner of life and the habit of attending the sacraments. There are now fifty regular beatas, thirteen novices, thirty women (who are Indians) who are kept under restraint, twenty Spanish girls under training, and four negro women. Every year some Spanish women, and many Indian and mestiza women, go into retreat there, in order to perform the 'spiritual exercises' of St. Ignatius, from which result much profit to themselves and much benefit to their respective villages. What has always aroused my admiration is, that although these women are so many in number, and all Indians or mestizas, and ruled by themselves, yet in more than sixty years they have not given any occasion for gossip in the city; rather, they have given it the utmost edification by their devotion, humility, application to labor, and assiduity in the spiritual exercises." Mother Ignacia dies on September 10, 1748; our author pays an admiring tribute to her ability, virtues, and piety—among other things, praising her because "she conquered, with most unusual perseverance, three kinds of sloth which are very arduous and difficult [to overcome]: that natural to the country, that inborn in her sex, and that which is congenital to this nation in its inmost being."]32

1 From Murillo Velarde's account of his order in the Philippines we extract such matter as describes their missions, their general labors in Manila for both Spaniards and natives, their methods of work, and some occurrences of special importance to them as an order. The "edifying instances," and biographies of the Jesuit fathers, and other devotional reading it is necessary to omit here, as our limited space forbids its presentation.

2 The papal concession for this jubilee of fifteen days had come that summer, and had been announced on November 18, just before the appearance of the comets.

3 The word Moreno is used by the earlier writers rather confusedly, and applied to more than one race, whether pure or mixed; but in later times it apparently refers chiefly

to the swarthy-complexioned people from the Malabar coast and to their descendants.

4 The Tagálog word for "bridge."

5 Spanish, sermones de tabla. The tabla is the list kept in the church sacristy which designates on what days certain functions are to be held; it is the tabella of the Italian sacristies, the church calendar of ours. Cathedrals and even lower grade churches (as collegiates, nunneries, hospitals, etc.) had their sermons (d'occasion, as the French say) on certain set days as marked in their local calendars, or tablas; these were always very grand, and delivered by renowned preachers and orators; many of these I have heard.

The phrase "endowed feast" (fiesta dotada) is used also in Italian and French. It was a custom, which I presume still holds, in all those countries (as I often saw in Italy), that a municipality, society, confraternity, or indeed any body of persons, had its feasts on set days in the year—for instance, feasts of their patron saints, or of thanksgiving, etc. Fairs also were endowed; that is, bequests (perhaps centuries old) provided that on set days the people were to have a fiesta, with music, fireworks, games, sermons, etc., with an alms for the poor—all paid for, as also would be the premiums for the fairs. These were occurrences always of great festivity and merriment; and in Italy, at least in the part where I lived, the smallest towns and hamlets had their fiestas dotadas.— Rev. T. C. Middleton, O.S.A.

6 The Exercitia spiritualia of Inigo de Loyola, founder of the Jesuit order; it has long been a text-book therein, and a manual of devotion for persons under direction of the Jesuits. See account of the examination of conscience prescribed in it, in Jesuit Relations (Cleveland reissue), lxviii, p. 326.

"In Europe it is customary for persons at particular seasons to retire for a time from the world, to give themselves up entirely to prayer and meditation. Some part of the season of Lent is generally selected for this purpose; and many, for the sake of more entire seclusion, take up their residence during this time in some religious house. This is called 'going into retreat.'"—Kip's Jesuits in America, p. 302.

7 That is, "headland of Bondoc" (or Bondog); a mountain 1,250 feet high, at the southern end of the peninsula of Tayabas, Luzón. (U. S. Gazetteer of Philippines, p. 397.)

8 Marinduque is an island off the coast of Tayabas province, Luzón; it is round in shape, about twenty-three miles in diameter, and has a population (Tagálog) of about 48,000. It has some good harbors; and it produces abundance of rice, cocoanuts, and abacá. (U. S. Gazetteer of Philippines, pp. 643–647.)

9 Theriacs were held in great estimation during the middle ages. They were composed of opium flavored with nutmeg, cardamom, cinnamon, and mace—or merely with saffron and ambergris.

10 Aornis (or Aornos), a lofty rock in India, taken by Alexander the Great; thus named, as being so high as to be inaccessible even to birds.

11 That is, as alternate or substitute for Encinas, in case of the latter's disability or death.

12 Interesting information about Lake Lanao is given in the following letter from the Jesuit Juan Heras to his superior, dated at Tagoloan, October 6, 1890; it is printed in Cartas de los PP. de la Compañía de Jesús, cuad. ix (Manila, 1891), pp. 254, 255.

"Desiring to furnish to your Reverence as accurate information as possible regarding the lake of Malanao, we sent again for some men who lived there many years as slaves. They are an intelligent family. The father is a Tagálog, captured when he was a mere youth; he was carried to the Lake, and later married a girl, also a Tagálog who had been enslaved. They had three children, and when one of these was ten years old and another one somewhat older, they made their escape, in the year 74. The father and mother lived at the Lake more than twenty years; they settled in Jasaán, and lived there very happily after their children had been baptised. The father has traveled entirely around the lake by the highroad, and the second son had gone half-way round, from the northeastern end to Ganasi. The information, then, which they had given us—precisely the same both tunes, for they had been questioned previously, last March—is as follows:

"The length of the lake from north to south—or from the mouth of the Agus River (which empties near Iligan), to Ganasi, the point of departure for Lalabúan, which is on Illana Bay—is 24 hours of straight sailing, with steady rowing and the wind astern. The breadth from east to west is half the length. It has many promontories, which form large curves [in the coast]; and the shore is steep and rocky at Lúgud and Tugua, at which points vessels cannot find anchor. The lake contains four islets. A good highroad runs around the lake, which is interrupted only near Taraca, by the extensive mud flats which form the rice-lands (or *basacanes*). Taraca is the principal town, and the sultan lives there. The places which are noted as villages [*i.e.*, on an accompanying map?] are not really such, but are the jurisdictions of the dattos. The settlement is one continuous street, with houses on both sides of the highroad almost all the way round the lake.

"The population is a large one, as several married couples live in the same house, and there are many dwellings. The people who have the reputation of being the bravest are those of Unayan, Bundayan, Ganasi, and Marántao. From Ganasi the highroad goes toward Lalabúan; it has no steep ascents or descents, nor does it cross large rivers; and by following this road Lalabúan is reached in one day. Halfway on this journey is the village of Limudigan, the sultan of Poalas, the richest of all those in the Lake region. Our informants state that the cannon are kept in Ganasi, in a large shed, to a considerable number. The places where the people have most guns are Maraui and Marántao; the number of firearms cannot be exactly stated, although these men say three are many of them. From Maraui one can go to Ganasi in three days, by taking the road to the right, and in four days by going to the left; it therefore takes seven days to make the trip around the lake—but the circuit of the lake is probably somewhat exaggerated. It is said that those people have many mosques. Maraui is on the Agus River, quite near the lake; these men say that there are many horses there. As to the exactness of these data, it is evident that we cannot be altogether certain; but it is certain that each of our informants has confirmed the other's statements."

In the same volume of *Cartas* is a valuable appendix by Father Pablo Pastells, in which he sets forth the importance of the plan formed by General Valeriano Weyler (governor of the islands during 1889–91) for completing the subjugation of Mindanao to the Spanish crown, and presents a brief historical sketch of the Spanish conquests in that island, and an account of conditions therein and of the natural resources of the country. He argues that the forcible expulsion of all its

Mahometan tribes would be impossible, and that the proper way to hispanicize Mindanao must be the slow one—but sure, if the results of the labors of Jesuit missionaries among the Moros be considered—of education, the introduction of civilized modes of life (especially by the cultivation of the soil), a political organization like that already in vogue among the Tagálogs and other christianized peoples, the influence of the Christian religion in displacing their superstitious and false beliefs, governmental protection to the peaceable natives, and the promotion of migration of Filipinos from the northern islands to Mindanao, thus gradually colonizing the latter with industrious, civilized, and Christian inhabitants. Statistics are added to Father Pastells's memorial, showing that the (Jesuit) missions of Mindanao contain (in 1892) a total Christian population of 191,493 souls; this number he compares with the list given by Murillo Velarde (1748; including all the missions of the Jesuits in Filipinas), which foots up to 209,527 souls. At the end of the *Cartas* is a map (dated March 19, 1892) of the "second and fifth districts"— *i.e.*, those of Cagayán de Misamis and Cottabato—on a scale of ten kilometers to an inch; it contains the latest geographic data up to 1892, and is especially full in the Lanao region and the course of the Pulangi River or Rio Grande, the headwaters of that great river almost interlocking with those of the Cagayán and another large stream which empties into Macajalar Bay. The map also shows the native tribes that occupy the region which it depicts.

13 Gabe or gabi is the native name (Tagal, Visayan, and Pampango) for the roots of Caladium esculentum (also known as Colocasia antiquorum), which are used considerably as food. This plant is frequently cultivated in the United States for its foliage, and is popularly called "elephant's ears," from the shape of the leaves.

14 A bay or inlet at the southwest angle of Iligan Bay, extending 12 miles southwest, its inmost point lying but 13 miles from the northern extremity of Illana Bay, which is on the south side of Mindanao. The fort here mentioned must have been at the mouth of Lintogut River.

15 Spanish, tierra de S. Pablo; but no information is available for its identification.

16 One of the very rare allusions to this mode of conducting commerce, as used among the Moros, which—although common enough in all parts of the world from very early times, and practiced by most peoples who have risen beyond the savage condition—seems to have been even to the present time undeveloped among the Moros, partly on account of their fierce natures and the feuds among them, partly because of their habits of piracy, plunder, and bloodshed. Of especial interest in this connection is the account published in the New York Outlook, December 23, 1905, of the "Moro Exchange" established at Zamboanga, Mindanao (July, 1904), by Captain John P. Finley, governor of Zamboanga district. Intended from the outset to replace slavery and piracy by honest labor, it has gradually gained the respect and coöperation of the Moro chiefs; and by taking advantage of their talent for trade is exerting a wide and strong influence in the development of industry and peaceful relations among them. This exchange even in its first year had a volume of business amounting to $128,000; and now its daily transactions run from 500 to 800 pesos, while in the Zamboanga district it has fourteen branches.

17 Spanish, al reir del alba, literally, "at the smile of the dawn."

18 Limbo (from Latin, limbus): in scholastic theology, a region bordering on hell, where souls were detained for a time; hence, applied to any place of restraint or confinement.

19 The lists of Augustinian friars in the Philippines record the names of some thirty members of that order who became insane or demented; and probably similar lists could be given by the other orders. Perez's Catálogo (Manila, 1901), and Gaspar Cano's Catálogo (Manila, 1864) present biographical information regarding all the members of the order who labored in the islands from 1565 down to their respective dates of publication; Pérez enumerates 2,467 for the term of 336 years from 1565 to 1901, and of these 1,992 belong to Cano's period, ending in 1864. Cano names thirty friars (two of them being lay brothers) who died in a demented condition; the first of these was Fray Francisco de Canga Rodriguez (1616), who was 55 years professed. Pérez mentions but twenty-seven of Cano's list, but adds four others for the years following Cano's record (1865–1901), a total of thirty-one names. Both these compilers record the facts of dementia among the friars in varied phrases;

and Cano speaks (p. 20) of "the many things which there are in Filipinas to cause the loss of one's mind." Zúñiga, in his Estadismo, refers to the liability of the missionaries in the islands to suffer mental alienation from homesickness, solitude, and lack of congenial companions, especially in districts where the natives were of low intellectual calibre. When I was a student in Rome, Pope Pius IX had a college (the Pio Latino) opened for Spanish Americans (from Mexico and South America); this was about 1860. The Italians said that the young students from those countries seemed to be especially given to excessive homesickness (nostalgia).—Rev. T. C. Middleton, O.S.A.

20 That is, "Go ye into the whole world, and preach the gospel to every creature" (Mark xvi, v. 15).

21 Thus characterized, because this long account of the hardships and dangers of missionary life is inserted in the midst of a sketch of Father Francisco Paliola, martyred in Mindanao in 1648.

22 "And the earth was corrupted before God, and was filled with iniquity" (Genesis 6, v. 11).

23 The Jesuit Diego Luis de San Vitores had just arrived (July, 1662) in Luzón with fourteen companions, in a patache, sent from Acapulco by Conde de Baños, viceroy of Mexico.

24 "Through evil report and good report" (II Corinthians vi, v. 8).

25 Tagálog words, meaning young men and girls of marriageable age. Barbateca does not appear in the standard lexicons.

26 See note on the masses, in VOL. XXXIX, p. 246, note 148.

27 "Saying: 'Holy, holy, holy, Lord God Almighty, who wast, who art, and who art to come.'"

28 After citing numerous examples from the customs of various nations, Herbert Spencer concludes—Ceremonial Institutions (New York, 1880), pp. 128–131: "It seems that removal of the hat among European peoples, often reduced among ourselves to touching the hat, is a remnant of that process of unclothing himself by which, in early times, the captive expressed the yielding up of all that he had."

29 The provincial of the Society of Jesus in the Filipinas Islands, in a report to the king dated June 20, 1731, declares that the Society reckoned 173,938 souls in the 88 principal villages and some visitas which they were administering. This number, compared with the estimate for the preceding period of six years, showed an increase of 11,886 Christians; by this may be seen the increase which the population is steadily gaining—except that of the Marianas Islands, which has decreased. (Ventura del Arco MSS., iv, p. 307.)

30 Spanish, azicate; "a long-necked Moorish spur with a rowel at the end of it" (Appleton's Velázquez's Dictionary). The Latin quotation means, "He who spares the rod hates his son."

31 Spanish, lolios y zizañas. Lolio is an old form of joyo; and both joyo and zizaña (modern, cizaña) refer, according to Appleton's Velázquez's Dictionary, to the common darnel, or Lolium temulentum.

32 Spanish, la inata del Pays, la conatural al sexo, y la congenita entrañada en la Nacion.

CONDITION OF THE ISLANDS, 1701

Remonstrance addressed to the governor and captain-general1 of the Filipinas Islands, on October 7, 1701, by the provincials of the religious orders, in regard to the wrongs and abuses that are committed in the said islands.

The Christian desire so proper to our obligation of attending to the preservation of the holy faith, in all the places and persons in which by the goodness of our Lord it is found already established, and to its propagation and extension in the persons and places (which are many) that have not been reached by the light of the holy gospel; and the strict religious observance of our profession, which at least for charity's sake constrains and obliges us to endeavor by all means that injustice and oppression shall not be suffered by any of the Indian natives of these islands—the spiritual administration and instruction of whom has been placed in our guidance and care by both Majesties, the divine and the human, entrusting, to the zeal that we are under obligation to exercise, not only the steadfastness in the faith and the good morals of all the natives who have been already conquered and brought back to the bosom of the holy Church, but also the promotion of new reductions and conversions: these are the motives, truly lofty ones, which impel us to set forth plainly to your Lordship the causes (of the utmost importance and gravity, and everywhere at work) which are producing lamentable effects in impairing the Christian native population, inflicting on them violence and injustice, and almost closing the door on that most desirable expectation of new conversions, and of the general relief for so many poor vassals [of the Spanish crown] who, as if they were fugitives from these islands, are engaged in foreign provinces with grief and almost ruin to their souls, among the infidelity of the heretics and the barbarous nations—whither are going, as from their own countries, their wives and their children, leaving only the memory of and pity for them.

The objects of this memorial are two: first, the honor and glory of our Lord, and the exaltation and increase of His holy faith; and second, the hope that the Christian zeal of your Lordship will, by all the proper means that will present themselves to your great intellect, furnish effective control of evils so serious and so general, and cause them to cease—so that the Christian faith and justice may again flourish, the people who formerly possessed these islands renew their abundance of population, and the increase of our faith continue its progress, with the reduction of the infidels. With especial reason [may we expect this], when the remedy for all the evils which are stated in this memorial is [already] provided by the Catholic and pious laws contained in the "Recopilacion de las Yndias;" and if perchance they omit the medicine for some of the said evils, that is likewise anticipated and provided by the decisions of the Councils for Mexico and Lima, confirmed by the holy Apostolic See, and inviolably observed in these islands.

It is taken for granted, Sir, as a maxim which experience has shown to be infallible in all America, that the means for the preservation and extension of the Catholic faith are the same as were employed for its first introduction, which was most prosperous because the ardent zeal of the gospel ministers was united with the power and arms of his Majesty (whom may God preserve), by which the progress of the faith was assured. [On this ground] it is very evident that in these regions it is not possible to improve, or even to preserve, the peoples who are already conquered and reduced, because no attention has been paid to maintaining the military posts, or building any new fortifications; on the other hand, in some places and provinces even the little forts that they possessed have been entirely removed, and in others the number of officers and soldiers designated for their defense from any hostile invasion has been diminished. The effect of this retrenchment, and of not reëstablishing the old military posts with the number of soldiers that is judged necessary, and with the military and food supplies which necessity and natural law prescribed for a suitable defense, is the reason why great destruction and losses from infidels and apostates are suffered and lamented. This has been experienced in the provinces of Cagayan and Zambales, as it appears, for the lack of the arms and defenses which in former times were sufficient for the defense of the faithful converts, and for attacking the hostile infidels—and even for chastising sometimes their wicked acts, as the rigor of justice demands. Today the converted Indians and other vassals of your Majesty are exposed to the dangers of fire and death and captivity which have been experienced in these past years, nor have our people had any other way [of escape] than to contract for the payment of a certain amount of tribute every year to the hostile Indians—an agreement in every way unbecoming and injurious to the reputation and credit of his Majesty's arms, so entrusted [to our Spaniards] by his royal self. There is this same lack of arms and supplies in the provinces and military posts of Yloilo, Cebu, Caraga, Calamianes, Yligan, and other forts; and from this the only benefit that can result is the very small one that his Majesty will save the expenses of reëstablishing posts and paying soldiers, and put a stop to another evil (likewise a small one), which is the losses occasioned to the poor by the idleness and license of the soldiers—but if this had to be attended to, there would be an end to all the military posts and garrisons which are maintained for the general welfare, the protection of the vassals, and the warfare (offensive and defensive) which natural law permits. Moreover, it is an obligation [and] characteristic of princes that they do not seek or desire the trifling evil mentioned, and as little the advantage of avoiding some expense—which cannot be done without violating that same royal obligation, especially when hitherto in all these islands there have been military posts and the necessary forces, not only in the interior of the country but also on its coasts.

From this grievous neglect it results that it is impossible for us to carry out our desire for the new conversions and reductions so earnestly charged by his Majesty; for if at present even our own preservation is difficult, how can any new conquest be easy? or how can it be right for our zeal to consider the acquisition of new Christian communities while leaving those that are now in our charge exposed to every invasion by the enemy and to total ruin? One thing that has contributed greatly to this wretched state of affairs is, that the expeditions for converting infidels and conquering apostates have ceased which in other days were made by the orders of your Lordship's predecessors, in accordance with the royal laws, after having consulted the royal court of justice—in whose decisions the hopes that were entertained of the great usefulness of those expeditions were not mocked. It seems as if that experience would incline [the government] to renew the said expeditions, which for some time have been neglected; and in this very island there is so great a number of infidels, who are confirmed in their very infidelity and iniquity because they know that there is never any effort to subdue and conquer them, just as if his Majesty (whom may God preserve) had not the right to do so.

From these deficiencies grievous results have followed, in depopulating the islands, which at present lack their former abundance of the peoples and sources of wealth that are native to them. Confirmation and proof of the truth of this statement is especially furnished by the five provinces near to this city. As for those which are more remote, it is known and is evident that all the coast of Tayabas, which extends from Sariaya to the headland of Bondoc, was formerly very populous and rich, but now it has hardly a village that can be called such; there are [only] some groups of huts jumbled together, inhabited by some Indians who are kept there by their desire of obtaining some petty commodities of the country, such as wax, skins, and pitch. All are destitute of churches and ministers; for their churches have been destroyed at various times by pirates and Mindanaos, and no attention has ever been paid to reëstablishing those places anew as military posts, and with the means of defense that were necessary in order that the great number of people that were in that region might be able to maintain themselves as Christians. It is also a fact that there have been [other] very weighty causes for the depopulation of the islands: the building [of ships] within these five provinces; and the excessive and rigorous exactions in the collection of the tributes, and the excessive polos2 and personal services [required]. The sad thing is, that all those who leave the islands are ordinarily apostates from the faith, and live and die among heretics, Mahometans, and other barbarous people; and no reparation has ever been made for this great evil, nor has any obstacle been placed in the way of men passing freely [from these islands] to foreign kingdoms, even those who are well known to be married.

The [requisitions for] the cutting of timber for the construction of the galleons constitute an evil that is necessary and unavoidable, since on these depends the entire preservation of these islands; but this necessity is equaled by the destruction and the injuries which that work has caused in these provinces, in the diminution of their population and products. For this so oppressive and heavy yoke has almost always been imposed upon the said five provinces without extending it to others—to which, without doubt, the silver that his Majesty expends in the said woodcutting would be of public advantage; and at the same time the said provinces that are now burdened would take breath and become prosperous with such a rest, an end to which it greatly contributes that the shipbuilding yards are not limited to the village of Cavite alone. With this easy distribution [of labors] in the shipbuilding, the damages arising from the said woodcutting would no longer be repeated in the same provinces, which, having been thickly populated and abounding in produce, are now ruined and barren—their inhabitants forsaking them for remote provinces, and for lands of infidels and heretics, and sometimes retiring to the districts within the mountains. The reason for this is that, although the building [of a galleon] costs his Majesty the amount of 40,000 pesos for the wages of the Indians, besides the poor of these provinces, [they] carry among themselves a burden of more than 100,000 pesos—or even more, because those who are designated for the repartimiento of the woodcutting search for others who can take the place of each one; and the cost of these substitutes usually reaches five or six pesos, and sometimes ten. For the payment of this, the former pledge, or sell, or enslave themselves; and from this cause result very serious evils—thefts, withdrawing to the mountains to roam as vagrants, and other crimes. Other burdens which the natives miserably suffer, and which ordinarily fall on the poorest and most wretched, arise from the fact that the alcalde-mayor who makes the apportionment of men adds to it a greater number than is necessary, and those who are thus added redeem themselves from this oppression by money; and then the [list of the] repartimiento goes to the gobernadorcillo, in order that the heads [of barangay] may summon for the woodcutting six or eight men, even though only four may be necessary. The gobernadorcillo collects in money that amount in excess, as a redemption from an imaginary woodcutting, a proceeding which does not impair the number of those assigned. Still more, after all the men go to the woodcutting, if any are lacking the [native] overseer pays the superintendent of the work at the rate of two reals a day for the failure of each man. To this is added that the superintendent himself is wont to grant exemptions of his own accord, with unjust benefit to some, to the great injury of the main work, [the burden of] which falls on those who remain; moreover, he usually establishes shops, and thus the fund which his Majesty provides to aid these poor people by the purchase of some of their commodities remains therein. His Majesty orders that the men be called out and paid for one month; but many poor creatures do not get away from the woodcutting in a month and a half, during which time they are so overtaxed and harassed that they hardly have time to eat, and of sleep they will have some three hours, as a result of their labors on the account of his Majesty and outside his account. Such is the sorrowful course of the experiences and the unjust acts which they encounter in the woodcutting, [a labor] so carefully guarded from these by his Majesty— whose royal and innate piety adorns his crown with his clemency toward the poor, and with the justice of the many laws which he has promulgated in their favor. In presenting thus in general these transgressions of the laws, these crimes, and these oppressions of the poor to your Lordship, as to their judge and father, it is not our intention to blame all the head overseers of the woodcutting; for some have been known who with Christian zeal, the utmost assiduity, and entire disinterestedness have begun and ended their terms of woodcutting with treating those poor people with compassion and justice.

In these provinces near Manila there are a great number of Indians whose mode of life may appropriately be compared to that of the gypsies in España; for they go from one village to another accompanied by some women, and, without labor, they travel, eat, and are clothed; while they prove to be the authors of many murders, robberies, rapes, and other iniquitous deeds. Of the same sort are a great many of the slaves from Manila, who have fled from their masters and go about in bands through various districts; they ravage and destroy fields and farms; they lord it in the houses of the poor Indians; and there is hardly an evil deed that their rash boldness will not perform.

The tribute of the half-annats which his Majesty commands to be paid by the public offices which enjoy honor and salaries is a burden on many provinces (and especially on that of Leite, in which these half-annats, recently raked up [suscitadas] are collected)—although it is a fact that the [native] governors of those provinces do not receive salaries or desire such honor; rather, they shun it on account of their poverty. From [the attempt at] constraining them the following results ensue: first, they flee to the mountains; second, those who do not flee are compelled to remain slaves, or else bind themselves for their whole lives, in order to find means for paying this half-annat, so grievous a tax and so against their wills.

His Majesty has given orders to fortify and repair the village of Cavite, because on it depends, in truth, the preservation and guardianship of this city, the safety of the castle of San Felipe, and that of many intrenchments and various houses, and of the royal storehouses, which his Majesty possesses there. [Moreover,] a large Christian community has gathered in that place; and there are four churches, and three houses of religious orders, with a considerable number of citizens. All these things strongly enforce the necessity of executing the said royal decree of his Majesty, for the preservation, promotion, and protection of all those religious orders and vassals—although our opinion inclines to suppose that there must have been reasons more important than these for suspending the royal mandate of his Majesty; and if these do not exist it surely seems that this state of affairs calls to your Lordship for amendment.

The most holy and awful sacrifice of the mass depends on the pious and punctual provision which his Majesty has made in having wine brought here for the celebration of mass; and this wine, as for the rest, cannot be sure. It seems that in recent years it has been required [from Mexico by the officials of Filipinas] in so small quantities that often not even the amount ordered by his Majesty is delivered; from this it results that, as this deficiency cannot be made good, there is a failure in saying many masses. Even in the oil for the lamps that burn before the blessed sacrament there is a great deficiency [in the supply], for two reasons: either because it is not delivered, or because it is delivered in places very far away. These two matters are, without doubt, worthy of your Lordship's most careful attention—from whose Christian veneration for the blessed sacrament and well-known piety our solicitude desires and expects an entire and complete remedy.

It seems as if in most things the principal object of the alcaldes-mayor in the provinces, and that in which they proceed with most assiduity—excepting many who conduct themselves with entire integrity—reduces itself to a rigorous and excessive collection of the tributes; and their other aim is the utmost attention to their own personal advantage. These two aims are most injurious and prejudicial to the public welfare and to the poor people of the said provinces—because, when there is no produce [with which to pay the tributes] the alcaldes-mayor either compel the headmen to search for it, and even to bind themselves to do this, or regularly make the headmen responsible for amounts which they not only will not but cannot collect. Another reason is, that the said headmen, with cruel injustice, compel Indians to pay tribute before the age which his Majesty commands and fixes, and this they do under the compulsion of the alcaldes-mayor; likewise, the said headmen exact more than the amount of their obligations for the conveyance of the tributes. In the other aim of the said alcaldes-mayor (that is, their own private advantage) is seen a monstrous hydra with many heads of injustice and iniquity. One of these is their compelling the Indians to labor in construction and other works which do not belong to his Majesty's service, although even for those [for the crown] the royal law spares and exempts them [from service] during the times when they sow and harvest their crops. The alcaldes also appoint certain Indians who are intimate with them, and who have influence among the other natives, to whom the latter deliver the commodities which they carry to the provinces; and these Indian agents, fixing the prices of goods at their own pleasure, compel the said Indian chiefs to supply them, either by sale or in exchange for other wares. From this results a most flagrant inequality in the prices and the exchanges of goods; and the loss in all these dealings always falls on the mass of the poor people, because the alcalde-mayor and the said petty chiefs or influential Indians always conclude their bargains with profit, and never with loss. Some alcaldes-mayor have gone to such an extreme of violence that, in case the said petty chiefs are unable to dispose of the goods which are thus committed to them, the alcalde compels them to assume the obligation, and to bind themselves to take the goods. Thus some of the Indians are constantly bringing upon others irreparable consequences and losses that are worthy of redress—all springing from the first injustice of compelling those to buy who neither possess nor can take charge of such commodities.

The assessment for each tribute is regulated at ten reals, and it includes two tribute-payers, the husband and wife; nevertheless, the Indians who have no fixed abode are burdened with the requirement that each individual taxed shall pay an entire tribute of ten reals each—although it is believed that this increase was imposed as a penalty, and in order that certain people might be reduced to villages and barangays; for it is evident, from the method of [planning] the tribute, that the imposition or the increase of the tributes is one of the peculiar and exclusive prerogatives of the supreme sovereignty belonging to his Majesty. These injuries, Sir, and these oppressions which extend through all the provinces, to the destruction of the poor, are certainly worthy of action [on your part], and constitute a legitimate obligation on your vigilance, and on the high office which his Majesty entrusted to your Lordship.

Probably it has contributed much to these pernicious results and this neglect of sacred things that in these recent years the principal aim and object of the supreme government of these islands, as well as of the alcaldes-mayor, has been only the increase of the royal revenue—actually reversing the royal orders, which decree that the first attention must be paid to religion, and to the ecclesiastics and their affairs and maintenance; and after that to the civil government and justice. But, contrary to these orders, it appears that in everything the first place has been attained by the [affairs of] the royal treasury, which ought to engage the later solicitudes [of the royal ministers]—and then without that excessive severity [of administration] which has been experienced in recent years, [and which has aroused our] pity and compassion.

In most of the provinces of these islands the gobernadorcillos are obliged, as are their [subordinate] officials, to accept, without their own choice, appointments to office; and as the cause of their shunning such appointments is the great expense of the year during which they serve, they suffer on this account great injuries in the provinces near Manila. It arouses pity in the hardest hearts to see and know by experience that nearly all the headmen enter office under compulsion from the alcalde-mayor, and, finding themselves perplexed to the utmost by the difficulties in rendering their accounts satisfactorily—either by the duplicate names on the registration lists, or the absences (which usually are many), or by the deaths [of those registered]—on account of the great poverty that is general in the villages these deficiencies fall back on the headmen, who are compelled to pay them or be imprisoned. This measure of imprisonment is carried out with so great rigor that many headmen are in prison, without any hope that they will be able to pay; and there are even cases in which the headmen have been imprisoned for many years for their indebtedness to the tributes in their charge, and, dying in prison, their burial was delayed for several days in order that their relatives might be able to find security for the dead man's tribute and debt. From this your Lordship can infer the excessive severity with which the officials proceed in the collections of the royal tributes; but in this no kind of severity can be proper, nor can it be decreed by the royal and liberal purpose of his Majesty.

The works and preparations for the equipment [of ships] which are made on his Majesty's account often make necessary various repartimientos and bandalas for the supplies of oil and rice, and other products, which the provinces furnish; and it is the continual and well-founded complaint from all of them that the amount paid for the said products is not according to their just price and value, but much less, from which follow the most serious wrongs to the poor. Of this precedent many of the alcaldes-mayor avail themselves for [their own] advancement, to judge by their unrighteous profits, with lamentable injury to the poor, which is general and well known in the provinces.

The royal decree of his Majesty provides that, for just and Christian reasons, Moors, Armenians, and other barbarous peoples may not remain in these islands as inhabitants and citizens; but for the last few years several ships from the Coast [i.e., India] have spent the winter here, and in consequence many Moors, Armenians, and other barbarians have settled without the walls of Manila, and in various provinces. These people have enjoyed (as they still do) free intercourse and trade with every class of people, and are causing notable injury to the spiritual welfare of the Indians—lording it over them, and setting a bad example in morals to all of them. Accordingly our affection and obligation [to the service of God] desire the exercise of your Lordship's justice and Christian procedure, that this injury, so universal and so opposed to the Christian and praiseworthy usages which they ought [to follow], and which our missionaries are endeavoring to introduce among all the natives, may entirely cease.

On account of the great facility (not experienced before) which there has been in cashiering soldiers, these evil consequences for the villages have resulted, with various unjust acts—according to what idleness, poverty, and many temptations have offered to many poor men who came here only to serve his Majesty in the employment of soldiers.

From the introduction of the vice of gambling are following the injurious results and the offenses against God which the holy fathers [of the Church] decry, and which experience places before our own eyes, in the shape of much cursing, poverty, abandonment of the wives and children of the gamblers, and the sinful waste of much time—in which occur quarrels, frauds, and other wicked acts appropriate to gambling and connected with it. Besides this, some of the alcaldes-mayor—who ought to be on the watch to prevent these things, according to the orders which they have from the supreme government of your Lordship—are the very ones who secretly give full license and permission for gambling games, in consideration of the money which they receive every month for the said license. As a result, the villages and their grain-fields are inundated with gambling games (of cards, dice, and cocks, and many other kinds), with the aforesaid effects—all against the will of God our Lord and of his Majesty, which is always impeded and seldom executed by the alcaldes-mayor.

The experience of many years with the Chinese nation has made it very evident that it was necessary to prohibit to the Sangleys, especially the infidels, trade and intercourse with the villages and provinces of Indians, and keep them out of Indian houses and grain-fields, and thus it is provided and ordained; but unfortunately this prohibition is neither obeyed nor respected. It is, however, a fact that only when they are married, and compelled to make their abode in the chief town [of the province], where the alcalde-mayor resides, or when they are settled in a certain Parián, does his Majesty permit them to reside among the Indians—who from communication with the Sangleys obtain only superstitions, frauds, and the loss of the habits of morality in which we are trying to instruct them. The administration of the Christian Sangleys is in charge of the two holy religious orders of St. Dominic and the Society of Jesus; and as these people are for the most part the poorest [of the Sangleys], we do not consider it foreign to our obligation to attend to them, in such manner as is possible and right. It is only just to direct your Lordship's attention to a custom introduced within the last few years, which is that the tribute that they pay for licenses [to remain in the country] has been increased—although it appears that the laws favor the Christian Sangleys, providing that their tribute shall be only ten reals; but at present they are paying the same amounts of tribute as do the infidel and heathen Sangleys. Your Lordship, with your clear judgment and ready comprehension, will be pleased to consider whether it is in accordance with the lofty purposes which his Majesty has for propagating the faith, and for lightening the burdens of those who are converted to it—in which his Catholic piety has so earnestly striven—that the said tributes should be extended and increased among the Christians; and whether they do not deserve to be relieved from so grievous a burden.

So great is the sorrow of our hearts at seeing and realizing how easily and quickly the Indians who are apostates from our holy faith retreat to the mountains, and the obstinacy which the infidels show in not coming out of them, that we cannot neglect to remind your Lordship a second time of the urgent necessity that expeditions into the mountains [by our troops] be continued, like those that were made in former times with success and useful results. We entreat and charge your Lordship that to this remedy which has been already tried on other occasions the piety of your Lordship will be pleased to add [another,] that of prohibiting to the Indians who are already Christians intercourse and trade with the infidels; for the regular result of this is, that the said infidels withdraw more and more from the mild authority of our holy religion. That religion is considered, by the said Christians, as intolerable, although it is not such, whether in itself, in its effects, or in the obligations which they assume by becoming Christians—which, in the feeble light of their understanding, is the same as being reduced only to subjection to the ecclesiastical minister, the alcalde-mayor, and the burdens of tributes and repartimientos.

Finally, Sir, our lofty desire for the general welfare of so many provinces, and the pleasure which we shall all feel in the prosperity and success of your Lordship—which, as [that of] the first and principal head [of this colony], must overflow in all its parts and subjects—impel us to point out to your Lordship how worthy of all assistance and effort in your Christian government is the pitiable condition to which the Christian villages are reduced, now one of poverty and barrenness, even of the native products. And those villages to which, it would seem, their age (which now is more than a century) must furnish greater abundance of produce and wealth rightfully their own, are in the same condition and the same poverty as are the villages that are more recent and less encouraged by the ecclesiastical ministers and the civil officials of these islands; and they can never enjoy any improvement, spiritual or temporal. The remedy for this—which ought to be effective, prompt, and steadily continued—in our humble opinion, is made up of various measures: some for the amelioration and redress of all the evils and difficulties already related to your Lordship, whose peremptory and executive orders must render them effectual; and others which, it seems to us, ought to be charged upon the alcaldes-mayor, and upon the proper ministers who are closest to the Indians themselves (who are the ecclesiastics), in order that they may by every means arouse and animate the slothful natures of the Indians, by instructing them in industries that will be useful to themselves, and in application to an [object of] desire that is honorable and advantageous to the public or to individuals of all the villages. This depends on and consists in not allowing that very abundance and fertility which our Lord has given to these islands to be destroyed with waste and negligence; for it is evident that the enormous sum of silver which necessity, against the royal orders, transfers to foreign kingdoms ruled by infidels and heretics, could remain in the islands themselves, and be converted into property, profit, and the acquisition of wealth for many poor persons. For there are found in these islands, as is well known, abundance of gold, amber, tortoise-shell, various cotton fabrics, wax, and many other native products, even omitting those that concern the sowing of the fields. If these were multiplied in both amount and kinds, it cannot be doubted that they would contribute to the villages, with considerable abundance, wealth and products; and that all the beneficial effects which can be desired would result, in favor of his Majesty and of the public welfare. The chief of these are: first, that all the painful burdens, unavoidable and necessary, which the natives have to bear, and which they lament, would become more easy and light for them, and that they would live a more social and civilized life; second, that their affection, loyalty, and obedience to his Majesty and to your Lordship in his name, as the authors of their prosperity, repose, and advantage, would be enormously increased. Third, all the Christian Indians would be more steadfast and rooted in the holy faith, and would become effective and most suitable instruments for [gaining] new conversions of infidels [and] apostates, the infidels themselves beholding the abundant wealth and profit, and other benefits, of the Christian Indians; for it is the temporal welfare evident to their senses which, as experience teaches us, strongly influences both classes of Indians, to be converted or to maintain themselves in the Christian faith. This same object will be greatly aided by inducing the Indians to settle and form villages; for, in the mode of life in which they now are found, in most of the provinces and villages in which the minister who instructs them is stationed and resides a certain number are destitute of houses, and all the rest of the people live so far away and so scattered that many are obliged to travel three or four leguas in order to be present on a festival day at the church—from which remoteness it also follows that, without any fault of the said ministers, many persons die without receiving the holy sacraments.

Such, Sir, are the evils, and such are the remedies which our consciences, our charity, and our zeal have dictated to us as being most worthy of gaining the attention of your Lordship—at whose feet, through the means of these lines, so many poor Indians approach to prostrate themselves. Neophytes, and bereft of all human protection, they have recourse to your Lordship, not only as to their governor and judge, but also as to a kind father—in whose term of office they hope that peace and justice will again flourish; and that the rights of the poor, and redress for their oppressions, will often obtain a hearing from your Lordship. This, it appears, has not been the case in other times, certainly at the cost of many tears, which were little heeded and never dried by the sovereignty and power that ought to do so. In their name, and only for the objects pointed out at the beginning of this memorial, and that by it we may unburden our own consciences, we are under obligation, at least according to charity, to solicit for them aid and justice.

We humbly entreat that your Lordship will be pleased, in regard to these points, to carry out what his Majesty ordains, and to take such measures as your Lordship may deem most suitable for prompt execution, most easy to be obeyed, and most conformable to the royal will; and we expect that what your Lordship shall judge to be most expedient will be in every way the best, since his Majesty has entrusted to your care, zeal, generous nature, and nobility the supreme government of these islands. Manila, October 7, in the year 1701.

> Fray Jose Vila, provincial of the province of Santissimo Rosario.
>
> Fray Francisco de Santa Ynes, provincial of St. Francis.
>
> Fray Jose Lopez, provincial of the Augustinians.
>
> Luis de Morales, provincial of the Society of Jesus.
>
> Fray Bartolome de la Santissima Trinidad, provincial of the discalced Recollects of St. Augustine.

1 That is, to Zabalburu, just one month after his entrance into office.

2 Polo: a personal service of forty days in the year.

EVENTS OF 1701–1715

[The following summary is made from Concepción's *Historia de Philipinas*, viii, pp. 299–391:]

[Don Fausto Cruzat y Gongora is succeeded, after eleven years as governor, by Don Domingo de Zabalburú y Echeverri, a knight of the Order of Santiago; he was appointed in 1694, but does not take possession until September 8, 1701. Finding considerable money in the royal treasury, he employs it on important public works. He constructs wharves at Cavite, completes the royal storehouses, and rebuilds the powder-factory lower down from Malate, with suitable fortifications for its defense; and he pays careful attention to the construction of galleons for the Acapulco trade-route.

A quarrel arising between the petty kings of Mindanao and Joló, the former (named Curay) is slain, and his successor asks Governor Zabalburú for aid against the Joloans, which the governor prudently declines to furnish. In the year 1705 the Manila galleon "San Xavier" departs from Acapulco, and is never heard from, being lost with all it contains, to the great sorrow and loss of the citizens of Manila. One of the auditors goes (1702) as official visitor to the province of Camarines,1 and disturbs its affairs with his "scandalous proceedings," especially his accusations against the Franciscan friars who are in charge of the Indian villages there. In consequence, they hasten to Manila to secure the aid of the courts there, leaving their charges without spiritual ministrations; the Franciscan provincial is therefore despatched to that province with orders to station ministers therein. Those missions had previously been for forty-five years in the hands of the Recollects.]

[In September, 1704, arrives at Manila the papal legate Carlos Thomas Tournon, on his way to China for the settlement of various ecclesiastical difficulties there; he treats the governor and other officials2 with arrogance, refusing to exhibit his credentials, and exercises ecclesiastical jurisdiction to such an extent that he antagonizes the religious orders and infringes on the royal prerogatives. These proceedings are tolerated by both governor and archbishop, although manifestly improper and objectionable; but when they are reported at Madrid the king is greatly displeased, and decrees that the governor be removed from office, and disqualified for holding it, and those of the auditors who assented to his acts be punished. Archbishop Camacho also incurs the displeasure of the king, which is increased by his having meddled with the affairs of the royal seminary of San Phelipe, and used at his own pleasure certain ecclesiastical revenues properly in charge of the secular government; and the governor fails to check him, and even to notify the home government of these unwarranted proceedings, which are reported at Madrid by ecclesiastical channels. Camacho is accordingly removed from his see, and transferred to the bishopric of Guadalaxara in Mexico.3 (He is regarded by Concepción as a very zealous and charitable prelate; he collected from various sources more than 40,000 pesos, which he spent in the adornment and improvement of the cathedral church at Manila, and for this and other pious purposes he incurred debts amounting to over 20,000 pesos more. He promoted the missions of Paynaan and San Isidro, going in person to persuade the Aetas (or Negritos) to be converted.) Zabalburú, having undergone his residencia, leaves Manila in the year 1710, and, after having suffered shipwreck in the Bahama Channel, reaches Spain, where he dies after a few years. In 1707 the Acapulco galleon "Rosario" arrives, "with so much silver that it made that fair [at Acapulco] famous;" it also brings a new archbishop, Fray Francisco de la Cuesta, "a professed religious in the distinguished monastic order of San Geronimo," who wins golden opinions from all.4 Before long, however, the old question of the right of episcopal visitation of the regular curas again arises; Cuesta tries to enforce this right, but with little result.5 A full account of this is given by Concepción, with the arguments adduced therein.]

[In 1709 the new governor arrives, Conde de Lizarraga (appointed in 1704); he is equitable, upright, and of affable manners. He finds an undesirable surplus of Chinamen in the islands, and sends back many of them to their own country, although many others buy permission to remain in Luzón.6 During his term occurs the controversy between some of the friar orders and the bishop of Nueva Segovia, Fray Diego de Gorospe y Irala (himself a Dominican), over the claim of the latter to include the regulars in his official visitations. The matter is carried to the Audiencia, the decision of which is unfavorable to the bishop; he dies soon afterward (early in 1714?), after having occupied his see nine years. Little else appears to mark the official term of Lizarraga, who dies in 1715.]

1 This was Francisco Gueruela; see summary of his report on this visitation, in VOL. XLII, p. 120.

2 "Except the master-of-camp Endaya, who charged him nothing for the house in which he lived, and spent more than twenty thousand pesos in maintaining him and all his retinue. Endaya made all these demonstrations because he had taken refuge in a church, and the patriarch [i.e., Tournon] condoned all his offences and enabled him to leave his asylum—without any one saying anything to him; nor did the judges dare to lay hands on a man whom the legate a latere had pardoned." Other favors and honors were conferred on Endaya by Tournon. (Zúñiga, Hist. de Philipinas, pp. 412–413.)

3 Archbishop Camacho was appointed in 1703 bishop of Guadalajara; and early in July, 1706, he went to take possession of that see (which he retained until his death in 1712), abandoning his diocese of Manila. He left as ruler of that see Don Francisco Rayo (who was not a member of the cabildo), despite the protests of the chapter-members. On August 19 the cabildo declared the see vacant, and chose as its provisor the archdeacon Doctor José Altamirano y Cervantes. At first his title was contested by Rayo; but the latter was finally induced to give up his pretensions, and by August 28 "the cabildo remained in peaceable possession of its government and vacant see." (Ventura del Arco MSS., iv, pp. 247, 248. In the same volume, pp. 135–206, is a detailed

account of Camacho's controversy with the orders and the papal delegate, with a royal decree on that subject, dated May 20, 1700.)

4 "As soon as he took possession of his archbishopric, he began to busy himself with the building of the seminary of San Phelipe; and the first error that he committed was, to place the arms of the cabildo on the front of the edifice together with the arms of the king, which he placed on one of the stories. He also drew up the instructions for this collegiate seminary; and when he came to the admission of students he did not remember the [rights of the] royal patronage, and arranged for their admission without mentioning the vice-patron. The king's fiscal, who saw therein one of his Majesty's prerogatives wounded, strongly opposed the exercise of the archbishop's claims, and from this ensued some mortifications to his illustrious Lordship; but the college was completed, and the seminarists were appointed, as the king commanded." (Zúñiga, Hist. de Philipinas, pp. 417, 418.)

5 "Because of the controversies which Señor Camacho had had with the regulars about subjecting them to the visitation, the pope issued a brief, in which that subjection was decreed; it came endorsed by the [Spanish] Council, and it seemed as if, in virtue of a decision so clear and explicit, no reply was left for the religious save that of the submission which Señor Cuesta desired; but their ingenuity found a mode of escape from this strait. They replied that this brief was a declaration of the rights of the archbishop, which they did not deny; and that their only proposition was, that it was not expedient to execute this decree in these islands (in regard to which his Holiness ought to have given a hearing to the religious orders). They asserted that it was, so far as concerned the point at issue, obtained surreptitiously; for it was staled therein that there were entire orders who were willing to come to these islands in the position of subordinates to the bishops—which was false, because the only authentic thing about it was, that the vicar-general of the Recollects had promised a hundred religious who should minister in Philipinas as subject to the visitation and the [royal] patronage; but when this was known to the general of the calced Augustinians, he had censured this proposal and compelled its withdrawal. The orders therefore petitioned that the execution of the papal brief be suspended, until

appeal could be taken to his Majesty. Señor Cuesta, who was a very peaceable man, and averse to disputes, agreed to this, and sent a report to the king. The representations of the regulars were considered in the Council of the Indias, and it was decreed that the regulars must submit; but his Majesty, being informed by a member of his Council of the injurious results which might follow from this visitation, approved the proceedings of Señor Cuesta, and ordered him not to annoy the religious in this matter until further orders." (Zúñiga, Hist. de Philipinas, pp. 418, 419.)

6 "He sent away most of the Chinese, and retained only those whom he deemed necessary for the mechanical offices and the service of the public; in this matter his reputation suffered somewhat, for it was reported that he had a share of the proceeds from the licenses of those Chinamen who remained in the country. However that may be, his decision was a very sagacious one, and advantageous to this country; for the Sangleys who come to Manila are more slothful than the Indians themselves. They remain here [pretending] to cultivate the land, and on account of this pretext licenses are given to them; but there is not one in each thousand of the Chinese who applies himself to this labor. The rest of them are all devoted to trade, a mode of life well suited to their idle dispositions and to the [social] system of their nation—where it is a received idea that he who is most deceitful is most clever. The Sangleys adulterate everything—coins, measures, sugar, wax, and whatever they can thus handle without the fraud being known. Every one of them is a monopolist; they all secrete their wares, even those of prime necessity, and sell them at the price that they choose to ask. The oddest thing is, that by dint of presents they are able to gain protectors, who defend them; and even if sometimes a fine is imposed on them, on that very day they plunder [people] in their trading, in order to pay for their losses. In this way they become rich in a short time, and send much money to their relatives in China, or else go back with it to their own country, defrauding the Philipinas Islands of this silver." (Zúñiga, Hist. de Philipinas, pp. 422, 423.)

THE GOVERNMENT AND DEATH OF BUSTAMANTE

[A brief summary of the events antecedent to and connected with the government of Bustamante is here presented, obtained from the very detailed and prolix account in Concepción's Historia de Philipinas, ix, pp. 183–424.]

[The Conde de Lizarraga, who began to govern the islands in August, 1709, dies at Manila on February 4, 1715; and the vacancy in his office is, as usual, temporarily filled by the Audiencia, Auditor José Torralba assuming charge of military affairs. In the Tournon affair of 1704, the senior auditor, José Antonio Pabon, had not resisted Tournon's unwarranted assumption of authority, and had therefore inclined the displeasure of the home government, being deprived of his office and fined. He thereupon petitioned for a reversal of this sentence, and restitution to his office and salary, which was granted by a royal decree of April 15, 1713; this document arrives at Manila during Torralba's rule, who declines, on various pretexts, to reinstate Pabon, and even attempts to obtain evidence damaging to his official character. Pabon therefore is obliged to take refuge in the Augustinian convent at Manila, and remains there until the arrival of Bustamante; the latter brings suit against Torralba to compel him to obey the royal decree in favor of Pabon, and to pay all moneys due to the auditor. Torralba had also instituted proceedings against another auditor, Gregorio Manuel de Villa, and two officers, Santos Perez Tagle and Luis Antonio de Tagle, on the charge of their having aided and abetted the Castilian Recollect religious in their revolt against their superiors in the order. (After the dissensions between the religious orders and Archbishop Camacho, resulting from his attempt to enforce episcopal visitation of the regular curas, the despatch of missionaries to the islands is greatly diminished, partly on account of those dissensions, partly because the "seas are infested with English and Dutch squadrons." All the orders therefore suffer from a scarcity of laborers; but the Recollects are fortunately reënforced by a mission band, conducted by Fray Joseph de Santa Gertrudis, of fifty-seven religious, "among them the flower of the province of Castilla." Later, in the distribution of the ministries and offices of the order in the islands, strife arises; the older members of the province — mostly from Aragón, with some from Valencia and Cataluña — secure all the best offices, as against the Castilians. When the provincial chapter meets, the latter present their claims, but are rebuffed; thereupon they convene a chapter of their own, in the convent at Bagumbayan, and elect a provincial and other officers. This throws all the business of the order into confusion, and Governor Lizarraga persuades the two parties to refer the controversy to the head of the order in Europe and to abide by his decision, which finally recognizes as legal the chapter held at Manila. Various difficulties arise in attempting to enforce this decision, but Lizarraga, who favors the Castilians, induces the provincial to leave them with their students at Bagumbayan. After the governor's death, Torralba aids the provincial by sending troops and bombarding that convent, to bring back the recalcitrants to Manila.) Torralba, having arrested Villa and the Tagles, keeps them in rigorous confinement, and hinders their appeal to the Council of the Indias; both sides send to Madrid statements of their respective claims. By royal decrees of August 18, 1718, all of Torralba's proceedings against them, as well as against Auditor Pabon, are declared null and void, and they are restored to their respective offices. Bustamante assumes the governorship on August 9, 1717; his first proceeding is to investigate the condition of the royal treasury, which he finds in bad condition, with large sums due to it and unpaid by the citizens. He takes severe measures to compel the payment of these debts to the government—among them, laying an embargo on the cargo of the galleon which comes this year from Acapulco, in which large amounts of goods and money have been brought illegally, to avoid payment of duties. A complete investigation of the ownership and registration of this wealth is ordered, the governor placing it in the charge of Andres Fernandez de Arquiju and Esteban Hizguiño. As a consequence of the governor's energetic measures, within the first six months of his government the sum of 220,671 pesos is placed in the royal treasury, besides the situado for that year, which amounts to 74,482 pesos; and the balance of accounts on February 1, 1718, shows that the treasury actually contains 293,444 pesos, besides jewels and other valuables deposited for debts to the crown. Concepción gives the principal items of revenue and expense at that time. An embargo is also laid on the silver which comes in the galleon of 1718, but little advantage therefrom results to the treasury. This financial investigation also shows that Torralba, during his government, and the royal officials had mismanaged the royal revenues, shown great carelessness in the bookkeeping, accounts, and allowed funds to disappear without any satisfactory accounting; Bustamante therefore imprisons them all, and seizes their goods.]

[At various times the Christian natives of the island of Paragua ask the Manila government, through the Recollect missionaries in whose care they are, for a Spanish fort and garrison in their island to protect them from the Moro pirates; but no action is taken on this until 1718, when Bustamante orders a fort to be built at Labo, near the southern point of the island.1 The Recollect province contributes to this enterprise 500 pesos, which are due to it from the royal treasury. About the same time the fortress at Zamboanga is also rebuilt, Bustamante insisting upon this work, against the advice of many of his counselors. He sends an embassy to Siam, to establish with that king friendly and commercial relations; the Spaniards are received with great pomp and lavish entertainment, and rich presents are exchanged in behalf of the respective monarchs of Spain and Siam; and land is granted to the Spaniards on the bank of the Chow Payah (or Meinam) River, for the erection of a trading factory. "It is the place that formerly was called Campo Japon, and is named Nuestra Señora de el Soto ["Our Lady of the Grove"]; it is sixty-four brazas square, on the east side of the river, and distant from it a hundred brazas." It is also a convenient place at which to make arrangements for the building of ships, and the Siamese will supply them with lumber (including teak wood) and iron for this construction. The Spaniards return to Manila in August, preceded by a Siamese embassy; but Bustamante is so preoccupied with other matters that he pays no attention to the strangers, and they are even badly treated. They return to Siam angry and resentful, and desire no further dealings with the Spaniards.]

[In 1719 the royal Audiencia is broken up by the lack of auditors: Torralba being imprisoned in Fort Santiago, two others—Julian de Velasco and Francisco Fernandez Toribio—being held in confinement, and Pabon being not yet reinstated in office. "Only Don Gregorio Manuel de Villa was in possession [of the auditor's functions], through the death of the fiscal, Don Antonio de Casas y Albarado; but as Señor Villa did not agree with the harsh and violent opinions of the governor, he retired to the convent of Nuestra Señora de Guadalupe, distant two leguas from the city." At this time Bustamante is told that a general conspiracy is being formed against him, "of all the citizens, and all the religious orders, and the clergy, influential persons being pointed out who were allying themselves with the Sangleys, who were to commit the parricide." Thereupon, Torralba begins to hope for release, and Bustamante talks over the situation with him, asking his advice. The result is, that the governor transfers Torralba to the government buildings, nominally as a prisoner, but rehabilitates him as auditor; with Doctor José Correa as associate judge, and Agustin Guerrero as fiscal; and they contrive various measures against their enemies. Many persons are arrested by this quasi government, and many others through fear take refuge in the churches. Among the latter is a notary-public, Don Antonio de Osejo y Vazquez, who carries his official records to the cathedral, and refuses to surrender them. A decree is therefore issued by the temporary Audiencia requiring the archbishop to see that the records are given up and returned to the proper place; he promises to obey, but delays doing so; upon being ordered a second time to attend to the matter, he answers by presenting the opinions of the two universities, which the prelate has consulted in this emergency, and which support him in declining to allow the right of sanctuary to be infringed, and in regarding the so-called Audiencia as illegally constituted. The governor issues a proclamation ordering all able-bodied male citizens to present themselves, armed, in the palace when a certain signal shall be given. The archbishop excommunicates Torralba for his proceedings against the ecclesiastical immunity; he sends notification of this punishment by Canon Don Manuel de Ossio and Doctor Fuentes, who force their way into Torralba's apartment, late in the evening of October 10, and force him to listen to the reading of the censure; but he contrives to get hold of a sword, and drives them out of the room. The next morning the governor calls the citizens to arms, and causes the arrest (in virtue of decrees made by his Audiencia in the night) of the archbishop, his messengers to Torralba, the superiors of the religious orders, and many other ecclesiastics. At this, a tumult arises among the people; an interdict is laid on the city; and a conspiracy is formed against the governor. "The religious of St. Francis, St. Dominic, and St. Augustine (both calced and discalced) came out from their convents, each as a body, carrying in their hands crucifixes and shouting, 'Long live [Viva] the Faith! long live the Church! long live our king Don Phelipe V!' Perhaps also resounded such utterances as in these cases are peculiar to the common people and to a tumultuous populace. These religious were joined by those who had taken refuge in the churches, and by a great number of people of all classes, and they went in this array to [the church of] San Agustin. Those who had taken refuge there, who were among the most distinguished citizens, filled with fear lest they should be taken from their asylum and put to death, joined the crowd, and promoted the sedition, all providing themselves with arms. A page of the governor, hearing the confusion and yells, entered his master's apartment, and in alarm gave him the news that various religious were coming toward the palace, conducting a mission. The governor, greatly disturbed, sprang up, and ordered the guards to keep back the crowd; he went to a window, and heard that from the corner of the cathedral tower thirty men were asked for to check the people, who were marching through that street. He despatched an order to the fort to discharge the artillery at the crowd; but he was so little obeyed that, although they applied the match to two cannons, these were aimed so low that the balls were buried in the middle of the esplanade of the fort. Without opposition this multitude arrived at the doors of the palace, the Jesuits following at a short distance, with many of the common people and many boys, the entire crowd, with deafening yells, repeating the vivas of the religious. As for the soldiers of the guard, some retreated in fear, and others in terror laid down their arms. The mob climbed up by ladders, and entered the first hall, the halberdiers not firing the swivel-guns that had been provided, although the governor commanded them to do so; he now went forward to meet them, with a gun, its bayonet fixed, and gave confused orders to his retainers to seize the weapons which by his order had been taken from them. One of the religious presented himself to the governor, and tried to set forth to him the misfortunes into which he was rushing headlong; but at the first words that he uttered, the governor, already furious, said to him, 'Go away, Father!' He attempted to discharge his gun at a citizen standing near, and it missed fire; then the governor drew his sabre and wounded the citizen; the latter, and with him all the rest at once, attacked the governor. They broke his right arm, and a blow on his head from a sabre caused him to fall like one dead. His son the sargento-mayor, who was in command at the fort, seeing the great throng of people who were entering the palace, mounted his horse to go to his father's aid. Entering the guard-room, sabre in hand, he wounded several persons; but as he was not sufficient for so many, he was attacked by them and fell from his horse in a dying condition, and they left him there. Some life still remained in the governor, but he gave no sign of it; and, supposing that he was dead, the people occupied themselves with imprisoning some and releasing others." Concepción mentions the ministrations of the Jesuit Otazo (whose account of the affair follows this), to Bustamante, and states that the dying man suffered many indignities at the hands of the mob; they even dragged him along, in a hammock, to thrust him into a dungeon, and while doing so a slave stabbed Bustamante twice near the heart. Finally they leave him stretched on a couch in the chapel of the royal prison, and without any medical care; the dean of the cathedral (who has just been freed from Bustamante's prison) summons a surgeon to attend the dying governor and his son, but he is destitute of bandages and other appliances, and when he returns with these the governor is dead.2 Concepción describes this episode indignantly, as "an abominable crime," which was discredited by the upright and honorable citizens, and relates the excesses committed by the mob, who broke open the prisons, and set free the worst criminals. At the beginning, they had liberated the imprisoned ecclesiastics; and now they insist that the archbishop, Fray Francisco de la Cuesta, shall act as governor ad interim. With great reluctance, and yielding only to the clamors of the people, the need that some one who can quiet them shall assume authority in this disturbed condition of affairs, and the advice of the leading ecclesiastics in all the orders, Cuesta accepts this charge, and takes the usual oath of office as governor until the king shall make another appointment. He forms an audiencia with the legal auditors still remaining—Velasco, Toribio, and Villa; and they together organize the temporary government, Pabon also being reinstated, later. A public funeral is given to the two Bustamantes, for which a thousand pesos are taken from the goods of the deceased, the other four thousand being allowed by the royal officials for the maintenance and the passage to Mexico of the governor's six remaining children (their mother having died soon after reaching the islands—according to Torralba, through Bustamante's neglect of her in a serious illness); the funeral is so ostentatious that in it are consumed seven and a half quintals (or hundredweights) of wax.]

[The archbishop3 sets on foot an investigation into the riot and the murder of the governor and his son; the substance of many of the depositions made in this matter is related by our author, but little information of value is obtained from them; no one will admit that he knows who dealt the fatal blows. Torralba4 testifies against the governor, condemning his fierce disposition, tyrannical acts, and "diabolical craftiness." According to this witness, Bustamante was carried away by greed, and appropriated to himself the goods of many persons whom he imprisoned; resentment at this was general throughout the islands,5 and caused a revolt in Cagayán, from which resulted another in Pangasinán, in which the alcalde-mayor, Antonio de el Valle, and other persons were killed. The auditors propose to investigate also the persons who had taken refuge in the convent of San Agustin, and afterward joined the mob; but they are advised by Doctor Ossio that this proceeding will too greatly disturb the community; that to proceed against these persons will be to cast odium on and grieve nearly all the citizens, since the commotion was so general; that all those who went out on that occasion did so "in defense of the ecclesiastical immunity, the preservation of this city, the self-defense of its inhabitants, and the reputation of the [Spanish] nation;" and that to carry out this plan would be likely to cause some disturbance of the public peace. The officials accordingly suspend the execution of the decrees that they had issued, and send to the Madrid government a report of all their proceedings in the matter, with copies of all the documents. In Mexico, however, the affair is viewed differently. The guardian of Bustamante's children, Balthasar de Castañeda Vizente de Alhambra, brings criminal suit before the viceroy, Marqués de Valero, against four of the citizens of Manila for the murder of the Bustamantes. Two of these men—Juan Fausto Gaicoechea y Gainza, and Diego de Salazar—are consequently arrested at Acapulco (March, 1721) and imprisoned, their goods being seized. The inquiry at Acapulco is equally fruitless, but Castañeda presses it before the viceroy, making definite accusations regarding the murder, and claiming that the authorities at Manila have slurred over the investigation of the murders, through undue influence of interested parties, and have made only enough effort to find the culprits to preserve their own reputation at Madrid; and he brings forward various evidence in support of his claims. The viceroy finally refers the case to the new governor of Filipinas, Marqués de Torre Campo, sending to him the accused persons, and Gregorio de Bustamante, nephew of the late governor. In January, 1720, the fort at Labo in the island of Paragua is abandoned, notwithstanding the entreaties of the Recollect missionaries there that it be maintained and reënforced—a measure for which Concepción accounts by the hatred felt toward Bustamante, who had established that post; and by the readiness of the Manila government to keep up the fort of Zamboanga, under the pressure exercised by the Jesuits, whose "astute policy" secured votes for that action, desired by them for the protection of their missions in Mindanao—an influence which the Recollects lacked. As soon as Labo is abandoned, the Moro pirates begin their raids on the northern islands, even going to the vicinity of Manila; and they undertake to form a general conspiracy against the Spanish power in the archipelago. The kings of Joló and Mindanao, however, profess to decline to enter this, finding their interest in an alliance with the Spaniards. On December 8, 1720, an attack is made by Moros against the fort at Zamboanga, but it is repulsed; those from Joló and Mindanao then come, professing friendship, but treacherously turn against the Spaniards and attack the fort; after a two months' siege, they are finally driven away, with considerable loss.6 The Moros afterward ravage the Calamianes and other islands, carrying away many captives, and killing a Recollect missionary, Fray Manuel de Jesús María.]

Letter from Diego de Otazo, S.J.

I will not omit sending a relation to Madrid, on this occasion when letters are sent from Manila to that court, of the tumultuous changes [here], of which your Reverence probably knows—if perchance (even though my influence be little and my authority less) my letter, when communicated to the father confessors of his Majesty and Highness, may contribute to the greater glory of God, and the welfare of these islands and of the souls who are converted in them, and those who may yet be converted when this community is established in tranquillity and order; it is this alone which I regard as the only object for which I can and ought to strive, since this alone has brought me to these islands.

Father Procurator: Don Fernando Bustillos y Bustamante (whom may God have forgiven) began his government of these islands with so much violence that, as he carried it to the extreme, this very thing deprived him of life. Blinded by the two mighty passions, greed and pride, and exercising the absolute power that the government of these islands confers on him, and taking advantage of the great distance from his sovereign master, [the result was that] all the citizens had to follow him and comply with his purposes, which were directed to his own interests, and measured only by his own desires. The dungeons of the jails and castles came to be filled with those persons who opposed or might oppose him; and the churches and convents were full of those who had sought refuge there, dreading lest they too might be imprisoned. The few Spaniards (and they were very few) who were outside went about—let us say, by way of explanation—with one foot on the street and the other in the church; and with the fear that if they lay down at night in their homes they would awake in a dungeon.

The archbishop, impelled by his conscience, undertook to employ some means—advising the governor like a father, and with the utmost possible circumspection, and after having consulted others—to see if he could check what was already dreaded; but, when he gave the governor his first paternal warning, the latter had become entirely blind, and determined to expel from Manila his illustrious Lordship, the superiors and professors in the religious orders, and the secular priests in the cathedral who had high positions and learning.

This fatal controversy began to find expression on the ninth or tenth of October, his illustrious Lordship desiring the governor to cease his intimacy with [*quitarle de su lado*] the auditor whom he held a prisoner [*i.e.*, Torralba]—with whom, while thus a prisoner, he was drawing up, at his own pleasure, and without any possibility of objection, the royal decrees which he judged necessary to his purpose. The archbishop sent the doctoral canon of the church and another prebend in order that, after the canonical warnings, they might notify [the auditor] of the excommunication which he had incurred by complying with so exceedingly illegal a proceeding. What occurred there when the doctoral canon carried this message I am unable to say; but the result was that they treated the canon and the other prebend badly, confining them as prisoners, and this was the answer that the archbishop received; the fact itself is known, but nothing else.

At daybreak on the eleventh his illustrious Lordship, in much anxiety, sent out to summon to his palace the superiors of the religious orders and other learned ecclesiastical persons, in order to hold counsel with them; but hardly had they assembled with him when they found that the archiepiscopal palace was besieged by armed soldiers, who had orders not to allow any one to depart, or any others to enter. One of the officers, entering the apartments of his illustrious Lordship, informed him that he must immediately go with him, by order of the king, the royal assembly, etc.; and thus, surrounded by soldiers, they carried the prelate to the fort on the plaza. In the same way they proceeded with the rest, his lambs, and, separating them from their shepherd and from one another, led them away and confined them in different divisions of the prison and the house of the Audiencia.

The interdict was published, and the bells began to toll, which disquieted all the people—religious, ecclesiastics, and laymen. Those who had taken refuge in the sacred buildings thought that they were ruined, and those outside felt deprived of the asylum of the church. This disturbance lasted from eight to twelve o'clock; at the latter hour the turbulent crowd proceeded, without order or concert, to the palace of the governor, and entered it without opposition from either the outposts or the soldiers of the guard. Shouting, "Long live the Faith and the Church!" they rushed upstairs, and at that same hour fell upon the governor with weapons, until he fell on the floor with wounds, and demanding confession, and they left him for dead. Then his eldest son arriving—who had been going about the city arresting the priests, and busy with other orders of that sort—the mob killed him also, which occasioned the death of a poor Indian. All these events occurred in about a quarter of an hour, so that by a quarter past twelve even the boys were in the plaza, celebrating the event [cantando la victoria]; the misfortunes [of the people] were at an end.

At the news of the tumult the father minister [of the Jesuit residence] sent several fathers from the house, that they might help to pacify the minds of the people and be ready to hear confessions, according to what necessity demanded; among those assigned to this duty I was one. On the way I met several persons, who told me that the governor was already lying dead; and as one who had gone out only to assist those on whom misfortune might have fallen—which, it was thought, would include many, as is usually the case in such tumults—I hastened my steps to the palace. Finally I found him whom they had considered as dead; he was lying in an apartment, the blood dripping from his wounds, and surrounded with people; and at his side was a religious who had attended him in order to give him absolution. I asked the latter what [had occurred], and whether in his opinion that poor man was in full possession of his senses; he answered that he did not know, but that he had absolved him sub conditione [i.e., conditionally]. When the religious asked me to try to find out in what state he was, I began to say to the dying man what the Lord inspired in me, in order to prepare him for being again absolved—which was done several times by the religious, with full absolution, and without any condition; for such were the tokens [of penitence] afforded by the expression of his face, and his sobs and sighs, and even tears, and his pressing to his lips the crucifix which I placed at his mouth, and so tightly did he press my hand when I asked him to, that he spoke to me more clearly thus than if he had answered with cries.

It was my opinion that he could speak; and, availing myself of an opportunity when I saw the people about him somewhat removed [from his side], I made no little exertion to secure an utterance from him. I spoke close to his ear, in a low voice; and he, recognizing my intention, answered me, saying: "Alas! my father, all this is little compared with what I deserve for my sins, which I confess are infinite; and this which is happening to me is the kindness of God. I do not complain of any one, and I will kiss the feet of every one. I only ask your Grace that you will not leave me until I die, and that you will be my companion until death; and that, if it be possible—so that I may die far away from this noise, and be able to pass in quiet the little time that may remain for me to live—they will carry me to the hospital; that of St. John of God would be the best. But in any case, do not leave me, your Grace, for the Virgin's sake; and care for my soul, that it be not lost." This was what he said to me, in substance, and even literally, the first time when he was able to speak.

Hardly had he said this to me when the people again came around us, in a clamorous crowd, and I turned to contend with them. I made every possible effort to provide for him what comfort I could, but I could only secure this, that they carried him, with me, to a room farther within the house; and there, now trying to restrain the tumult, and now assisting him, I found him always in the same excellent frame of mind. Sometimes I began to hear his confession, in coherent and detailed form; sometimes the confession would be interrupted because the doors at times were opened—until I could, by the aid of some persons whom I knew to be influenced by the fear of God, keep the doors closed for a time. I spent the time thus until about six o'clock, when he died. In that time extreme unction was given to him; and Doctor Rayo, who held delegate authority from the archbishop, absolved him etiam in foro externo [i.e., "also in the outer court"] from the excommunication. I omitted no effort in order that he might use well the time for the benefit of his salvation, regarding which I can state two things. [Here follow long pious reflections, which may be left to the reader's imagination.] Finally, God punished him there for the violence which he had employed with others— not allowing them even the comfort and consolation of communication with their confessors, as some desired; and it was not permitted to them except only to make them comply with the [requirements of the] Church; for when he desired to prepare himself at leisure, and to pass quietly the time which remained to him, with the confessor who was aiding him there, there was no way of securing this. On this account it is my opinion that God chose to punish him in this life in order to pardon him in the other one. This is my opinion; oh, that it might agree with that which God has! for then the salvation of this poor man would be certain.

It has seemed best to me, Father Procurator, to relate this in order that it may be known that this man, however much people undertake to say against him (much of which will be false), met a Christian and Catholic death. And I say further that, although his passions hurried him on to do such outrageous and reckless things, they never separated him from the [Christian] faith or the Catholic religion; and therefore, whatever your Reverence can do to prevent those in Madrid from believing what will be reported in this matter, do it, for God's sake—in regard to the former [i.e., Bustamante's Christian death], acquainting the father confessors with these facts. Moreover, it is not right that such things [as are said against him] should have influence, when the only result will be infamy for him and for the six or seven children whom he has left behind.

On the other hand, it would seem to me desirable that his Majesty command that in the residencia which will be taken of this poor man's government there be no discussion of his personal character, or of his proceedings which have not been injurious to others; and that those which are such be considered only in so far as is necessary to satisfy, so far as is possible, the injured party—or even, putting all this aside, that action be taken only in regard to the goods which at the time of his death might be found to be in his name, secretly and through the agency of others, like those which he has in the ship and patache which this year went to Nueva España. These are going in the name of other persons, but on his account, and amount to a great deal—so much, that if in Mejico the just, prompt, and honest measures were taken to have these goods sold at the ordinary fair, like the rest, and if the proceeds were safely deposited, and his Majesty and the judge of his residencia here were notified of the amount thus realized, I believe that with this alone the king, the bondsmen, and the private persons who should prove themselves to be his legitimate creditors could satisfy their claims against him. [Add to this] the goods that may be found in his house, and those which may be on his account from the coastwise commerce, in order that, when these are converted into money, their just value may be distributed equitably, according to the plan which is prescribed in matters of restitution when there are many creditors.

This precaution will be very necessary in order to prevent many difficulties which must follow from other charges [against him], some being involved in others; and from these will result no greater gain than disturbances in the community, mutual hatreds, the rise of many falsehoods founded in malice, endless delay in ascertaining the truth, relics of quarrels left for the future, the disappearance and destruction of the aforesaid goods of the deceased which can be obtained, and finally the destruction of the wealth of some persons without any benefit to others. This is what I feel in Domino, having considered matters coram ipso [i.e., "in His presence"], and near at hand. Therefore, my fathers, there is nothing more expedient for the service of the two Majesties and of souls than the measure of burying in oblivion [hecharle tierra] all the rest concerning him, especially the suits that he brought against others—since he cannot have authority distinct from that which he must assume on account of his office, as representing the king, and it was not for himself that he demanded justice against the subjects whom he prosecuted, for the good man proceeded against all who opposed him, as seditious traitors—and this it is necessary to lay aside, for it is an intricate affair and will become more so.

Also [I recommend] the approval of what was done in the formation of the government and Audiencia that were organized after the fatal event; for it did not seem that anything else could be done, either as a matter of policy or in conscience, or that would be more agreeable to the wishes of the king, in such circumstances, to do what was right and prudent, without being declared presumptuous.

And who doubts, after reflecting on the event and its antecedent circumstances (and, when one considers what human nature is, it seems as if the event were the natural result of those circumstances)—or, to speak more correctly, on the especial providence of God, and His justice—that also it would be most expedient for the tranquillity of this colony to bury in oblivion likewise the tumult and what occurred in it; and that attention be paid only to taking such measures as will be proper to prevent, so far as that shall be possible, the occurrence of such troubles in the future—or at least not to leave the future so exposed to peril from them?

But what [a task] will that be? Oh, holy God! there is no doubt that it is very difficult. For, as the principal root of these tumultuous excesses and quarrels—inextricable entanglements, which it is impossible to clear up from Filipinas—[is the enormous distance] at which the islands are from the court of their sovereign (who is the one who must supply suitable and timely measures), and this it is impossible to get rid of; it consequently seems also impossible that these regions can ever be protected from difficulties of this sort. The only thing, then, that seems possible is, that these be prevented by a method which will in some way supply the nearness of the sovereign which is necessary for preventing check, in order that they may not occur with such them in time; or that will establish some sort of facility.

But what can this be? I suppose that the politicians will plan the matter much better; but I say in the Lord that I do not find any more convenient way than to establish at this very time an ordinance which, with the royal authority, shall serve to prevent in time the principal difficulties, those which bring on the rest.

Here, my father, the governor takes away and establishes, gives, commands, unmakes and makes, more despotically than does the king himself; and more, in himself he would join in one the royal and the pontifical authority. Royal decrees are not sufficient; for either he hides them, or he does not fulfil them as he ought. The Audiencia does not serve [as a check] on him, for he suppresses and he establishes it, when and how he pleases; nor do other bodies, whether chapters or [religious] communities, whether military or civil; for he does the same thing [with them]. And never do there lack pretexts for doing thus, even though such bodies are appointed by the king; and with the pretext that account of the matter has already been rendered to Madrid, what he has begun remains permanently done, or else he proceeds to change it, as seems good to him.

Assuming this, [it would be best] to maintain here a council, which would be stable and permanent, and to whom, as being supreme, all the decrees and despatches of the king should come addressed, the council distributing these as might be required. No failure in the entire fulfilment of the despatches and decrees of the king should be allowed, save with the agreement of this council; and the governor should not be authorized to appoint or remove officials, or hinder them in the performance of their duties, whether civil or military; they should be appointed by the king, as now are the chief and principal ones, the auditors and fiscal. For the citizens there should be six or eight perpetual regidors, from whom should be elected, according to custom, their alcaldes-in-ordinary. [The king should also appoint] the royal officials who belong to the royal treasury; and, of military officers, the two wardens of the castle in this city and that at Cavite de la Punta, the master-of-camp of the Manila garrison, the sargento-mayor of the plaza, and the lieutenant-general or the general of the artillery. Even if the cause were, in the opinion of the governor, so pressing and evident that he demanded the arrest or suspension of any one of these whom I have mentioned, without waiting for the decision from Madrid, he should not do so without giving account to the said council, or without its consent; and if the case were so urgent that it should be necessary to arrest any one of those persons before giving account to the said council, such account should be furnished immediately afterward—by the governor, or, if he cannot do it, by the fiscal of his Majesty; and, if neither of them do it, the president of the said council, when he learns of the facts (in whatever manner he may obtain such knowledge), shall demand that he be given the motive and cause for the decision reached with the official who is imprisoned or banished, or deprived of the exercise of his office, in order that his council, when informed of the case, may take action. If the decision of the council is contrary to the resolution made by the governor, the official shall continue in the exercise of his functions until the final decision shall come from Madrid. And if perchance the governor disobey this rule, and do not render account of the motive and cause which has influenced him to take that course with the officer whom he is treating as a criminal, the president of the council, with its advice, is authorized to replace, and shall do so, the said official in the exercise of his office. In this particular, all the other officials of the king, and his soldiers, must obey this president, and not the governor, under such penalties as his Majesty shall see fit to impose upon them.

Item: If any one of these persons appointed by the king fail to act, by either death or any other accident, another person shall not be appointed in his place by the governor alone, but he shall do so jointly with the auditors and military officers above mentioned, if the ad interim appointment is to a military post; and if it is municipal, the electors shall be the governor, the auditors, and the other regidors. If the appointment is that of a royal treasury official, [he shall be chosen] by the remaining members of that body, with the governor and the auditors—among whom I include, for all the elections, the fiscal of his Majesty—and the person who receives the most votes shall be chosen; and in case the votes are divided among two or more, the lot shall decide. He who is thus elected shall remain as a substitute in the vacant post until the king shall appoint a proprietary incumbent, and shall possess the same privileges as the others have, besides that of continuing under the protection of the said royal council.

As for those who might compose this council, I cannot find any who would be better—in order that it might be durable, and most free from prejudice; and that its proceedings might be most prudent and reasonable, judicious and learned—than the following: for president, the archbishop of Manila, and in his absence the dean of the holy cathedral church of Manila; for its members, the dean, in case he is not president—and, if he act in that post, in his place shall come in the senior prebend, by vote of those in the council; and besides these, the doctoral prebend of the same church, and the rectors and prefects (or the regents) of the two universities, Santo Domingo and that of the Society, or those who shall take the place of all these. Those who occupy the chairs of Institutes7 and laws in the university (which have been recently established) shall not have place in this council, for I do not know whether they will be permanent; and because, even if they are so, these professors must be included in the number of those who are under the protection of the said council, as being officials appointed by the king and subjects of the government here. The decision of the members of this council must go out in the name of the whole body, and will be that which shall receive the most votes from the six councilors; and in case of disagreement among them the decision will be that to which their president shall agree, out of those proposed in the council—each one of these councilors giving his opinion in writing, which opinion must be a decisive vote, and not merely consultory.

And because the chief mate [*capitan maestre*] of the galleon is the one who has charge of the royal mails, it would seem desirable, in order to make sure that this official conducts himself with entire fidelity in surrendering them to the said council, that he who is chosen for that post shall [not] be selected altogether by the governor, but must be approved by the council, as protector of the royal decrees and officials of Filipinas, which is the sole employment that the said council will have. Thus that official, once he is chosen and approved, must remain under the protection and jurisdiction of the said council until he has fulfilled his commission.

And because this council will remain entirely free from the possibility of being disturbed by the governor, and because the most scandalous controversies which have occurred in these islands have proceeded from the abuse of the royal prerogatives, the governor with the Audiencia seeking by force to deprive the archbishop and the ecclesiastical judges of the secular revenues—for sometimes they overstep the bounds in the essential part, and in other cases exceed the limits immoderately in their mode of procedure—it would be expedient and even necessary for his Majesty to forbid them to do so, and deprive them of authority to enforce that. They should be allowed only to ask for it, and, having given information of it to his Majesty, await his royal decision in order that that may be accomplished, in reality and in the mode of procedure, which always will be just and reasonable, and carried out to the letter, as his Majesty shall ordain for the service of God and for his own.

In this manner my poor mind has planned, having considered these matters in the Lord, in order that some means may be employed to make up for the distance [from Madrid], and to place some check on the despotic sway which, on account of the distance, the governors of these islands possess; for, as I said above, not only do they act more despotically than could the king and the pope if those rulers were at the same time united in one being, but also they are the whole [government] and all the offices, since every one must do and does only what the governor desires, with reference to the offices which the king entrusts to him.

It is clear that, for the object that is desired, that which will contribute most of all is the judicious choice of the governor and the other officials, [who should be] worthy, upright, unprejudiced, disinterested, having the fear of God, and zealous for His honor and the service of the king—as well as for their own honor, which is established by this very effort. But qui sunt hi, et laudavimus eos?8 I see it, forsooth. On this I will only say that the governor in any case should be a soldier, honorable and experienced, to whom the government is given on account of his merits; and not one who may be a merchant or trader. Still less should he be one who has secured the post of governor with money, and not with merits. [In order to secure] for the other officials men worthy by their merits, fitted for their positions, having the fear of Cod, and honorable, an important means, without doubt, is care in their selection.

I see that your Reverences will tell me that I am tiring myself uselessly, and that nothing of this concerns me. This may all be true, but I believe that in the presence of God this my labor will have, if not reward, at least excuse, since I have undertaken it With an aim to the welfare of the souls in these islands, and to the progress in them of our holy faith, [objects] which are hindered by misgovernment here.

In regard to the other matters [here], I know that every one is sending in accounts of them, and I am sure that each one will give such information as he feels is true; as for all those who are doing this officially, who shall say that they will not report according to what is right, and with weighty arguments? I, at least, cannot persuade myself to think otherwise; for all the said persons I regard as truthful and God-fearing men. The one with whom I am better acquainted than with any of the others is Don Francisco Fernandez Toribio, an auditor, and now fiscal, and a [university] professor of the Institutes; and I can at once inform you that what he may say can be believed, that it is his own opinion, and that in saying it he will be governed more by reason than by prejudice. He is a man indeed, since he is so good, upright, disinterested, God-fearing, and truly honorable; and although he and others like him would be good for these places, yet they are not good for men of this sort. God preserve your Reverence for many years, as I desire. Manila, November 19, 1719. The humble servant of your Reverence, etc.,

Diego de Otazo

I.H.S.

Letter from the archbishop of Manila

I had given to your Paternity account [of affairs] last year, by way of Mejico, of the wretched condition in which this commonwealth and these islands were, and of the unspeakable grief with which I was living at seeing the lawlessness, tyranny, misgovernment, and insatiable greed of the new governor, Field-Marshal Don Fernando Manuel de Bustillo Bustamante y Rueda; and afterward in the same year, by the Eastern [India] route, I also sent to your Paternity an account of the commotion [here] and the violent death of the said gentleman, who perished on the eleventh day of October in the same year. Nevertheless, as the latter route is so irregular, and it may have happened that the said letter of mine has not reached your hands, it has seemed to me prudent to repeat my last letter, and send it by the galleon which is now sailing for Acapulco, in order that your Paternity may be fully informed about that event (although summarily), on account of what may yet occur.

The said gentleman reached this city on the thirty-first of July in the year 17; and from the outset it seemed, with his disposition—unquiet, changeable, petulant, and with inordinately bad tendencies—that he directed all his efforts to the ruin of these islands. He persecuted the citizens, arresting some, exiling others with pretexts of embassies, conquests, and new expeditions, and causing others to seek refuge for themselves, fearful of his harsh treatment; and he fattened on the wealth of all the people.

To these evil beginnings corresponded like ends; and from so mischievous causes were experienced the effects in the unlooked-for and miserable death which he, with his eldest son, encountered on the eleventh day of October in the past year. At that time the common people rose in rebellion, and, going to his palace, deprived him of life, without his having at his side any person who would defend him, even among his own servants. This is a proof that he was hated by all; and it is notorious confirmation of the truth of this statement that the great precautions which he had taken since the tenth [of that month] for his safety in his own palace availed him nothing; he had provided soldiers, both infantry and cavalry, who, as they affirmed to me, numbered more than three hundred. In the general opinion this success [in killing the governor] was gained by especial permission of His [Divine] Majesty, who by this act of providence, through His lofty and venerable judgments, chose to furnish relief when it could not be looked for so soon from human sources.

This tumult was caused by the arbitrary nature of the governor's proceedings; for, without conforming to laws, either human or divine, it seems as if he had—according to my judgment before God, in whose presence I speak—no other law than his own will, from which proceeded his despotic decisions, directed to his own advantage and not to the general and public welfare, which ought to have been his chief care.

With this consideration [i.e., his own advantage], and in order to find the goods of the master-of-camp Don Esteban de Higuiño (whom he had kept a prisoner since the beginning of August), he gave orders that the chief notary of the municipal council of this city should demand, at the end of September, the official records of a notary-public who had taken refuge in my cathedral on the same day when the arrest of the said master-of-camp occurred. The consultation which he held and the petition which he presented to the ad interim fiscal of the Audiencia were merely formal; the matter was referred to the royal Audiencia, without stating whether it was by a consultory or a decisive vote; and the papers were considered in the royal Audiencia, which was composed of only one official, who had for associate judge the counselor [asesor] of the government. This auditor was commanded to despatch officially a royal decree for the surrender of those notarial records; and I was notified of this on the twenty-sixth of September, and the papers offered to me with a view of the decree of August 11, in which the said auditor was qualified for [transacting] the business of the Audiencia—a copy of which decree I send with this. There were various difficulties in regard to the fulfilment and observance of this decree9 on account of the serious injuries which might result to the administration of justice in the ecclesiastical estate, and to the sheep of my flock. Obliged as I am in conscience to attend to their relief, I conferred regarding these doubts with persons in whom I had confidence, and with the [heads of the] two universities of this city—in whose opinions I tried to find ground for the decree which enabled this single auditor to have his abode in the royal hall [of justice]; because for this he had exchanged the imprisonment in which he had remained in the fort and castle of Santiago. Their uniform reply to me was, that I ought not to consider the Audiencia which was formed in this manner as a royal Audiencia, or the decree which was issued [by it], with the royal name and the seal of his Majesty, as a royal decree. I did not [at once] come to a decision in a matter so important, and on which so many things depended; and moreover, in order to show my profound veneration for the royal prerogatives of his Majesty and my earnest desire for the public tranquillity—to which I have given attention from my first entrance into this archbishopric, as also to the amicable relations which I have maintained with the royal officials of his Majesty (especially with the governor of these islands), since this contributes much to the service of God and of his Majesty—I presented my doubts, with a copy of the replies given by the universities, to the said deceased governor, at a conference which was held on the seventh of October. I charged him as his friend that, considering these questions with the careful reflection which is demanded by the strict account of our deeds which we must render to God, he should do what was most safe for the discharge of our consciences in the service of God and his Majesty. To this advice he gave me no answer, either written or verbal; and when I was waiting for one, in order to choose the safest [course] and avoid consequences which always are injurious to the public welfare, on October 8 (which was Sunday), a little before twelve o'clock, I was annoyed by a second royal decree—in which, professing not to understand the reasons which I had for doubts, he insisted on the surrender of the said records. Having answered that in order to make my decision I was waiting for his reply, I pressed him for it [on the next day,] the ninth, with another [written] communication of substantially the same tenor as the first one, exhorting him to make the best decision, that is, the one which he would at the hour of death wish to have made; but he declined to receive it for that morning, on the pretext that he was ill—although it was plain to me that he was well [enough] to hold conferences with the single auditor of whom the Audiencia was composed. In the afternoon, he gave orders to receive my communication, at the repeated insistence of the chief notary of my archbishopric, who carried it; but he would not allow the notary to enter the palace or to see him.

From this stoppage of friendly relations and lack of civility which I began to experience in regard to this matter, and on account of the news that I had of the repeated deliberations that he held [with the auditor], I could only expect very evil results in the banishment of myself and of the ecclesiastics—which I mistrusted from the twenty-seventh day of September, when I had sent my provisor with the cura of Balayan, for them to certify to the said governor the information which on this very point had been privately given to the said cura by an alférez named Antonio de Torres, who had much familiar intercourse with the said governor. This information was reduced to the statement that a certain alférez had told how his Lordship had resolved to banish me from this city by the middle of October, because he had made ready to demand from me, about that time, that he might remove to the most distant of these islands all the persons who had taken refuge in these churches, both within and without this city; and, taking for granted, at the start, that I would not permit it, with that ground for action he would proceed to carry out the said banishment. When I learned that the said alférez, when summoned to the governor's presence, confirmed his statement, although he exculpated himself with frivolous pretexts; and when I did not see any punishment inflicted on him for this insolence, and knew, moreover, that they only gave him orders that the matter should be kept secret (as it was): I had sufficient grounds for the said suspicion. And as it was quite consonant with prudence to prevent the dangers and obviate the measures from which might result these evil consequences, having assured myself of the only arguments10 with which I could prevent this act—to command the single minister in this Audiencia and his associate, under penalty of major excommunication and [a fine] of five hundred ducados in silver, to abstain and refrain from sitting as judges and transacting the affairs of the Audiencia, the formation of which, in my judgment, had been invalid—I acted accordingly, in conformity with the opinions for which I had obtained confirmation by the vote of my cabildo and the superiors of the holy religious orders. Availing myself of this means for ending the controversy, as conducive to the public tranquillity for which I was striving, without intermeddling with the governor I issued two monitory decrees, in which I gave orders as above, in order that at the very same time they might be notified, to the said minister and his associate;

and I committed this business to the doctoral canon of my church, in order that, as a discreet and capable person (since he is morning professor of canon law for his Majesty), he might conduct it with the judgment and the precautions which are desirable in a matter so delicate. He went to execute this commission in the hall of the Audiencia, in which building this single minister of that court has his abode, abandoning the obligations of his rank, and trampling on both human and divine laws. Hardly had he heard my name, when the notification of this decree was begun, when he snatched it from the hands of the doctoral canon and tore it to pieces; he demanded a sword and buckler, and the protection of the king; and he uttered so many cries, and left his room with so much noise, that he disturbed the entire palace of the governor. He goaded on the governor so that, without any warrants and without a session of this so-called royal Audiencia, he seized the said canon and the prebend Doctor Don Juan de la Fuente, who accompanied him, in the porch of the court prison; and there they remained, surrounded by soldiers with pikes and naked cutlasses, during all the night of October 10. At that time he gave orders to surround his entire palace with a guard of infantry, and would not allow that three ecclesiastics should go up to see him, whom I sent with a courteous message, in order to obtain information as to the motive of this singular proceeding. The governor gave orders to detain them in the guard-house, where they remained among the rabble of soldiers, exposed to the inclemency of the wind and of the rain which fell that night, until the morning; and then they locked up the ecclesiastics in a small room which was connected with the guardroom of the halberdiers, without any food—at which the city began to be disquieted. The doctoral canon and the prebend were conveyed by an escort of soldiers with an officer to the castle and fort of Santiago, where the castellan kept them confined under a guard of his soldiers, and without any communication [with other persons]; and as soon as they reached this place, at daybreak, the military watchword was changed, [accompanied] with [the firing of] a cannon loaded with balls, and [the beating of] war-drums; and the bells were rung as a summons for the entire city. Disturbed at this signal—which, by an edict published in the preceding year, was given for their attendance at the royal palace—all the citizens gathered there; and when they were assembled the late governor addressed to them a vigorous exhortation that they should defend the royal jurisdiction, which he assumed that I had injured and usurped. He censured the opinions of the two universities, and berated the persons who signed them, saying that they did not understand the laws, and that they were disturbing the church just as one Molinos11 and one Luther had disturbed it.

After six on the morning of Óctober 11, as it was evident to me that the notification had been actually made—by the information which by my order was received; and by a brief letter which they brought me from the said doctoral canon and prebend, in which they assured me of their imprisonment on account of the notification to the single minister of the Audiencia of the monitory decree (which was made ipso voce) warning him that his name would be placed on the list of excommunicates [tablilla]— as also to the eldest son of the governor (who was sargento-mayor of this army) and his adjutant, I gave orders that they he posted as publicly excommunicated, about seven o'clock in the morning.

At that hour the superiors of the holy religious orders, with other prominent religious who were under their direction, assembled at my archiepiscopal palace in order to console me in the trouble that had come upon me from such noisy preparations and violent demonstrations; and while we were discussing these matters, and inferring from these premises the evil consequences which openly were dreaded for the ecclesiastical estate, through the doors of my archiepiscopal palace (which were open) entered military officers, armed, with a great number of soldiers; and, having filled the palace and surrounded it with infantry, the officers came upstairs, with the adjutant who had been publicly excommunicated, until they reached the room where I was with the said superiors and religious. A captain named Don Pedro de Velasco said that he came in behalf of his Majesty, and by order of his governor and captain-general, in order that I might go with him to the royal court; and he would not accept the reply which I gave him in writing, assuring me that he was under penalty of death if he acted differently. Although I did not consider the court to which he summoned me as the royal court, since the single auditor who composed it was execrable, I resolved to go (as I solemnly declared) in consideration of the public tranquillity and the respect due to the royal name of his Majesty. But as soon as I left my palace, the military officers and soldiers surrounded me; and when we reached the door of the governor's apartments, by which I had to enter, I saw that it was locked. I recognized the deceit and malicious subterfuge by which they had drawn me [from my house]; and I declared this, as well as that I would not go of my own will to any other place than the royal court. I tried to shelter myself in the royal seminary of San Felipe, in order not to be wet by the heavy rain that was falling, but the military officers would not allow me to do this; and therefore I leaned against the lintel of a door that stood open in a private house. The sargento-mayor, who was a son of the governor, apologized for taking part with his father in this deceit, since it was required from him. Don Benito Carrasco, an alcalde-in-ordinary, came to tell me of the order of his Lordship that I must go wherever the military officers and the soldiers carried me. They, seeing my unwillingness, lifted the chair in which I was sitting, and by force carried me to the public street, where my sedan-chair was—which I had to enter, in order to avoid even more disgraceful, scandalous, and sacrilegious acts; and I allowed myself to be carried—surrounded by armed soldiers, as if I were a criminal who had committed atrocious offenses—through the public streets to the fort and castle of Santiago. There they delivered me as a prisoner to the castellan, Don Ygnacio Navamuel, and he received me as such, and kept me in his dwelling-house; nor would the sargento-mayor, who remained in command at my archiepiscopal palace, permit them to bring me the bed and small chest of clothing which the members of my household tried to send me for my personal comfort and cleanliness.

After seizing me, they proceeded to convey other prisoners with a guard of soldiers: my secretary, who was confined in the same castle; the commissary of the Crusade; the schoolmaster and a prebend of the cathedral; the commissary and secretary of the Holy Office of the Inquisition, with two other religious of St. Dominic; the prior of the convent of San Agustin; the rector of the college of the Society of Jesus, together with the master Father Avina; and my provisor—placing them in the infantry barracks and the quarters of the royal accountancy, with orders that no one should speak to them.12 They would have carried away, in the same manner, all the persons who were in my palace, if the common people had not opposed them; for it seems that the intention of the governor was, as his corresponding secretary has deposed, to seize all the persons who signed the opinions which the universities gave me.

For this so execrable deed there was no cause on my part, since I did not prosecute any determination of my own that was opposed to the royal laws of his Majesty; nor was the monitory decree of that character, which was notified to the single auditor of whom the royal Audiencia was composed— for with that document I aimed, as a prelate, to deprive the governor of the pernicious means which he was employing in order that he might not have in his government any other law than his own ambitious and depraved will. Nor for carrying out my seizure, under the pretext of banishment, did he previously take the steps which the royal laws provide; for the royal writs were not issued which should have been, to know whether there had been any failure of obedience on my part—a proceeding which is required in order that the penalty of [loss of] the temporal revenues may be applied to ecclesiastics—as the auditor himself and his associate have testified. For it was resolved, in a session which they held on October 9, that an official of the royal Audiencia should go to confer with me over the difficulties about which I had consulted the governor; but this formality was not carried out. On the other hand, availing himself of his administrative13 power—to which, at the time, they likewise agreed—for use in case of any emergency, when that arose of the outcry which this single auditor made at the time when he was notified of the said monitory decree, the governor compelled them [i.e., the auditor and his associate] to dictate an act, assuming that it was one proceeding from the royal court (although it was not such), on the night of October 10, in which they decided that what had been agreed upon the day before should be carried out, in regard to the use of the [governor's] administrative power against my person and those of the other ecclesiastics. Although, in order to excuse themselves for the many offenses that they committed in this so discordant session [acuerdo], they undertake to avail themselves of the fear and coercion in which they say the governor kept them, I know not whether this evasion which they use as an excuse can assist them, when as Christians they know that they ought to die rather than sin; and when, since they could have availed themselves of the privilege of sanctuary (as others did) to prevent injury to their souls, they did not do so, through caring for the comfort of their bodies.

After the unfortunate event which I have related had occurred, all the people hastened to the castle where I was, and, without my being able to resist their impetuosity, they liberated me from that place, generally acclaiming me as their governor in the name of his Majesty. This was the greatest blow that could happen to me, and I protested against it before God [saying that], if my imprisonment and its previous hardships could serve as a mortification to me, this demonstration grieved me far more, without comparison, as being so entirely contrary to my own judgment and disposition. But the people, who still remained under arms, cried out that they would not lay down their weapons, until I should accept, in the name of his Majesty, the government over them. At this I made all possible protests, and efforts to resist this, with the prominent and learned persons of the city, not only ecclesiastics but laymen; but as they were unanimously agreed, with the general feeling and opinion that I ought in conscience and justice to accept this post, for the sake of quieting this community which otherwise would run great risk, and the disturbances would increase, and be the cause of greater misfortunes and more violent deaths—I was obliged to accept14 the said government, sacrificing my own [mode of] life to the service of God our Lord and that of his Majesty (whom may God preserve), and for the welfare of the people.

It is impossible, even with the greatest care and attention, to relate this affair with all its circumstances, so marvelous and mysterious were many of them. Likewise, it is impossible to explain the ruined, wasted, and unsettled condition in which everything remains; therefore, I will only say to your Paternity that I ask you to have compassion on me, and that you will earnestly commend me to God our Lord in your prayers, that He may grant me light, and judgment, and strength for the great task in which I am engaged. I remain, as I should, entirely at your Paternity's orders, continually entreating that His [Divine] Majesty may preserve you for happy years, as I desire. Manila, June 28, 1720.

[Francisco, archbishop of Manila].

1 Zúñiga says (Hist. de Philipinas, pp. 443–445) that the Moros of Joló and Mindanao, although their rulers were nominally at peace with the Spaniards, had frequently ravaged the islands, the sultans pretending that they could not restrain their subjects; Bustamante accordingly decided to rebuild the fortress at Zamboanga, but when he laid this plan before the junta of treasury officials they refused it by a vote of ten against seven—on the ground that the fort was of no service against the Moros, and would cause extraordinary expense. "As a matter of fact, the entire situado of that military post amounts, in supplies and money, to about 25,000 pesos, which only serves to enrich the governor, who is sent from Manila every three years. Against the majority of votes in the junta the governor gave orders to reëstablish the post, exasperating people's minds, and giving occasion to the malcontents to exaggerate his despotism. The Recollect fathers, who had returned to the province of Calamianes because the secular priests—whom the bishop of Zebú had stationed there when the Recollects abandoned it—could not maintain themselves there on account of the Moros, erected with the money of their province some little forts, hardly deserving that name, which did not shelter many places in those islands from the pirates; and they requested the governor to establish a post in the island of Paragua, at Labo, hoping that thus they would be freed from those annoying enemies. The governor consented to this, and established a post [there] at much less cost than that of Zamboanga, but equally useless."

2 The Jesuit Delgado says of this (Hist. de Filipinas, p. 205): "I was at that time in Manila, and saw the bodies of those unfortunate men, dragged along, stripped of their garments, and covered with some old rags; and I was obliged, in order that I might enter the anteroom of the palace, to step over the

body of the governor, which was lying across the threshold of the door." The editor of Delgado reproduces in a footnote Otazo's letter (q.v. in this volume, post), with the following remark: "Don José Montero y Vidal, in his Historia de la piratería, t. 1, p. 254, asserts that Don Fernando de Bustamante was assassinated in a tumult at the head of which the Jesuits placed themselves. The following document will show that gentleman the falsity of his assertion."

3 Archbishop Cuesta surrendered the government of the islands to Bustamante's successor, the Marqués de Torre Campo, who took possession of it on August 6, 1721. The home government censured Cuesta for too little strictness in investigating Bustamante's murder, and transferred him to the bishopric of Mechoacan, Mexico. He arrived at Acapulco January 11, 1724, took charge of his see on April 18, and died on May 30 following.

4 "The long residencia of the persecuted auditor Torralba—imprisoned sometimes in Cavite and sometimes in Manila, and always loaded with taunts and annoyances—was settled by the Council of Indias, who condemned him to pay a fine of 100,000 pesos, besides the 20,000 previously imposed, with perpetual deprivation of office and exile from Madrid, and Filipinas. He was reduced to such want that he had to beg alms to support himself; and when he died, in 1736, he was buried as a pauper in [the church of] San Juan de Dios." (Montero y Vidal, Hist. de Filipinas, i, p. 436.)

5 According to Zúñiga (Hist. de Philipinas, p. 443), the hatred of the citizens arose from the fact that Bustamante's harsh collection of the debts due to the royal treasury, many of those who owed the king having died, or being in great poverty, obliged the bondsmen to pay those debts; this was so resented by them that the citizens of Manila began to hate the governor.

6 In the Ventura del Arco MSS. (Ayer library), iv, pp. 433–435, is a letter, apparently by one of the Jesuits, describing this attack; it differs from that of Concepción in some points. The attack was made by Malanaos, from La Sabanilla, under the chief Balasi; and warning of it was sent to the governor, Sebastian de Amorena, five days beforehand, by Prince Radiamura, brother of the sultan of Mindanao. The attack was made by the "king" of Joló and Buhayen, with 104 joangas, and a force of 3,000 men by land and

sea. In the fort were not more than 200 men—Pampangos, creoles (probably "Morenos," that is, Malabars, etc.), and a few Spaniards; but they fought so bravely that the enemy could accomplish nothing in a siege of three months. Finally Radiamura sent a force of 1,090 men to aid the Spaniards, and at this the enemy raised the siege and went back to their homes. The above document is preceded by an account (pp. 409–432) of affairs at Zamboanga from its rebuilding to 1721, also from a Jesuit hand. The writer says that 3,000 men were sent for this enterprise, who built a town in a few months, although under the greatest difficulties, the former buildings being destroyed, and the site overgrown with shrubs and trees. By that time Bustamante seemed to have forgotten the undertaking, and they were neglected and left without aid. Of the soldiers, "some had but small wages, and most of them none; and the workmen were almost all obliged to serve at their own expense." Desertions ensued, so that "at the end of six months, hardly 300 men remained; and of these no small number died and many of them were sick, overcome by labor, or hunger, or the unusual difficulty of working the hard soil." So great were their miseries that they talked of abandoning the fort and returning to Manila; but in the following February several Jesuits arrived at Zamboanga and brought tidings that a new governor (Amorena) was to come with reënforcements, and supplies of money and food. This was accomplished in June, when 200 soldiers arrived from Manila; while in May the Jesuit José de Zisa had brought from Cebú supplies of money and food, with 200 Boholans—who, however, "are very much afraid of the Moros." Governor Cuesta sent orders for the old soldiers at Zamboanga to return to Manila, and for the Boholans to go back to their own villages; thus the garrison was left in poor condition to withstand an enemy, which probably emboldened the Moros to attack the fort in the following December, as is told above. The writer here mentioned states that the Jesuits had succeeded in making a surprising number of conversions, almost 600 persons being baptized in the Zamboanga district.

7 Spanish, Instituta, i.e., the compendium of Roman civil law compiled by the emperor Justinian. The mention of "the

university" in this sentence is presumably of San José, the Jesuit institution.

8 Thus in Ventura del Arco; but the indicative form in the second clause seems hardly satisfactory. One would rather expect a subjunctive with ut, making it read, "Who are they, that we may praise them?"

9 Cuesta here alludes to the decree ordering the surrender of the records, and to its encroachment on the ecclesiastical immunity.

10 In text, malos fundamentos; but malos seems improbable, as applied to the archbishop's own measures. It may be regarded as probably a copyist's error for solos.

11 Miguel Molinos was a Spanish theologian, born at Zaragoza in 1627. He was one of the mystical thinkers, and attracted a considerable following, not only in Spain but in Rome, where finally he settled. He there published a book entitled Guia de la piedad, in which was taught the doctrine called "quietist;" this was condemned by Innocent XI, who caused him to be placed in the dungeons of the Inquisition, where he died (1696). An interesting account of him is given in the historical romance by J. H. Shorthouse, John Inglesant.

12 When Archbishop Camacho attempted to enforce the episcopal right of visitation of the regular curas, the superiors of the orders replied to him "first verbally and afterward in a written statement, which was composed by the Jesuit Father Avina, who had been an auditor of the royal Audiencia of Manila." (Zúñiga's Historia, p. 398.)

13 Spanish, economica potestad; but the word economica is here applied in an unusual sense, which is not made apparent by the definitions in the lexicons. It is possible that, as used here, it is derived from ecónomo, "he who is appointed to administer and collect the incomes of ecclesiastical posts that are vacant, or are held in trust" (Barcia)—the governor, as possessing this power, endeavoring to force a vacancy in the offices of archbishop and others, that he might use that power. Or, economica may mean "reserve," applied to powers placed in the governor's hands in reserve, only to be used in emergencies.

14 "Never has there been seen a tumult [of the people] in which ambition was less dominant; all were content with their own offices, and at seeing themselves free from unjust and violent imprisonments. Only the archbishop, who had risen to the post of governor, was disturbed and uneasy; but his mind was somewhat calmed when he received a royal decree in which his Majesty commissioned the archbishop to restore the royal Audiencia to the same footing which it had before, and to set free Señor Velasco; and, in case he should be hindered by the governor, to suspend the latter from his office and himself assume the government in person—which was almost the same as what had just been accomplished, so far as this uprising concerned him." (Zúñiga, Hist. de Philipinas, p. 463.)

LETTER BY A SPANISH OFFICER

Cousin, friend, and sir:

At the coming of the galleon which arrived here from Nueva España at the end of July in last year, 1729, I received two letters from your Grace of the same tenor, dated April 19, 1728. While they gave me most special pleasure, on account of the consolation which is afforded me by all the letters from your Grace which I am so fortunate as to see, I have not been and am not able to express my feelings at the news contained in them of the grievous illness, the inflammation in the chest, from which your Grace has suffered for so long a time; and I am very anxious that you should continue to improve, so that your Grace may be entirely free from it (as I hope you now are), and restored to the excellent health which I earnestly hope you may experience for many years. In the midst of so much vexation as has surrounded me, God has been pleased to grant me the favor of good health, so liberally that it seems as if He had cast me in bronze; for He has preserved me in the midst of so much trouble without the slightest headache, contrary to my usual condition, for which I give thanks without number to His great goodness—remaining, as I always shall, so devoted to your Grace as you must well know.

The governor of these islands, Don Fernando Baldes Tamon, arrived here safely in the above-mentioned galleon, and accordingly took possession of this office, in which he continues to show the earnest zeal which, with a desire for what is most conformable to right, actuates him. From the place from which the mails which came in the same galleon were despatched to this city he wrote to me—on account of the news which they gave him there of my troubles—with very cordial expressions of affection; and as soon as he arrived here he began to confirm this impression, not only by his confidences on various matters, and by having cared for the comfort of some of my dependents—about whom unfortunately, doubtless on account of my lack of means, I am nevertheless being undeceived, by experiencing [from them], in return, that ingratitude which always more than abounds here—but by manifesting to the public that he valued above others [even] my uselessness. [He did so] in such a manner that, recognizing this, envy and prejudice were aroused, especially that of the licentiates and auditors, to see how they could deprive me of this gentleman's protection. Not only to show my gratitude for his kind intentions above mentioned, but in order to carry out the prudent counsel which your Grace is pleased to give me, I endeavored to follow from those beginnings the line of returning his kindness, as is proper, manifesting my feeling of obligation as well as I was able, and even in the midst of the many pecuniary losses that I have experienced—which have been caused not by extravagance, since I have tried to live as plainly as a religious, but by the unfortunate result of fairs in which everything has been lost, besides the unlooked-for destruction of property1 when the galleon was wrecked in the year 726. The day before he took possession of the government, I waited on him with a batôn [of office] made of gold, with a diamond which I caused to be set in its tip, which was valued at more than six hundred pesos. Don Fernando still continues in his kind regard for me, although these knaves have not relaxed in their perverse designs. Your Grace may rest assured that, on my part, not only will not the slightest cause be given to him for growing cool toward me, but I shall, on the other hand, endeavor to secure the opposite result, in whatever concerns the behavior that is due him. Your Grace will please say the same to all your honored friends, who, influenced by the [same] affectionate loyalty [fina ley] which I acknowledge toward your Grace, have always favored us, pledging themselves to advance my interests with him— especially Señors Legarra and Maturana.2 The latter himself has told me that Don Fernando is under obligations of great friendship to them, and that they will take especial pains to talk with him in my behalf. While on my part I give them grateful thanks, suited to the extraordinary obligation to them under which I shall always remain, I am meantime fulfilling that obligation without [unnecessary] delay, for the next galleon (since the [brief] time does not give me leisure for this one), in attending to the affairs of the above-mentioned gentlemen, Señors Legarra and Maturana—and in regard to the others. In virtue of the knowledge that your Grace can do me the pleasure of facilitating those which are, I trust that you will be pleased to continue to me the much that I owe to you, and for which I shall always remain under great obligation to you, by asking them that on the first occasion, or in reply to this, they will deign to confer on us the new favor of returning thanks to this knight; for that will be a circumstance which will gratify him, and will certainly be very apropos. And in case they consent to bestow on us this new honor, I trust that your Grace will please arrange that the letters come through my hand, in order that I may deliver them to him.

By the letters which I wrote to your Grace, in the aforesaid last year, you will be fully informed of the extraordinary quarrel in which I was involved by the bad counsel and selfish designs of the father of my wife Doña Maria Josepha, encouraged by the mischief-making partisans that he has. On this topic I ought to add that, soon after the galleon which carried the aforesaid letters had sailed from this place, the said Doña Maria Josepha with great eagerness made known her desire to return home with me, urgently entreating that I would enable her to do so as soon as possible. Such being the relations between us, and the lawsuit being then near its final limit [estar en terminos de concluirse] (since all the evidence [necessary] for deciding it had already been furnished), and since, to judge by what was coming out in the suit, much annoyance could be occasioned by my side to her father, in order that it might serve as a warning and correction to the malice and evil design with which he undertook this quarrel, I resolved, responding to the good-will of the said Doña Maria Josepha, to give her the satisfaction of [granting] her petition. By way of correlative [to this], I performed the feat of overlooking, in regard to that same father of hers, the injury that in every way he has tried to do me; so that, although I could, while awaiting the decision [of the lawsuit] which, as the saying goes, was already in my hands—inflict on him most grievous injury, notwithstanding all this, from that time I formed the steadfast resolve that in case Doña Maria Josepha and I were reunited, as we were expecting, not only would I do my share to secure that from it not the slightest [harm] should result therefrom to him, but that we should maintain such harmony that this matter should no longer be remembered. In pursuance of this resolve, and because it seemed to me that this was the best way in order to live in conformity to the commands of God, I spoke upon this subject to the former governor, and to the archbishop3— who, on account of their earnest desire, as heads of the commonwealth, that this result might be secured, were unspeakably delighted that Doña Maria Josepha and I should come to so good a resolution. Immediately they held a conference in regard to the measures that should be taken in order that this reunion might be accomplished as soon as possible; and as it seemed best to them that it should be done through a conference with her father, since she had asked me that the matter might be thus arranged, they agreed to talk with him about it; this business was attended to by the archbishop, in his own name and in that of the governor. Although that gentleman [i.e., Doña Maria's father] answered the archbishop with plausible arguments, to the effect that our union did not depend upon himself, but upon the aforesaid Doña Maria Josepha, but that he would, nevertheless, speak to her with the aim of promoting it, he acted so deceitfully that, in place of devoting himself to carrying out that promise, what he did was to go, a short time after he had left the presence of the archbishop, to the place where (as I told your Grace in my previous letters) Doña Maria Josepha was staying. [There], like a lion unchained—goaded by the idea of what the archbishop had given him to understand, to the effect that Doña Maria Josepha and I would certainly come together in a very short time, and by his own notion that we had been communicating with each other with that object—he began to threaten her in the most extravagant terms, in order not only to break up her purpose of reconciliation, but to prevent her from having the slightest communication with me. Not halting at this alone, his preposterous behavior went so far that he visited the provincial of St. Dominic; and the latter, being a good friend of his, and a man of so excellent judgment as he has shown in this affair, complied with his demand—which was, that the provincial should carry into effect whatever orders he [i.e., my wife's father] should give to the prioress of the house where Doña Maria Josepha was.4 The prioress obliged that lady to leave the rooms in which she was living, which had a view of the street, and placed her in others where I could not possibly speak to her on any side of them. They placed such constraint upon her that she experienced inexpressible affliction, through this and other most improper measures which they took—even going so far that [they would not admit] the daughter whom I had by Doña Rafaela (whom may God keep), when they learned that this girl had on previous occasions gone to that house on account of the request that the said Doña Maria Josepha had made to me, that I would send my daughter to her; for they made arrangements to deprive her of the pleasure of having the girl with her, availing themselves of the same means which Herod used when he published the edict for the slaughter of the Innocents, so that the death of Christ our blessing might be included therein. For, not shooting openly at the window they aimed at, in order to attain their object orders were given by the provincial that in no case should any young girl be allowed to enter the house—notwithstanding the fact that until then not the slightest objection had been raised to the admission of any of the girls who were of my daughter's age, and even when they had been going to that house for a longer time than she. When I learned of all these and other wrongful acts, I brought them to the notice of the archbishop, who was amazed—modifying the idea that he had formed of my wife's father from his previous actions, and being equally surprised at the provincial for his actions in contributing to proceedings in which he ought [rather] to feel so great scruples at following the lead of this man. The archbishop administered to him an exceedingly severe rebuke, nor was the provincial left without others, which to a person less carried away by passions would have served for his entire correction. At last, when the father of Doña Maria Josepha saw that these and other malicious and unusual measures—of which he secretly availed himself in order to attain the purpose which guided him to actions, in regard to the lawsuit, which were improper and unjust—were continually failing him, and that consequently the affair of our reconciliation was steadily taking such shape that it would very soon be accomplished, he yielded in outward appearance, through his fear that this would occur without his having the least intervention in the matter. Through the agency of that same provincial, the affair was discussed with the archbishop and the governor; and thus the conclusion of it was arranged, so that, a few days after the middle of July, Doña Maria Josepha and I were reunited, the former governor having brought about a reconciliation, two or three days before, between her father and myself.

Auditor Martinez—who, as I informed your Grace, had charge of the lawsuit, in virtue of the commission which the aforesaid former governor, Marqués de Torre Campo, gave him for that function—as soon as the news reached this city that the present governor was coming in the galleon, made on his part incredible efforts to have this affair settled. He eagerly endeavored, with especial activity, not only that this settlement should be effected, but that all the official acts should be burned—a proceeding which every one here [dis]approved;5 for without doubt the purpose that more than any other directed him was, that, knowing his own guilt in the mad acts which in his passion he had committed, he desired to repair it, or [rather] cover it up, by this means—fearing that if this business were not completed before the governor arrived here, the latter would do with it what was right; moreover, almost the same idea had been entertained on account of what concerns the preceding governor, by means of its having been known or found out in the same manner. The auditor exerted remarkable activity in the settlement [of the lawsuit] from the time when the said galleon usually met very little delay in reaching these islands, and did so with far more briskness as soon as he learned that the galleon, with the present governor, was already within them; and in fact, if the latter had arrived in this city before this affair had been settled, it is not to be doubted that he would have given them much trouble, by means of it and the knowledge which with great precision he obtained, from the time when he entered the islands, of the outrages and wrongs which had been practiced against me to judge by the great pain which he felt at these, and hinted to me on the first occasion when I went to see him. This was immediately after he arrived outside the walls of this city, where he was obliged to remain until he took possession of the government, in consequence of the custom which prevails here in this regard.

The director whom my wife's father had for the [business of the] lawsuit, or for drawing up his allegations in court [escriptos], took refuge in one of the churches near the city, as soon as he knew that the governor had arrived here. The latter, having understood the many wicked acts which this man had committed, besides those that he practiced in that affair [of mine], desired that—since for the present he could not be punished in proportion to what he deserved, on account of his being in that asylum—he be sent to some military post, not only in order that this might serve as a correction to him, but with the intention that this community be freed from a person of so utterly perverse practices, and that he be not given the opportunity to continue in them. He therefore held a consultation in regard to this point with the archbishop, who, having the same knowledge as the governor, in regard to the perversity of this man, and the great expediency of sending him to a military post, and assured that the sanctuary which he enjoyed would not be violated by another punishment, very readily agreed to the plan, and caused that man to be removed from that sanctuary in order to secure him (as he did) in the prisons of the archbishop. [There he remained] until he was carried thence, some two months ago, by command of the same governor, to the military post that is most remote in this jurisdiction. The efforts which this knave made to see whether he could escape being sent away from here were many; and they were so singular, unusual, and culpable that they seem incredible—as your Grace will recognize from one of them. This is, that he feigned that he was sick, and so skilfully that, the governor having sent two physicians to examine him, they were persuaded at seeing him that really he must be very ill. At that time he practiced the stratagem of having acted the part of a dying man, so skilfully that they even tolled the passing bell for him; but the fact is, that a little while after this had been done—when the physicians had gone away, as also had a religious who had been summoned and had hastened to him—it was learned that he ordered the women to bring him some food, and that he performed his part as well as a good gravedigger could. This trick caused much amusement here as soon as it was discovered, as might be expected from its singularity.

The father of Doña Maria Josepha frequently came to our house after we were reconciled, and consequently I went to that in which he lived, and on my part showed to him the same kindness as before—not only because my good-will had forgiven him, but on account of the promises that we had given each other on the occasion when the previous governor made us friends, or rather reconciled us, that we would go on in the future without the least change. Notwithstanding this, [he acted strangely]—I know not whether it were because his perverted mind was, as a result of the ill-success of his evil designs, permanently impaired; or because he had formed the opinion that I had some share in the removal of the above-mentioned director of his from the church, in order to banish him to the military post. This [latter] idea was contrary to the facts in the case; for it is certain that I had not even the slightest shadow of complicity in that incident. It is he [i.e., my wife's father] who (at the time when the said his director was in the aforesaid archiepiscopal prison), coming on foot through a street in which I was riding in a forlon6 on the opposite side [from him], began when I approached close to him to fling himself about like a madman, and to utter such insulting terms that, although I could not, on account of the noise made by the forlon, distinguish what he meant by them, they compelled me, notwithstanding that I was going forth on pressing business, to order that the forlon halt, in order to ascertain what was the cause of that outcry, or what was the matter with him. Immediately he advanced like a wild beast to the side of the forlon, where he began, with the same wild behavior as before, to break out in extravagant utterances, such as "What knavery and wickedness is this?" with others that were equally or even more disrespectful. When I saw this, although I could not help growing hot within [at conduct] so unusual, discourteous, and besides without cause, I maintained outwardly a countenance without the least change; and in that attitude I expostulated with him—saying that he should tell me what caused him to act thus, since I was ignorant of the cause; and that he must endeavor to moderate his behavior, and not apply such language to me, but must use such terms as were proper. With these and other arguments, and the mild way in which I stated them to him, it was to be expected that he would, unless he were blind with passion, cease from his mad behavior; but he was so contrary that he displayed even much more excitement, and broke out into even wilder utterances. Notwithstanding that so great provocation was enough to have made me alight without the least delay from the forlon in order to obtain satisfaction from him, I was so patient that I again expostulated with him aiming therein to avoid all violence, and for my part to keep the promise which at the time of the reconciliation we had each given to the governor and also to the archbishop, in order that there should not be the least trouble between us. The return that he made for this was, to tell me, still more angrily, to alight from the forlon, and that down there I would find out what I wanted to know. At this new and extreme provocation, [given] in his evil and malicious manner, my patience was exhausted and I sprang out of the forlon; but before I had set my feet on the ground he came toward me with a naked short sword [espadin] which he wore, with a blade of the size prescribed for a sword, as was afterward found. At this I drew my own sword (which is one of the regular style); but as it was necessary for me to make unusual exertions in using it, as it was quite rusty, he wounded me at this time with his weapon, in two fingers of the left hand. We made thrusts at each other several times, during which—either through the blindness in which his furious passion kept him, or for some other reason, I know not what—he several times afforded me sufficient opportunity to have taken his life, if I had chosen to do so. Notwithstanding this, as I had drawn my sword with no other intention than to defend myself, and not to injure him seriously, I behaved toward him accordingly; so I proceeded to disarm him, and, throwing him to the ground, I drew my own short sword, in order that he might more clearly recognize the kindness that I was doing him. At this point different persons came up to separate us; and the governor, when he heard of this occurrence and the excessive provocation which I had had, gave orders to the sargento-mayor to convey my antagonist to the castle of this city. As for me, on account of the legal formalities [necessary] until the judicial investigation of the affair was made, he sent me a message directing me to remain under arrest or detention at home. Before the said sargento-mayor could reach him [i.e., my wife's father] to conduct him to the castle, the professor of laws who is an honorary auditor—a native of Leganès, of whom I told your Grace in my previous letters, and who was a great friend of his—carried my wife's father, half-covered with mud as he was, to the presence of the governor; and he pleaded so urgently that in place of sending him to the castle they should transfer his prison to his own house, that the governor had to comply with his request. [Santisteban's account of the settlement of this affair is too prolix to be repeated here in full. The substance of it is, that an investigation was made by Auditor Martinez, and by him referred to the Audiencia, where it was decided that the difficulty should be smoothed over, and the parties again reconciled to each other; the governor is obliged to agree with this decision, but remains the firm friend of Santisteban. The latter is willing to forgive his assailant, but wishes to avoid the recurrence of such troubles; he confers thereon with the archbishop, who promises to arrange matters with the governor, but dies before he can attend to this matter. Later, Santisteban and his father-in-law are nominally reconciled, but with the proviso that they do not go to each other's houses; but Santisteban is obliged to be on his guard against the secret machinations of the other.]

A little while after the governor took possession of his dignity, the necessity arose for making a change in one of the offices in the regiment, for a reason which rendered such a change unavoidable. On this occasion the governor directed that I should propose three names of meritorious persons whom I should find to be suitable tor that position, in order that from these he might select the one whom he thought best—determining that in future this practice should be observed in regard to all the military offices to which he had to make appointments. Although this regulation is so eminently proper—not only because it had been the usage here until, in the last few years, the inexperience and despotism of some of the governors broke up this method of procedure; but because it is in all countries the inviolable usage that the masters-of-camp or the colonels (which is the same thing) have always proposed [appointments for] the vacant posts in their organizations—it caused much surprise (or, to speak more correctly, envy) in the licentiates or auditors. For, as soon as they heard of it, they went to see the governor, and with as much energy and eagerness as if some great advantage could thus result to them, addressed him, endeavoring to dissuade him from the observance of this method—availing themselves, in order to incite him not to allow this regulation to take effect, of the artful argument that it was opposed to his own authority. But the governor, knowing their good intentions and how very proper are those proposals of names (as above stated), sent them away more offended than they were when they came into his presence, on account of his answer to them that he could not permit the appointments to be made as they wished, since it was the prerogative of all masters-of-camp to propose them—saying that no one could have a better knowledge than these officers have of the merits and fitness of persons for their command, in order that those who were necessary for military employments might be judiciously selected. From this your Grace will understand how far the prejudice of these licentiates can extend, and their exceeding ill-will, and that I shall find myself badly off and can ill remain here with these and other knaves, who are in more than abundant numbers in this goodly land, and of so evil, or even worse, intentions; and the good intentions of those licentiates not stopping at this only, I will relate to your Grace another case in which they show no less their proved enmity.

The former bishop of the province of Zebu in these islands, Don Fray Sebastian de Foronda, had done me the favor of lending to me six thousand pesos for the payment of a debt. That gentleman having died, the licentiates began to make arrangements for the collection of his expolios,7 in this usurping the governor's jurisdiction; for it appears that this business belongs to the control of the superintendency of the royal treasury, which exercises [that control]. They issued an edict directing that I, making acknowledgment of the promissory note which they found, which I had made in favor of the said bishop, must immediately make the payment of this amount. I replied to this that the note was made by me, but that, as I had not the funds, it was not possible for me to pay the note then, but I would do so as soon as I could. At this, they issued another mandate in which their ill-will in regard to this affair (which, in general, has existed a long time) began to make itself fully visible—which contained these expressions: "We command you, every official with appointment as deputy of the alguazil-mayor of this court, that when you see this present you proceed immediately and without any delay to require General Don Manuel de Santistevan to deliver up the sum of six thousand pesos, which he is owing to the goods of the expolio of the very reverend master in Christ Don Fray Sebastian de Foronda, deceased, late bishop of Calidonia, and apostolic ruler of Zebu; and if he shall not pay the said sum, you shall proceed to levy on his person and goods up to the quantity necessary to make up the said six thousand pesos, the tenth,8 and the costs of collection, in the usual form. For this command is given by an edict issued by us, on the past fifteenth of September in this year." Such are the expressions in the decree. When the friend who on other occasions, as I have informed your Grace, has directed me in all my lawsuits (whom, before replying, I consulted on this affair) comprehended the artful manner in which this mandate was worded—for while my office was stated therein as "general" (which, although I was one, I was not accustomed to style myself, as others do here), the document said nothing of my office of master-of-camp; and, as it was more important to misrepresent the former judicial point than to set aside the latter, it was a consequence that whenever such [word illegible in MS.] should come to be seen here, it would follow that the auditors could arrest me with this title, and without recourse to the governor, who is the one authorized to do so, when cause arises—this friend thought it best to attack them with a counter-mine. This was to reply to them (as was done) that the said decree or mandate could not concern me, because not only on account of my noble rank I could not be imprisoned for debts, but I was also excepted therefrom by being master-of-camp, so that in no case could this seizure of my person be made without the consent of the governor. It seems that they had, before his eyes, issued another decree, saying that this measure should be duly carried into execution—with the statement that it must be ascertained whether in the office of the court notary of that same Audiencia my title was registered, or there was evidence that I was such master-of-camp; and that in the latter case the governor should be notified before they proceeded to carry out the decree, in order that he might give the orders which would prevent perplexity among the soldiers whom I keep as my guard. The governor was sorry for these attacks on me, and partly on this account, and because he desired that such a precedent should not operate generally, and partly in order to avoid on that occasion the disturbance that might arise from his defending his own jurisdiction in the aforesaid matter of the expolios, which these subordinate officials were usurping from him, and seeing that I had not the means for paying this amount, he showed me the special favor of furnishing to me five thousand four hundred pesos—part in the salary which to that time was due me, and the rest in cash, which he ordered his steward to give me. With this, and six hundred pesos more which I obtained in other ways, the whole of that debt was paid into the royal treasury; from which it resulted that, as the auditors had not been able to secure the execution of this last decree, in so far as concerned my person, on account of this deposit or payment, which forestalled their attempt to compel me to have experience in the court of justice, when they heard of it those fine snobs [buenas alajas] of licentiates were left more than amazed; and the grievous vexation which they experienced through the fact that their malicious cunning and procedure had been frustrated was increased no little by their learning that the greater part of the amount furnished had been given by the governor, who will send to the king or to the Council of the Indias, on this occasion, or when the galleon shall sail for Nueva España, an admirable document—which has been prepared by the friend who, as I have already stated, has directed me in my legal business—in which, relating this action, he proves by forcible arguments that those auditors acted illegally therein, and makes it very clear that they could not and ought not to meddle in that business.

I am fully informed of the reasons which made your Grace regard it as not expedient to present in the Council the sworn statement which I sent you, in the year 725, of what had been done up to that time in regard to the affair of the jurisdiction of the small fort. Considering that, although the governor has known and knows the injury that was done me in that matter it will please him that the revocation of the sentence which, ill-advised, his predecessor pronounced should come from there [i.e., Madrid], I trust that your Grace, on receiving this letter, will be pleased to arrange for presenting in the aforesaid Council the sworn statement of the whole of this lawsuit which I sent you in the year 727; and make all possible endeavor to secure that, if the affair result as is just, the decree which I mentioned on that occasion be sent here. Also such measures should be taken as will lead to Auditor Martinez, who was the chief cause of so unjust a sentence, being given the condign punishment that corresponds to his fault; and that the same be done as concerns Alcalde Vermudez, on account of his having thrust himself into usurping the jurisdiction of another.

In regard to the subject of boletas,9 it is also important to continue [our] importunity, so that (as I hope) a decree may come, assigning me definitely at least ten toneladas in each galleon, which are eighty piezas or boletas. This is a number so moderate as may be understood from the fact that it is hardly half of the amount with which in the past it was usual for my predecessors to compensate themselves out of what was allowed in the galleons by the latest regulation of his Majesty to the entire body of citizens, [and] was that which was commonly assigned to them on those occasions. This arrangement will be very desirable, so that the prejudice arising from differences in the persons who are associated in the distribution of space [repartimiento] each year cannot, with what each one will have, attempt to change the allotment of what should be given to me; also because the governor, although he may desire to favor me in this particular, cannot do so by himself alone, as he has only one vote. Besides, if we consider former instances, it will not be strange if the plebeians10 with their arts induce him to do what they wish. [A note on the margin, evidently added as an afterthought, reads: "If this matter of boletas proves difficult to secure (although it is so ordinary an affair that even to a half pay sargento-mayor named Don Franzisco de Cardenas a decree came last year, which decreed that they should provide for him here with fifty boletas), and the favor of the government can finally bring it about (if on the other hand it does not turn out as I hope), your Grace need not trouble yourself over this question of boletas."]

This gentleman, the governor, has told me that your Grace gave him the duplicates (which he has brought here) of the reports which I made and sent to you in regard to the absurd speeches which have been habitually made here. I have been much pleased at this precaution (which was a very proper one), not only that he might come here with full knowledge and information about affairs, and because of the benefit which he has derived from them (which he has personally acknowledged to me), but because since his coming he has proved the truth of all that is contained in them.

I am very thankful to your Grace for the news which you send me in regard to the condition in which affairs are there [i.e., in España]. I cannot express my feelings at the death of the Count, not only because I know the same things that you mention, but on account of the especial circumstance of the personal favor and affection for which I owe him the gratitude for which I shall always be under obligation; and I am equally grieved that it happened thus, in the prime of [his] life, on account of what concerns Don Pedro his nephew. For the present, then, since for lack of time it is not possible for me to write, your Grace will please present my condolences for both these casualties to the lord Count Mozo, and to my lady Doña Ge[r] trudes, assuring them that I sympathize with them very sincerely. Will your Grace please also convey my kind remembrances to the other acquaintances and friends who favor us, as also to all our relatives—and especially to our Don Matheo, and to my lady Doña Antonia, telling them how sorry I am for the impaired health that they have suffered, and that I shall be exceedingly delighted if they regain their health.

A little while ago, God took away the eldest child of Don Luis and Doña Rosa, after a tedious and lingering illness with diarrhœa. They are exceedingly grateful to your Grace for your expressions of kindness, which they very cordially reciprocate; and Don Luis places at the disposal of your Grace [whatever he can do for you in] the new office which he holds, that of chief notary (in proprietary appointment) of the cabildo of this city, with accompanying rights of privilege therein. In order to secure this purchase (which he made here from the crown), he was aided by a schedule of properties which he owns in this same city, [amounting to] some twelve or fourteen thousand pesos, for the post cost him that amount. Although it is certainly an excessive price, it is compensated by the advantageous circumstances attending it: he has authority to select a deputy who can exercise the office in his name, as is the case at the present time—the latter to be paid, according to what they say, 3,000 pesos each year—and it is a place of much honor and esteem, just as it is in all the cities of these kingdoms. These advantages he had borne in mind, for without them he would not have undertaken this office, even if it had been worth much more; [another consideration was], that whenever he may choose to quit it he can do so, assured that he will find some one else here to whom he can make it over, at very nearly the same amount which it cost him, since that office is sought for by many persons.

I render to your Grace the grateful thanks which I owe you for the diligent efforts that you made in order that the post of governor here might be conferred on me; and I now see how, on account of the reasons which you state, you could not gain the result that was desired—for which it is necessary to resign ourselves and be patient. By my previous letters your Grace will have learned the object to which my mind is directed, since learning that [my hope of securing] this office has been disappointed, and the other motives that I stated therein. Every day increases, if that be possible, my desire to indemnify persons here; and moreover I am certain that, instead of securing advancement [here], I can regard it as certain that I shall, on the other hand, become more embarrassed at every step—considering that I cannot hope in any direction for the least gain of [pecuniary] profit; and that my salary is so limited that, as I have stated on other occasions, it is not enough even for the absolutely necessary expenses of my decent living, moderate [as that is]. For all these reasons, I cannot help repeating at this time my urgent requests to your Grace in regard to this subject, entreating with almost the same energy which I could employ to escape from purgatory, if I found myself there—that you will, as also friend Arce (to whom also I have written at this critical time), continue your efforts until one of the posts of governor which I have mentioned to your Grace can be secured for me, either in the kingdom of Peru or in that of Nueva España. I suppose that the [door to such a] purchase is now closed; but if through a little good-fortune there is opportunity for one, you can render assistance in securing one for me, from the money which will remain from what I have sent, since all of it is now on the road thither [i.e., to España], according to the information which they have sent me from Nueva España. If this shall not be enough, I trust, in the great loyalty and affection which I owe to your Grace, that you will make up the remaining sum that shall be necessary, in such way as you shall find most convenient—[what is needed] not only for this purpose, but tor the rank of field-marshal; or, that failing, for the rank of brigadier. I will repay the amount that may be needed, with more than its proceeds amount to, as is just—assuring your Grace that the favor of aiding me to secure (as I hope) this relief will be so exceeding a kindness that 1 have no words to express suitably my inmost appreciation of it, nor, consequently, to show the gratitude for it which I shall always feel toward your Grace—whose life I beseech our Lord to preserve for me for many years, with all prosperity. Manila, January 28, 1730.

Cousin and Sir:

I am very sorry that the articles which I sent by Fathers Buena Ventura Plana and Joseph Bobadilla were lost, through an accident; for this has deprived me of the pleasure which I would have felt if they—as being things from this country, although of little value—had reached the hands of your Grace and other gentlemen to whom my gratitude and affectionate good-will had addressed them.

I think that the aforesaid fathers are now in Nueva España, on their return journey, and I do not doubt that in passing by way of the court there [i.e., Madrid], on their return from Rome, they exerted whatever good offices they could in my favor, on account of the special affection which I owe them, and [which], your Grace is pleased to declare, they displayed. And although I take into consideration the fact that at present the other fathers who reside at that court cannot accomplish much, for the reasons which you give me, I persuade myself that it will do no harm if your Grace will please to preserve (if you can do so without special trouble) communication with all those to whom you caused the letters that went from here to be delivered; for they will not fail to render aid in whatever may arise. Nevertheless, even without their aid I have entire confidence that your Grace will employ the other means which you have obtained through your great ability, and such others as you may find convenient, if one alone do not prove sufficient for the attainment of one of the governorships which I have mentioned. Again I assure your Grace—to say nothing of the fact that this hope itself affords me some pleasure—that it will be a favor so praiseworthy, and so great a kindness, for me to be able to escape as soon as possible from this chaos, this deep well, that (as I have already said) I shall not have words with which to express it, and therefore to manifest to your Grace sufficiently the gratitude which I shall always feel toward you. I flatter myself that at the same time there may come an order to the governor to give me the command of the galleon in which I shall have to make my voyage, for the reason which I have already explained to your Grace on other occasions, in order that in this way I can perform it with more convenience, and without so great expense. In case the granting of such order be refused (although I imagine that there will be no obstacle that can arise in the way of issuing it), it will be desirable to obtain letters from the secretary (present or future) in the general office of state who has charge of matters concerning the Indias, recommending to this gentleman [i.e., the governor of Filipinas] to be sure to grant me this favor; it would even be worth while for Señors Legarra and Maturana, and likewise Sargento-mayor Castro of the Guards, also to write to him on this subject.

[At this point the writer indulges in various half-anxious reflections on the uncertainty of his future, the delay in obtaining the benefits of a governorship even if he secure the appointment to one, and the possibility that all this delay may be time wasted; but he endeavors to bear these things in patience. He states that he has also written to one Patiño11 on these matters, and he hopes that these representations will lead to measures by the home government that will check the arrogance of the Manila auditors; and he urges his cousin to push his claims to a better post than he now has.]

I kiss your Grace's hands, as your cousin and sincere servant and friend, who earnestly desires to see you again,

Manuel de Santistevan

[*Addressed*: "To my cousin Señor Don Lorenso de San Tistevan."]

[On the margins of pp. 28 and 29 of the MS. appears the following, evidently a postscript to the letter:]

Cousin and Sir:

When your Grace may write to the relatives [Spanish, *Pa—*, *the rest blotted*; the context would indicate *parientes*], I trust that you will grant me the favor of explaining that, for the reason which I have already stated, lack of time, it is not possible for me to write until another opportunity (which I will try to do); and will your Grace please say the same to the mother of Doña Rafaela (whom may God keep), and convey to all of them, in my behalf, my affectionate remembrances.

This packet—of which I will send another copy by the galleon, being uncertain whether this may be lost on the way—is going by way of one of the colonies which in this part of Asia belong to the foreign nations, such as Francia, Inglaterra, Olanda, and Portugal. By this route letters usually go very expeditiously to that kingdom [of España], as also those come here which are sent thence by these routes, employing the method which I described in detail to your Grace in the years 723 and 24—a fact which many persons here have learned by experience, in the case of the letters which by these lines are sent to them from the court there, by the correspondents whom they have in it; for one, the governor obtained this satisfaction soon after his arrival in these islands, in receiving various letters, among which was the commission as warden of the castle of Santiago in this city, for a nephew whom he had brought, who in España had been an alférez of the Guards.

From the maternal grandfather of Doña Maria Josepha the authorities seized here 102,000 or 106,000 pesos—a sum which, as it had been sent from these islands to Nueva España as an investment by Don Fernando Bustillo Bustamante, the former governor of the islands, was therefore by order of the viceroy of that kingdom [of Nueva España] placed in the royal treasury of Mexico; as also another considerable amount, which the aforesaid governor had sent, was obtained from various other seizures which the viceroy had made. Although the executors of the said grandfather of Doña Maria Josepha obtained a decree that they should be repaid for the amount seized, there has not thus far been any way in which that could be done—either because there was a lack of funds, or because the person to whom this commission had been entrusted in the aforesaid city of Mexico was inefficient. The greater part of the amount thus seized belongs to the aforesaid Doña Maria Josepha; in order to ascertain what is legitimately hers, some measures have been taken in order to secure the division of all the goods; and if (as I hope is the case), this effort shall have succeeded [in time] for the despatch of the galleon, I will then send word to your Grace of the result, in order that your Grace and friend Arze may be so kind as to ask for a new decree in which the viceroy shall be commanded to see that the most prompt satisfaction be given for the aforesaid amount. With this and a strong letter of recommendation from the secretary for the affairs of Indias in the general office of state, addressed to the present or future viceroy, there will be no doubt that the collection of this money will be facilitated, as is necessary and desirable—and all the more if this order shall arrive at the time when, as I trust, [an appointment to] a governorship being received, I should go, as would be necessary, to that kingdom [of Nueva España], even though it might be for [an office in] that of Peru.

1 Spanish, lo que se llevó la trampa; literally, "what the trap carried away with it;" a variant of the phrase llevarselo el demonio. It is translated above in accordance with the definition in Caballero's Diccionario de modismos (2nd edition, Madrid, 1905), p. 744.

"Fairs" [ferias] here alludes to the annual sale or fair at Acapulco which took place at the arrival of the galleon from Manila; in this case the goods from Filipinas evidently were sold at a loss.

2 Apparently referring to Juan Ventura de Maturana, who was royal secretary in the Council of the Indias in 1734–35.

3 This was Doctor Carlos Bermudez Gonzalez de Castro, a secular priest, a native of Puebla, Mexico, and a prominent ecclesiastic at Nueva España. He arrived at Manila on June 29, 1728; displayed great zeal in his office, kindness to the Indians, and piety and charity in his personal character; and died on November 13, 1729, being nearly seventy-two years old. (Concepción, Hist. de Philipinas, x, pp. 167–170, 182–184.)

4 This house must have been, since it was under the control of this provincial, the beaterio of Santa Catalina, founded under Dominican auspices. Its first prioress was Sor Francisca del Espiritu Santo, who died on August 24, 1711, at the age of sixty-three years.

5 In the text, a cuya accion tuvieron todos aqui; but evidently some word is omitted after tuvieron—probably mal, as such a proposal could not be generally approved.

6 A sort of coach, with four seats: it was closed with doors; and the body was supported by heavy straps, and placed between two wooden shafts (Dominguez).

7 Espolios: property left by a prelate at his death.

8 Spanish, decima; possibly meaning a tenth part due to the crown.

9 Boleta: referring to the assignments of lading-space in the Acapulco galleon; each ticket giving its owner the right to ship one pieza of goods. See VOL. I, p. 63.

10 Spanish, Paysanaje, literally "peasantry;" applied here somewhat scornfully to the mass of citizens as distinguished from the nobility and military class, and especially to the merchants of Manila. Cf. French, bourgeoisie.

11 Probably referring to Don Joseph Patiño, then one of the ministers of the Spanish government, through whose hands much of the business relating to the Philippines seems to have passed (as mentioned in Extracto historial).

EXTRACTO HISTORIAL

Commerce of the Philippines with Nueva España, 1640–1736 (to be concluded). By Antonio Álvarez de Abreu; Madrid, 1736.

Source: This document is translated, partly in full and partly in synopsis, from the *Extracto historial* (Madrid, 1736), compiled by Abreu; it includes "Periods" iii–x, but on account of its length will be completed in VOL. XLV.

Translation: It is synopsized and translated by Emma Helen Blair.

COMMERCE OF THE PHILIPPINES WITH NUEVA ESPAÑA

PERIOD III

Occurrences from the year 1640 until that of 1702, and from this year until 1712.1

17. Although there is no evidence in the Expediente2 of what resulted from the commissions given to Señor Palatox by the decrees which may be seen at the end of the preceding "Period," one consequence was that the Philipinas trade with Nueva España was continued, in the form which we shall soon describe. For the viceroy of that kingdom, Conde de Paredes, when he was in office made remonstrances at various times from the year 1684 until 1686, in regard to the great confusion which always had been experienced in the valuations of the cargoes on the ships from Philipinas which arrived at the port of Acapulco; and he declared that none of the measures which had been employed had been sufficient, so that they could regulate the duties which the merchants of those islands ought to contribute, nor for preventing the illegal acts and frauds which were committed, to the injury of the royal treasury. He had therefore found it expedient to make the regulation (as he had done) that every ship of those which came to the above port of Acapulco should compound its customs duties [indultasse] in the amount of 74,000 pesos; and this had been the practice until Conde de Galve had gone to fill that viceroyalty, and he gave an account of this matter.

18. On receiving this information, despatches were sent on June 5, 1697, to the viceroy and Audiencia of Mexico and to the governor and Audiencia of Philipinas, informing them that the said arrangement had been revoked and annulled, since it was contrary to what had been commanded by laws, decrees, and royal orders, and for many other serious and just reasons. Both of these governments were commanded to cause the publication of the revocation and annulment of the above arrangement, and were ordered to take especial care in the administration and careful collection of the duties which the merchandise in that traffic ought to contribute—most strictly observing the regulation that no more goods should go from those islands than amounted to 250,000 pesos, nor should more than 500,000 be allowed

to go back as proceeds. Moreover, this commerce must be strictly confined to citizens born in Philipinas, and prohibited to those of Nueva España; for any goods which should be found belonging to the latter must be considered as confiscated, and those which should come outside registration, if they belonged to those islanders, must pay double duties. The declarations [manifestaciones] of these goods must be made within the limit of six hours, or at most of twelve, which was fixed as the utmost allowance of time. It was most strictly commanded that for the future they should no longer allow the declarations of [registered] merchandise which until then had been permitted, that the ships in that commerce should not exceed a burden of four hundred toneladas each, and that they must be the two which sailed each year to the port of Acapulco.

19. These orders having been received and published in Philipinas, the city and the merchants of Manila set forth the difficulties which were arising from the mode in which their trade was carried on. They entreated: first, that there should be only one ship in that trade, having a capacity of 1,200 toneladas, and not two, as had been decided; second, that the amount of 250,000 pesos, stated in the permission which had been granted them, should be increased; third, that in return should be brought back the entire amount which the merchandise should produce in Acapulco and the kingdom of Nueva España, and that it should not remain limited to the 500,000 pesos to which it had been restricted. They offered, for the regular voyage of each year, to make a contribution to the treasury [servir con] of 100,000 pesos, on account of the duties; and they asked that, when it should appear that these dues had been paid, neither the royal officials of Acapulco nor any other officials should meddle with the registration of the goods that were landed at the arrival of the ship, nor with the embarkation of the silver on its return voyage, but that both these should go free.

20. In order that the distribution of the lading-space which was made in these islands should be equitable, the decision was confirmed which in 1699 had been made by the governor of the islands at that time, commanding, in regard to the statement that this distribution was not made among the citizens, whose qualifications [for this] belonged exclusively to that city, that the municipality alone, without the intervention of any other official, must send the list of the citizens to the committee which met for this purpose; and that the said distribution should be made among the persons included in the above list of citizens, without that government or the Audiencia being allowed to have any discretionary power in this matter.

21. In view of this remonstrance, and of the demands made by the kingdom of Peru (in regard to opening to it the commerce by way of Acapulco), by the provinces of Nueva España, and by the consulate3 of

Andalucia—which set forth the weakened and diminished condition of commerce in these and in those kingdoms, through the excessive amounts of cloth and other commodities which were coming from Philipinas, in the ships allowed to them, to the port of Acapulco—the Council proposed to his Majesty in a report dated July 7, 1703, the measures which it regarded as expedient for the regulation which must be made in the commerce of Philipinas; these his Majesty was pleased to approve, and their contents may be reduced to the following points:

22. That in the Philipinas Islands two ships should be built, each of 500 toneladas burden, which should transport the goods permitted to that trade; that the citizens should be authorized to convey in these to Nueva España the amount of 300,000 pesos in their products and other commodities, and on the return to Philipinas to carry 600,000 pesos in silver, allowing 100 per cerft gain minus the duties and expenses. Among other things which they were commanded to watch over for the regulation and observance of the said commerce are the following:

23. That the city of Manila should itself make the distribution for the lading of the two ships, without the intervention of any official.

24. That the merchants and those interested in the trade should present within a specified time-limit the commodities, invoices, and articles which they were to send to Nueva España; that these should be placed in the royal storehouses, and the estimate of their value be made. This must be done by the agreement of two persons of experience, deputed by the city and the trade, with royal officials and the fiscal of the Audiencia of Manila, and the fiscal must superintend the entire valuation. If any merchant should feel aggrieved in the enumeration he should go before the committee [of distribution], in order that his just rights might be guarded; and if the committee did not take care of this, he should have right of appeal to the Audiencia.

25. That he who had no goods to lade should not be allowed to give up his right in favor of a third person, but it should accrue to the rest, a new distribution of that part being made.

26. That the registration be made by the royal officials, with the assistance of the fiscal; that the goods shipped and their valuation should be carefully ascertained; and that the decisions of the officials, or a copy of them, be sent to Acapulco for the use of officials there.

27. That in Acapulco must be ascertained the quantity of silver which should be shipped on the return voyage, and, if the goods sold should perchance exceed the 600,000 pesos, they [i.e., the Manila owners] should not be allowed to take away the excess in silver, but [must take it] in goods.

28. That if the sale of the goods shall not fill this amount of 600,000 pesos of the permission, the merchants of Nueva España cannot under any pretext, no matter how just, make up the deficiency, or place in the ship the remaining amount of silver, for this was perpetually prohibited by his Majesty from the time when these orders were issued; and whatever might be done in contravention of these should be punished with special severity. For it had been learned that under this pretext those born in Nueva España or resident there were steadily introducing their trade into Philipinas, thus causing most serious losses to the royal treasury, and bringing that commerce to the state which was acknowledged, with great detriment to the trade of España. In regard to this matter the viceroy was charged to devote himself with the utmost activity to the strictest fulfilment of this order, without overlooking the slightest thing.

29. That if it were found that any portion of silver belonged to a native or resident of Nueva España it should be regarded as confiscated, and applied in thirds;4 and, besides, the delinquent should pay to the royal treasury three times the amount thus confiscated. If he repeated the offense, the penalty should be imposed upon him of loss of goods, and exile from these provinces for ten years.

30. That thenceforth should likewise be prohibited the acceptance of declarations of goods [manifestaciones], nor should they for any reason be accepted, even if his Majesty should lose the double duties that belong to them, since on no account would he allow them to be tolerated.

31. That in order to avoid confusion in the decree of the year 1697 already cited (and leaving these points settled and in use, in such form that they should be permanent), if the governor and merchants of Philipinas in giving the 100,000 pesos, should come to offer it by way of adjustment [regulacion]5 of the duties in each voyage, and not under the name of indult [indulto], as had been proposed, they should be entirely released from payment of all the duties which they must make good in Acapulco, not only on the outward but on the return voyage. It was also declared that goods sold at that port or shipped from it should not pay alcavala on the first sale; for it was certain that the contribution of the 100,000 pesos from the permission would cost seventeen per cent, leaving eighty-three per cent gain to those who were interested in the trade. Moreover, as his Majesty paid the expense of the building, cleaning, and equipment of the ships, and supplying them with soldiers, provisions, supplies, and ammunition, without receiving more than forty-four ducados for each tonelada, it would not only be advantageous, but even necessary to the royal treasury to furnish a considerable amount for preserving their commerce and traffic to the natives of the island, which was all the favor which his royal munificence could exercise. If, however,

an agreement should not be reached by the trade in the adjustment of the 100,000 pesos, the royal duties must be exacted and collected in full, without excepting anything.

32. That in the enumeration of the traders should be included the Spaniards born in the country, and the military men stationed in the port of Cavite; and these might engage in that traffic—excluding, however, ecclesiastical ministers, whether secular or regular, and those who were foreigners to those Philipinas Islands.

33. That the master of each ship must make a book containing the freight list, and present it with the aforesaid documents at Acapulco to the castellan who governs that port and the royal officials, for the discharge of cargo. At the same time he must carry a duplicate of all these documents, to be sent to the viceroy as soon as they arrived, in order that he might examine them and communicate with the tribunal of accounts, in which a copy of it must be made to send to the Council.

34. As soon as the ships should anchor in Acapulco the castellan and royal officials of that port should station the guards necessary to avoid the concealment of goods or their clandestine introduction, causing the ship to be lightened and its cargo landed with the utmost promptness, and collecting the established duties or securing them by the goods themselves, according to the usage up to that time.

35. That when the goods had been landed and the amounts registered had been ascertained, the ships should be inspected; and whatever else was found therein should be regarded as confiscated, without allowing therein any claim or remonstrance. Half of the goods confiscated should be applied to the royal treasury, and the rest in two parts to the judge and the informer—excepting in the case when the value of confiscated goods should reach 50,000 pesos; for then the viceroy and the royal court of Mexico must allot to the judge and the informer such quantity as should be proper, leaving to the decision of the judges other penalties in accordance with the guilt of the offenders.

36. His Majesty having agreed to the proposals made by the Council, they issued on August 12, 1702, despatches in accordance therewith, to the governments of Nueva España and Philipinas, informing them of the regulation herein explained, and commanding them both to observe it strictly and inviolably. In consequence of this, the governor of Philipinas, in letters of June 21, 1705, and May 24, 1708 (in which he acknowledged the receipt of the despatch sent to him), reported that he had carried the decree into execution, and had made it known to the merchants in the city of Manila, who had offered to make good the burdens of expense which

would ensue if the two ships of 500 toneladas each were immediately built according to this command—in view of the fact that there were two galleons and one patache in the ports there; of these one might serve eight years, and the other a little less, and the patache four. For this reason the governor had commanded that the building of the two ships should be suspended until those which were then in use should be worn out.

37. That also it had been regarded as impracticable that the valuation of the cloth and wares which were to be traded should be made through the actual examination of the bales and their other goods, and that this should be carried out in the royal storehouses—considering that the crowded condition of those buildings, and the risk of thefts, fires, and other accidents, did not permit this method to be practiced, as was commanded by the decree that has been cited.

38. That to this was added that, as the Chinese do not gather at the fair [at Manila] until the end of May in each year, and the ships sail from those islands toward the end of the following June, the royal officials were unable in so short a time as one month to attend to the aforesaid examination, and to undertake the despatch and registration of the ships, on account of the great amount of work that they had to do in this. For these reasons it had been decided that, in the invoices that were brought forward, an itemized account should be given of the stuffs, their quantity, quality, numbers and marks, and the names of the consignees; and that the consignors should furnish samples of each article; and some bales here and there could be opened to ascertain if there were any fraud and punish it. And that, the aforesaid city and merchants having agreed to and accepted all the rest that was contained in the above despatch, the galleons had accordingly sailed for Nueva España in the years 1705 and 1706.

39. The Council, being informed of this memorial, agreed that the strictest orders should be repeated (as was done by decrees of December 12, 1712) for the exact observance and punctual fulfilment of those given on August 12, 1702, excepting that which concerned the opening of the bundles in the royal storehouses for the valuations. It was permitted that these should be made by means of invoices, which each one must present, swearing that the goods were his and that the bales contained no more than was set down on the invoices. The Council also decided that the traffic and commerce of those islands should be continued by the two ships already in existence, until they should become unseaworthy; in that case they must be laid aside, and the building of the two ships of 500 toneladas burden each should be undertaken, according to their former decision.

40. Inasmuch as in the year 1706 the galleon named "Rosario" had been despatched from Philipinas under the regulations made by the cited decree of 1702, and modifications in this had been proposed by the city and merchants of Manila, the viceroy Alburquerque6 had commanded (with the opinion of a junta which he formed for the reception and unlading of the galleon) that this cargo should not be admitted to the adjustment of the 100,000 pesos, which the above regulation provided; and that consequently the declaration of goods should be accepted, by the rules of valuation and of the payment of duties which had been observed on other occasions. The Council, after the statement of the fiscal and consultation with his Majesty, severely censured the viceroy, and the officials of the junta who had agreed with his opinion; and they returned thanks to those who were of the opposite opinion, who thought that the adjustment of the 100,000 pesos should be paid, as that was the most exact and accurate meaning of the royal orders issued in the year 1702.

PERIOD IV

Of the demonstration which was made in the year 1712, when the Duke de Linares was viceroy, of the illegalities in the trade permitted to Filipinas, and the difficulty of preventing them.

41. On May 27, 1710, a despatch was sent through the private correspondence office [via reservada], addressed to the Duke de Linares, viceroy of Mexico, directing him, on account of the pressing necessities of war, to grant indult of the penalties for the illegalities (specifying those which had been committed in notable transgression of the law) with which the Filipinas commerce had been and was still carried on—not only in the commodities which were shipped, but in the silver which was sent back for them—neglecting the rules and orders that had been given for that commerce. In consequence of this, by order of the viceroy, an investigation was made in Mexico by an auditor in the year 1712, of both the shipment and the returns; and as a result of this was shown the great illegality with which the stuffs from China had been traded. It appeared that the goods that came without registration were allowed to enter on the declaration of them; that, contrary to the permission, all or the greater part of the merchandise in this commerce belonged to citizens of Mexico, Puebla and other parts of that kingdom, and not to the native citizens of the islands; that while the permission limited the returns to only 600,000 pesos, the amount thus permitted had been exceeded in some years by two millions, and in every year by a considerable amount; and that no investigation had been made of the chests carried by the mariners of those ships, to see whether they contained more than 30 pesos' worth of goods.

42. Although with this investigation and the accompanying report of the auditor who made it (which he sent to the viceroy), and the opinion given by the fiscal of the Audiencia when he saw it, that court was of the opinion that the indult should be granted to the traders of Mexico who proved to be guilty, that body of traders refused such benefit, supposing that against its individuals such guilt would not be proved as to require compurgation [by the grace] of the indult; and the viceroy Linares, in a letter of August 4, 1714, in giving account of these investigations, made the following statement:

43. "By the last trading-fleet [flota] I informed your Majesty of the progress of the investigations which had been begun in regard to the commerce of Philipinas, and of the measures which I had taken with the merchants of this city in regard to the indult. They assured me that, as they were included in the offense, and the access to his Majesty's clemency was so open, they would avail themselves of this favor, in order not to suffer another investigation or expose themselves to an experience of the severity of the penalty, since it was easier to take refuge in the sovereign asylum of your Majesty in the indult. But as the opinions of men differ, and their fears are wont to range themselves on the side of their advantage, the notorious nature of the offense was not enough to convince them, or the prohibition of the law to persuade them, on account of their persisting in the belief that [this very] tolerance sufficed to keep them from incurring [the penalties of] guilt; and that the fact that the ships came [to trade] without conforming to the orders of your Majesty afforded to the [Mexican] traders a certain indult for not making any change in the custom [regarding it]—alleging that the tolerance [of the government] was a matter of convenience, and insisting that they had not traded directly in the islands. With this the merchants resolved in a special conference, convened for this purpose by the consulate, that they would not avail themselves of the indult, leaving in my hands the liberty to proceed against all of them, hearing them in [the courts of] justice.

"Having learned of this decision, and being certain that many of the merchants were refusing the contribution as a body, and covering the indults as individuals, in order to secure greater advantage to themselves, I directed the auditor who had had charge of this investigation to summon them—each so separately and independently of the others that even the knowledge of this proceeding could not be imparted to them; and beginning with those who were distinguished by either wealth or position, whose opinion might be either a guide or a check to the others, in order that, these having once accepted the indult, their submission and connivance might facilitate the acquiescence of the others.

"I was influenced to this opinion by the difficulty of proceeding against all of them; for, as they number almost five hundred, and among them are the most prominent merchants, any procedure against them would cause a great sensation in the community, even though the cause should justify it, especially [if it occurred] at the despatch of the trading-fleet. [Also I was influenced by other considerations,] knowing by experience the losses that the merchants suffer through the irregular condition of the trade and the failure of the mineral products to make these good; their valuing more highly the actual balance in their favor from some investments which give prompt returns than their hopes from others which [various] causes might naturally retard; [the desirability of] gaining the tranquillity of the commonwealth by the voluntary contribution of its individuals; and by this means rendering more worthy of their regard the royal clemency of your Majesty, and pledging them to gratitude at receiving as a kindness the indult which menaced them as a penalty.

"Those who probably are included in this infraction of the law may be reduced to three classes of persons: those whose wealth supplies them with funds for trading, and who therefore risk these for heavy investments, without fearing lest they be ruined or left without funds for other purposes; others of the middle class [as merchants], who under the protection of the preceding class expose to risk a part of what they possess, and content themselves with moderate gains, because their means do not allow them to make greater outlay; and still others (and the most numerous), who are very poor and are unable to hazard any money, but who go to the port of Acapulco and there purchase what they can for the comfort of their families and their own petty affairs — and these are the majority [of the transgressors], among whom are many who are [now] absent, dead, or bankrupt.

"In the books of the carriers7 in which is set down the silver which has been carried to the port [of Acapulco], and the merchandise which has been transported to this kingdom [of Mexico] — all money is included without any distinction, without specifying the coin which goes destined for the fair at Acapulco and that which must be sent to the islands; and this produces confusion, which it is very difficult to clear up. For if they [i.e., the merchants] are charged with this remittance of coin, they say that the money is for the fair, which is lawful and allowed; if they are obliged to admit that they are sending coin and are not receiving goods, they say that it is for the balances [due] on commissions from the citizens of Manila. As this traffic goes on under a confidence system [confiánza], in which there is neither written document which can certify the remittances, nor register in which the real owners can be declared, nor bill of lading by which the right of possession may be known — the result is, that the citizens of Manila send as their own the bales which belong to those of Mexico, and the latter send money as if it belonged to the citizens of Manila, produced from those bales which were not their own. And as this trade is carried on publicly with this dissimulation, and it will not be easy for any one to ascertain the inside of it and the agreements which are privately made, it follows from this that there will always be difficulty in proving guilt, and that the merchants will persist in trying to persuade the officials that the money which they send is intended either for the fair at the port, or for the payment of [debts to] its owners.

"From this confusion—the depth of which cannot be ascertained, because there is no kind of proof which will make it evident—there results only the suspicion against them, a possibility which has made this negotiation8 more opportune to them, not only because money makes it all easy, but because it is not supposed that very large investments can be made with a small remnant of funds.9 But as this remains a matter of supposition (although public report states otherwise), I must confine myself to judicial terms, in order [either] to acquit or to condemn. The proportion of the indult must always remain a difficult thing, because there has been no accurate rule for deciding it, nor could it be imposed in a definite amount, in order that the contribution might be calculated in accordance with it. For this reason, we estimated the amounts, averaging their judgment and my own, from which about 15,000 pesos have resulted; and the persons who have furnished these sums are secure as to the despatch of their affairs, in virtue of the powers which your Majesty confers on me. For this I send also the record of proceedings, in which appear [the names of] other individuals besides those included in the memorandum [minuta]. I must tell your Majesty that most of them are very poor, and that what they possess is not sufficient to pay a contribution in any amount; and it, after investigation, either then lack of means or their innocence rendered the exaction of the penalty impossible, I considered it best not to engage the [royal] authority in making extortions from the vassals.

"Your Majesty has given notice, in your royal decree of May 27, 1710, that frauds in the commerce consist in the excess of the shipments [over the amount permitted], and in what relates to the money which is transported by the ships of Philipinas to each of those countries, and that this irregularity depends on the judges who at Acapulco receive and despatch the ships. Although I must acquiesce in these judgments, and, no matter how much care the viceroys take to confer these powers on officials of zeal, intelligence, and energy, it is possible for self-interest to corrupt them, I also grant that it is difficult to ascertain their transgressions—because, as there is but the one official before whom the declarations of the goods and the registrations of the silver are made, it is very possible that he may have an interest in one or the other of these—either recording a smaller quantity of goods, in order that there may be smaller duties; or not registering the silver, which he can allow to be shipped outside the amount permitted. But as in both cases there is no one to make objection besides the very parties who are interested—and it suits these to be silent, because their profit depends on that—nor is there a witness to state what occurs, nor document to prove it, the transaction goes on, under a system of confidence to which neither proof nor even suspicion can be opposed.

"In some accounts, I have learned, certain sums have been credited to your Majesty, under the title 'Amounts in excess of the permission,' which is ten per cent of the excess over the 600,000 pesos which your Majesty allows to be transported; but whether these items are punctually credited or not, or whether under cover of these other and larger sums were received which were profitable to the judge, it is not easy to ascertain. I take abundant precautions to prevent these things from being done, but if they are done, or are hidden, I cannot prevent it; and I go on, sincerely believing that the minister [in whose charge this matter is], of whose fidelity I have had experience in other directions, will exercise that faithfulness in this also.

"For the future, your Majesty commands that the merchants refrain from transgressing in what is prohibited; but the very nature of the subject leaves some openings that cannot be repaired, through which the greed for gain thrusts itself, not only among the officials but in the merchants; and thus the most sagacious understanding does not perceive or suspect them, and thus does not correct them. I will specify some cases to your Majesty which will make this point clear.

"Your Majesty commands in law 12 on 'Navigation and commerce of Philipinas,' in the compilation of laws of the Indias: 'That those who desire to go to Philipinas must give bonds, for their residing in the islands for at least eight years; and the viceroy shall allow them to carry with them their wealth in money, besides the amount of the general permission.' In virtue of this law, cunning has discovered two safe and sure ways for perpetuating the commerce of this kingdom with those islands: the first, in the permission [here given] for carrying the money; the second, in [the assumption of] citizenship. For experience has shown that, on pretext of [maintaining] confidence and friendly relations, the merchants here send out one or more persons, the profits of them all being contracted for with these persons; the latter ask permission from the government, and display 50,000 to 70,000 pesos as their own, which actually are amounts entrusted to them by many persons. Under this supposition, they go over to Manila with the title of citizens, trade with that money, and regularly ship, as their own, the goods consigned to the citizens here [in Mexico], to whom belonged the money [carried by these agents]; and by remittances of silver and shipments of goods they continue to perpetuate that commerce—in such manner that, if efforts are made to learn who is the shipper, it is [always ostensibly] a citizen of Manila, in whom it is taken for granted that there is no fraud; and if the names of the consignees are ascertained, answer is made that they are his agents. But the latter are not agents, but owners, and the former are not owners, but agents; and in this way the order of things is reversed, by changing their names and the titles to property, and the profits remaining in the hands of those who are under prohibition.

"From this difficulty, authorized by the permission of the law, follow others. For, granting that these agents, even though they have actual residence in Manila, stay there not with the intention of becoming permanent settlers, but of living there only during the agencies which are patronized by the citizens of this kingdom, and that in virtue of the royal orders of your Majesty they are reputed as citizens: it [yet] follows that to them, as citizens, is assigned lading space in the ships, in accordance with the law, and with the royal decree of the year 1702; and thus they have the greatest facility for continuing in their trading, because no hindrance is offered to their shipments. They stand in the way of those who are really citizens and natives of those islands, whose remonstrances occasioned your Majesty's prohibition; but as this interference goes on under the shelter of so plausible a reason, the latter have no way in which to oppose it, nor can they avoid suffering from it; and what [the authorities] there decide to belong to the parties interested is, strictly speaking, what has been entrusted to them by the citizens of Mexico.

"From this result two other and irreparable losses to the commerce of Manila. The first is, that for the 300,000 pesos of the permission there is a million of pesos to be invested [therein]; and [these agents], in order to make the most of their remittances [from Mexico], and to secure larger profits on their commissions, pay for goods at excessive prices, and are preferred in the sales. This is what cannot be done with their own money by the real citizens of those islands, because they have not [sufficient] capital remaining to permit adequate gains with high-priced stuffs and enormous costs [for transportation]—especially when these [citizens] regularly sell [their goods] at Acapulco (whither they go exposed to loss of their capital), in order to have the relief of bringing back their wealth in the same vessel with themselves; and the others [i.e., the agents of Mexicans] ship to Mexico their goods, the owners of which store them away in order that time may give them value, for they do not need to sell these goods at once in order to continue the remittances of money [to Filipinas]. Thus, the former must necessarily lose, or at least not gain; and the latter must gain, or at least not lose.

"The second [injury to commerce]: although no more than the 300,000 pesos of the permission, in goods valued in the islands, can be shipped, experience has shown us that much larger amounts come thence; and the reason is, because the register contains the appraisements of the goods so exceedingly low that it is impossible, unless fraud intervene, that they could be purchased at first hand at those prices—but with the trick that all the reduction of price thus made on the goods is squeezed besides into the [amount of the] permission, and the real account comes separately to the owners. As a result, the greater part of the space on the ship is occupied by those agents, although with the pretense that they produce but small amounts; and all this springs from that original root of allowing citizenship, and the transportation of their silver, to persons who, without the intention of becoming settlers, continue there so long as it brings them profit. The fear of this abuse has led to an investigation at Acapulco, to learn whether the valuation of the stuffs is the actual value of them at Manila; and as the witnesses are necessarily from that city they frankly say that it is so, and enormous quantities of goods come thence under the pretext of the 300,000 pesos permitted.

"These considerations and the fulfilment of my obligation constrain me to inform your Majesty that although I have applied all my energy and watchfulness in order that what was decided by your Majesty should be put into practice, causing the royal decree of the year 1702 to be proclaimed in Mexico and Acapulco, and allowing two years of liberty in order that the transaction of this commerce with those islands may cease, the perversity and selfishness of the merchants is able to pervert the rule which is seen therein—in public giving out that they are conforming to the tenor of that decree, and in private and secret hiding under [their system of] confidence the prohibited transactions, which cause, besides the royal displeasure of your Majesty, serious injury to the commercial interests of Spain. For when there is abundance of the goods from Manila—which on account of their cheapness are more suitable for the common people—the value of those from Europe is impaired; and from this results the stoppage of the trading-fleets, the lack of purchasers, and the lowering of prices, because the people do not consider the European goods necessary for their supply [of clothing]. I know very well that in the islands a change is expected from regulating the commerce, as has been experienced this year, when the [Manila] ship came in ballast—the merchants perhaps fearing the threatened punishment of the confiscation of their goods (as I set forth to your Majesty in a separate report). From this will result the forced expenditure of the royal situado and the inefficiency of the royal exchequer; but as it is certain that those islands cannot maintain themselves with the situado alone, and that they need the traffic in their goods in order to obtain a balance of profits and to meet their obligations, they will have to continue in their shipments, conforming themselves to the [terms of the] permission, if they do not wish to experience the penalty of law in punishment for their frauds.

"This year of 1714 is the last one designated and determined by me for closing and finishing the mutual relations of both commercial bodies, taking into consideration, however, the capital belonging to Nueva España in the islands, and that the penalty ought not to be anticipated, considering the publicity of the prohibition; and, as nothing is coming this year, it will be necessary to abrogate it in the following one. All this I place before your Majesty, in order that in regard to what is contained therein you may be pleased to apply suitable measures."

In view of this letter from Viceroy Linares, and of other documents, whose contents do not concern this writing, it was agreed by the Council (after having listened to the fiscal), by a decree of the second of March, 1715, that this collection of papers [Expediente] should be kept until the commissary of Philipinas (who, it was learned, was coming to the court) should arrive; and that in the meanwhile all the previous documents which the Council might possess in regard to this commerce should be collected together.

PERIOD V

Of the information given by the commercial interests of España, in regard to the injuries arising from the Philipinas trade; and orders given by his Majesty in the year 1718 prohibiting the [trade in] the silk fabrics from China.

45. As the result of the memorial sent to the king by the consulate and commerce of Nueva España (which his Majesty was pleased to refer to the Council), in which they described the backward condition in which their trade was, and stated the arguments why the trading-fleets annually sent to that kingdom [from España] should not be continued, the Council agreed that the consulate and commerce of Sevilla should give a report upon their opinion of this memorial, calling together for this purpose in a general conference all the shippers and merchants who were in that city; and that their discussions, proposals, and joint opinions should be exactly copied, with the individual opinions which were offered, and the whole sent to the Council.

46. The body of traders having assembled in Sevilla on January 27, 1714, in order to comply with the order of the Council, and the importance of this matter having been discussed at length in the conference, it was

unanimously agreed that the injury arising from the notable, frequent, and large importation of foreign goods which had been made throughout America had been very pernicious to the commerce of Sevilla; and that it was impossible that that commerce should return to its former condition if those importations were not checked—which they had entreated his Majesty to do in repeated remonstrances, which they now made again, trusting that the earnest and truthful utterances of vassals so faithful as they could not be displeasing to the royal ears.

47. [They further declared] that the injury caused by the large amount of freight which was earned into Nueva España by the ships from China, rivaled, if it did not exceed, that from the other importations. For, although the merchants of Mexico did not touch on this point in their memorial, the silence in which they kept back this subject (although it was a more odious source of damage) readily explained what interests were concerned in tolerating and continuing those ships, at the same time when the latter had so injured and driven out the commerce of España that no words were sufficient to explain the grief and resentment [of the Sevillans] over the great losses which had been caused to it. For although the ships which were bringing in the cloth and other goods (a matter to which the consulate of Mexico attached much weight) were ruining the commerce of España, in those important lines of linen goods, and others which they were bringing in, [nevertheless] the knowledge, suspicion, or information of what they were could perhaps make the [resultant] damage to the Spanish commerce less serious, such knowledge causing the refusal to injure that commerce; but that could not be guarded against in the ships from China, for their cargo was composed of all the silks and other goods generally which could be traded in by the merchants of España, of those which are manufactured in these kingdoms; and, whatever might be lost in that region on the part of the commerce of España by reason of foreign importations, it lost everything through those from China.

48. That, his Majesty having granted to the island of Luzòn (in which was located the city of Manila) and to the other islands around it only this, that every year there should go to the port of Acapulco one ship to obtain the situado for the maintenance of the fortified posts, conveying only what pertained to white and colored cotton stuffs, pepper, porcelain, raw silk, and other similar commodities which are produced by the islands which obey [the king of España], and with the prohibition of every kind of woven silk stuffs as contraband—for which reason the latter have always been burned on account of the notion of their being made in China and Japòn (which are countries governed by idolaters, Mahometans, and heretics, who are not under the dominion of this crown)—the abuse of this permission

had reached such a state that the ship came with a lading of eleven or twelve thousand bales from China and Japòn, so dexterously packed by those infidels that the largest bale which the commerce of España was shipping to the Indias did not include the volume or the value that was enclosed in a bale of those silks, which was less than a vara deep. Moreover, they put therein imitations of all the satins, velvets, ribbons, mantles, hose, and every kind of silks, which were manufactured in España; [and these were] so showy and beautiful that, not only for this reason but on account of the very moderate prices at which they were sold throughout Nueva España, no other kind of silks were used than those of China. The result of this was that all the silk factories in España (which were paying so enormous duties to the royal treasury) had been broken up and destroyed; and the fortunes of those who were trading in the Indias were ruined by the great losses which they had encountered, since the Spanish commerce was deprived of a line of goods so important and rich as is that of the silk, in all its kinds of fabrics.

49. That this loss had passed over to the woolen goods, such as picotes, barracans,10 and others which were shipped in the trading-fleets; for those who had clothed themselves with these throughout Nueva España were now despising them, observing that for half of what a woolen garment cost them they could procure another of China silk—being apparently as well clothed, although in the quality of the goods they had been deceived. In this manner the Chinese goods carried out of the country three or four millions of pesos in each ship, which was but little less wealth than that carried by a regular trading-fleet.

50. That the damage which this illegal trade occasioned to the royal treasury and to the Spanish trade enabled one to judge of the great amount of property which those ships transported, of the treasures which they carried, of the loss which they caused to the commerce of España, and of the amount which they did not contribute [to the royal revenues]—augmenting by this means the power and wealth of those infidels, who are enemies to the Christian faith and to the crown. For this reason, and because the consulate and commerce of Sevilla firmly believed that this was the greatest loss and the greatest source and cause of the ruin of the trading-fleets, and that which most urgently called for relief with the most prompt and energetic measures: they concluded by entreating his Majesty that he would deign to give orders that the permission given to Philipinas be strictly observed, under the most severe penalties, commanding that its limits be restricted within the limits of its first concession, for this purpose despatching the most rigorous orders; and that the trading-fleets should go punctually

and frequently, each year. On this point they expatiated at length, and it is omitted because it does not belong to this subject.

51. In view of this information and of the proceedings in the Council (of which there is no account in the *Expediente*) it is found that by decree of January 8, 1718, his Majesty stated to the Council that, having been informed of the quantity of stuffs, silken fabrics, and other merchandise which the ship from Philipinas brought, by which the greater part of the silver of Nueva España was carried out of that country, he had decided to prohibit absolutely the trade in the aforesaid commodities. He declared that the only trade which could be carried on was in linen goods, porcelain, wax, cinnamon, cloves, and other products which are not carried from España, to such an amount of these kinds of goods as the Marqués de Valero should notify to the governor of Philipinas, which must be transported by one of the ships which for the last five years had arrived at Acapulco [from the islands]. His Majesty furnished with this a copy of the order to this purpose which he had given to the Marqués de Valero, the tenor of which is as follows: [Here follows a copy of the decree, dated at Madrid on January 8, 1718.]

53. By another decree of June 20, in the same year, 1718, his Majesty sent to the Council, for its information and guidance in the matters which belonged to it, a copy of another decree (which was issued to the Council of Castilla), prohibiting the importation and use of the fabrics from China and other parts of Assia, since this was to the injury of the manufactures and commerce of España; its tenor is as follows: [A copy of this decree is also given].

PERIOD VI

Of what occurred from the year 1718, in which the commerce of silken fabrics was prohibited, up to the year 1722, in which the merchants of Philipinas protested.

55. The Marqués de Valero, then viceroy of Mexico, in a letter of March 12, 1719—accompanied by a duplicate of another letter dated June 20, 1718, in which he acknowledged the receipt of the despatches in the private correspondence, dated January 8 of that same year, which prohibited all silks in the ship from Philipinas—considered the inconveniences which would result from that commerce being reduced to linen goods, porcelain, wax, pepper, cinnamon, and cloves, excluding stuffs, and raw silk and [silken] fabrics. For, he said, if this prohibition should be put in practice, the result would be the decay of religion, and the risk that it would be neglected, and its extension would be endangered and even exposed to ruin although this matter had cost his Majesty so much solicitude in promoting and assisting

the missions for preaching the faith. [He declared] that the Spanish families who were there would abandon the settlements, for they could not maintain themselves in those islands without the trade in the aforesaid commodities, since that in the merchandise allowed to them had no profit, on account of its low price and the little demand for it. That the natives of Nueva España were also included in the prohibition, since their usual material for clothing was the stuffs from China, on account of the moderate prices of these, and because they could not use the cloth from España, since it was more expensive—unless, if they are deprived of the former, it will follow that they consume the latter; for if their need and poverty would permit it they would use the Spanish cloth, since all value it more on account of its greater durability and better quality. That the arrival of the trading-fleets was welcomed by the rich merchants, but that most of the people in the kingdom were much more eager to see the ship from China; and, if its arrival were delayed, one did not fail to notice many expressions of regret. That the royal treasury was notoriously injured; for, with the duties which the silk merchandise yielded, the situado was forwarded to Philipinas and the Marianas Islands, and in default of those duties it would be necessary to make the remittance from the funds in the treasury of Mexico. That would cause arrears in paying the fixed charges which the treasury had to carry, and could hardly meet with all its income, and the royal treasury would also be injured by the loss of the ten per cent which was paid by the silver sent in return for merchandise; and, besides, the few commodities which were carried would not yield enough to cover the cost of the navigation.

56. The fiscal—to whom it was ordered to send these representations, that he might examine them and compare them with the Expediente—made his reply on January 10, in the year 1720, reaffirming the motives which had prevailed, since the discovery and conquest of those islands, in permitting to them the commerce with Nueva España, so far as it was necessary to their preservation. [He also stated] the infractions of law which had changed the amount permitted—250,000 pesos of principal, and 500,000 for the returns (which "Period i" mentions)—and what was ordained by the royal decree of August 12, 1702, for the regulation of the management and continuance of this commerce; and declarations made by his Majesty in regard to unsettled points which arose, in the meeting of the Council in 1712, from which despatches were sent on December 12, of that year (which are mentioned in "Period iii"); and the fact that the abuses with which the merchants of Peru had carried on commerce with Nueva España had made it necessary that in the year 1631 that trade should be entirely prohibited. He was of the following opinion: that the permission to trade ought to be continued to the citizens of Philipinas, for the damages to the commerce of España would be

avoided if that of Philipinas did not exceed the 300,000 pesos which were allowed to it.

57. That if this commerce should perish, trade and intercourse in those distant provinces would cease; and if they were cut off from communication with Nueva España they would remain exposed to seeking for commerce with the adjoining nations, and in imminent danger of trading away at the same time their own rights and customs, and of going to perdition—the Catholic faith being extinguished entirely or in part, the propagation and maintenance of which was and always had been the chief care of his Majesty.

58. That although in the royal decrees of January 8, 1718, there was reserved to the islands the trade in sugar, porcelain, linens (called "elephants"),11 and spices, these commodities were not adequate for maintaining a continued commerce, nor for producing the revenues which those islands needed.

59. That the government should not disregard the consideration brought forward by Señor Valero, of the damage which ensued to the poor vassals of Nueva España from depriving them of the privilege of supplying themselves at less cost with the fabrics from Philipinas; for if they cannot obtain these, and the poor are unable to meet the expenses of the Spanish merchandise on account of its high price, they would be exposed to the wretchedness of destitution. In conclusion, he said that advice should be given to his Majesty that the remonstrance of Señor Marqués de Valero was just; and that deference should be paid to it, by suspending the operation of the above-mentioned decrees and warning all the officials in those regions that they must conform without any variation to the orders given in the decree of the year 1702—with various provisions which he proposed, one of which was the total prohibition of the commerce in case the conditions of that decree were violated.

60. Having considered this reply of the fiscal, it was agreed by an act dated February 1, 1720, to advise his Majesty in accordance with all the preceding recommendations; and the Council was of opinion that it should reiterate the enforcement of [the commands in] the despatches of August 12, 1702, and December 13, 1712, with a strict stipulation that the ship could not be allowed to sail if the value of the 300,000 pesos of the permission were invested in silks only.

61. While this opinion was in the royal hands, an order from his Majesty came down to the Council dated September 5, 1720, in which—influenced by a memorial which had been presented by Don Manuel Lopez Pintado in the name of the consulate and commerce of Cadiz; and by a letter from Marqués de Valero just then received, dated March 8, in the same year—his

Majesty commanded that the Council should inform him of their opinions in regard to the prohibition of stuffs and silks from China in the Philipinas ship, after first listening to the memorial from the commerce of Cadiz.

62. The Marqués de Valero in the letter here cited of March 8, 1720, urging what he had set forth in previous letters in regard to the difficulty which he encountered in carrying out the decrees which prohibited the commerce in silken fabrics, also spoke of the new distress in which the islands were, on account of the plague of locusts, failure in their harvest of rice, and the scandalous proceedings of Governor Bustamante. The viceroy said that it seemed to him better for the service of God, and that of his Majesty, to delay the regulations which changed the method in which that commerce had been conducted, until his Majesty should make such decision as pleased him in regard to the viceroy's previous memorials; and he said in conclusion that he had also found it desirable to make this suspension of the decrees because the emperor of China had hindered his vassals for the last two years from trading with the islands—which had resulted in the galleon of that year carrying but few silk goods. Consequently, the greatest scarcity of that merchandise had been experienced, for, even before the arrival of the ship, a libra of silk spun [beneficiada] and dyed was worth 26 to 28 pesos.

63. In consequence of this order of his Majesty there were sent to the consulate of Cadiz copies of the decrees of the year 1718 and of the letters of the Marqués de Valero which have been noted, in order that the consulate might report in regard to its opinions, fully and clearly stating the inconveniences, or the advantages, which might follow the prohibition of the stuffs, silken fabrics, and other merchandise from China. They answered this in a letter of July 16, declaring that on this subject they had made on different occasions the representations which were contained in two official documents which accompanied, and that nothing occurred to them to be added to these (which are the ones noted in nos. 46 and the following, "Period v").12 Orders were given that the fiscal should examine the whole matter anew; and he in his reply of September 11, in the same year, 1720, taking into consideration what he had stated in another of January 10 preceding (which is the reply that is indicated in no. 56), added, that the consulate only complained in its memorial and in the remonstrances of its merchants of the illegal manner in which the commerce of Philipinas was carried on; and the fiscal asked that this be restricted within the limits of the permitted amount.

64. He stated that it was a mistake to assume that the permission was only for the products belonging to the native citizens of Philipinas, because the laws which permitted this commerce did not contain such limitation, and continual usage had excluded it; for always the islands had traded

in silken fabrics without hindrance, for with the products of the country it would be impossible to carry on an annual commerce to the amount of 300,000 pesos.

65. That the absolute prohibition of that commerce which the consulate proposed in its memorial (it is not in the *Expediente*), following the precedent of prohibiting the commerce of Peru with Nueva España, ought not to be considered. For the latter prohibition left both those kingdoms free to trade with Castilla, by which the lack of commerce between them was made endurable; but this result could not occur with Philipinas if the commerce of Nueva España were prohibited to them, since there remained no other of which they could avail themselves.

66. That, if the products of the natives of those islands were sufficient to make up the annual [amount of] trade to the extent of 300,000 pesos, it would be just and reasonable that the commerce in silken fabrics be prohibited to them; but as the aforesaid viceroy positively stated that those products were not sufficient for that purpose, it would not be right to deprive them of this privilege without further knowledge of the subject. The conclusion of the fiscal was, that orders should be given to observe the royal decree of August 12, 1702; and that the viceroy and Audiencia of Mexico, and the governor, Audiencia, archbishop, and royal officials of Manila, *should send in information very clear and detailed on the question whether the products of the country could fill up the amount, [of exports] assigned to that commerce.*

67. The Council, in view of all that is mentioned in this "Period vi," and of a summary of the context of the letters of the Marqués de Valero, and of the replies of the fiscal, were of opinion, in their session of September 23, 1720, that his Majesty should be pleased to command a repetition of the orders given for the fulfilment of the regulations issued on August 12, 1702, and September 13, 1712—with a strict stipulation that the Philipinas ship should not sail with an investment which should exceed 300,000 pesos, and that to be in the commodities which were specified [therein], with exclusion of every kind of silken fabrics; and with other measures and statements which are contained in the despatches that were issued for the enforcement of those decrees, dated October 27, following, of which mention will be made.

68. At this session it pleased his Majesty to make the following decision: "I agree entirely with what the Council proposes; and the corresponding orders shall be immediately given, with the most punctual and strict charge to the officials whom this concerns (and especially the viceroy of Nueva España) that all the above orders shall be carried out promptly, without any objection or alteration—with the warning that, if any neglect or delay in

fulfilling this decision is experienced, proceedings shall be brought against them as disobedient to my orders. And in order that those officials, as also private persons in Nueva España and Philipinas, may be fully informed of this determination, a decree shall be drawn up with the utmost clearness and precision, which shall include the whole of this business. This decree shall serve as an ordinance, in which, without reference to others, shall be expressly stated what every person must observe in this commerce, and the penalties which transgressors will incur, in accordance with what the Council proposes, to the end that, by placing an authentic copy of it at the heads of the registers on the ships from Philipinas and making it public, no one can allege ignorance. The Council shall pay especial attention to the manner in which proceedings shall be taken in this matter, not only in Nueva España but in Philipinas, in order to secure the punishment of those who disobey my orders, and of those who shall delay their execution."

69. In consequence of this decision the royal ordinance which was mentioned in it was drawn up, with date of October 27, 1720. It was addressed to the viceroy Marqués de Valero, and the Audiencia of Mexico; the royal officials of Acapulco; the governor, Audiencia, and fiscal of Philipinas; and the archbishop of Manila; and copies of it were given to the consulates and merchants of Cadiz and Manila, at their request, in order that they might print it. Its tenor is as follows:

70. [This decree is addressed to Marqués de Valero, viceroy of Nueva España. After rehearsing the arguments brought forward in previous letters received from Valero, the decree ordains the following rules for the commerce of Philipinas: Two ships shall go annually from the islands to Nueva España, each of 500 toneladas. "The value of the lading which the said ships are to carry from Philipinas to the port of Acapulco may be up to the amount of 300,000 pesos, which must come invested strictly and solely in the following kinds of merchandise: gold, cinnamon, elephants, wax, porcelain, cloves, pepper, cambayas and linens woven with colors [lienzos pintados],13 chitas, chintzes, gauzes, lampotes, Hilocos14 blankets, silk floss and raw silk spun, cordage, and other commodities which are not silks." These ships are prohibited from carrying silken fabrics, "satins, pitiflores, velvets, damasks, Pekin silks [Pequines], sayasayas, brocades, plain satins, grograms, taffetas; silver and gold brocades; embroidered pieces of silk stuff for [covers of] beds, the [hangings for] drawing-rooms [estrados], and women's petticoats; silken gauzes flowered with gold and silver; pattern pieces for petticoats, figured or embroidered; dressing-gowns, chimones, or made-up garments; hose, ribbons, or handkerchiefs; or any fabric which contains silk." The penalties for transgression of this order are confiscation of such goods, payment of three times their value (this amount to be shared

between the royal fiscal, the judge, and the informer), and perpetual exile from the Indias; and the confiscated goods are to be burned. Declarations of goods shipped are absolutely prohibited; those who are permitted to trade must be chosen by the city of Manila, without the aid of any official; the duties to be paid are fixed at 100,000 pesos for each voyage, with the express stipulation that this payment is to be called adjustment [regulation] of duties, and not indult; no religious person and no stranger may be allowed to ship goods; every shipper must present an itemized invoice of the goods sent; the ships must not be overloaded; no right to lading space may be transferred to another person. Provision is made for inspection, valuation, and landing of goods, and for the disposition to be made of such as shall be confiscated; and the limit of six months is fixed for the disposal of all Chinese silk goods that may be on hand in Nueva España when the decree is published, after which time all that are found must be burned.]

PERIOD VII

Of what was done in Manila on receiving the decree of October 27, 1720. Recourse to the Council by their deputies. Reply from the commerce of Andalucia, and what was decided in regard to this matter in the year 1724.

71. On August 2, 1722, the governor, Marqués de Torre-Campo, received at Manila the ordinance despatched on October 27, 1720, of which the preceding "Period" speaks. Having caused this decree to be published by a proclamation in that city, record of it was made in the offices, and it was communicated to the municipal council in open session. The cabildo protested against it, promising to obey, but resolving to set forth to the governor in the first place, and afterward to his Majesty, the damages and troubles which would result from its execution to religion, to the royal treasury, and to the greater welfare of those islands, from their not continuing to enjoy the permission to trade in fabrics of silk, which they had possessed for more than one hundred and forty years. They would therefore be obliged to entreat that his Majesty give them permission to retire, with their families, to the lands and domains of his Majesty which they should consider most suitable.

72. In a long memorial presented to the governor was set forth in detail the motives on which they based this action; and when orders had been given that the fiscal of that Audiencia should examine it, although he recognized that their statements were correct, and that the islands could not maintain themselves on the system of commerce which had been laid down, he demanded that orders should be given to fulfil the cited royal decree, and that the city and merchants should appeal to his Majesty who, there was reason to expect, would take care of his vassals there, and of the interests,

both spiritual and temporal, which were concerned in it—and the governor gave orders to that effect. Although the city and the merchants by a second memorial insisted upon a suspension of the above regulation, demanding that, in case there was no room for it and for continuing their trade in silks and stuffs as heretofore, at least he should declare that they were not obliged to invest their funds in the commodities which were prescribed to them, as it would occasion their total ruin (and they demonstrated this): nevertheless, the governor, bearing in mind that the damages to his Majesty would be no less, if the galleon for that year should go empty, commanded that, in accordance with the amount permitted by the cited regulation, they should make the distribution of the [permits to ship] merchandise as his Majesty had commanded. The city and the merchants, with the hope that his Majesty would give attention to the urgent representations that would be made by the commissaries whom it had been agreed to despatch to the court, agreed to continue the commerce meanwhile conformably to the despatch of 1720—sacrificing out of respect to his Majesty, and in order to maintain the religion established in those islands, their own wealth, which necessarily must be ruined and lost in a commerce so useless and unfortunate as that to which they were reduced; since the bulky commodities, on account of their abundance and poor manufacture, would not allow them to gain ten per cent, since the risks extended to fifty per cent.

73. The city of Manila, in order to render commendable and frame in more formal manner its appeal from the aforesaid decree of October 27, 1720, which it must bring before the royal person—not only for the continuation of the traffic in the silken fabrics, but also for the increase of its permission from the three hundred thousand pesos which it was enjoying to five hundred thousand—came before the Audiencia and presented before it the arguments and reasons in favor of both these requests. After explaining the losses that would arise from the desolation and depopulation to which the islands would come (which the Audiencia took into consideration in its memorial, as will be noted) the city added that when in Manila there were only 230 citizens (which was in the years 1636–37) returns of 500,000 pesos were permitted to them; but since in the year 1722 the city had 882 citizens, and there was an increase in the charitable foundations, which placed 150,000 pesos at risk on each galleon, the necessity was evident of increasing the permission to 500,000 pesos—350,000 pesos for the citizens, and 150,000 for the charitable foundations. This increase in the number of citizens made necessary the expansion of the permission, from the very fact that in the year 1702, in which there were only 400 citizens, his Majesty had permitted 300,000 pesos of investments, and 600,000 pesos in returns.

74. It was also expedient that permission be given to the seamen to transport in their own chests goods up to the amount of 40,000 pesos of investment, on account of the importance of interesting them in the defense,15 and in order to facilitate that in provinces so remote there should be Spaniards who would serve as artillerists and seamen, since their wages alone, in voyages so arduous and long, could not be sufficient incentive. In order that that commerce might be regulated and infractions regarding the lading be avoided, an arrangement was proposed to his Majesty in which the annual investment was reduced to 3,200 piezas of the regular sizes—half-bundles, bags, sacks, [churlos, balsas (for bolsas)] cakes of wax, and other like packages of bulky commodities, and three hundred half-chests of goods from China, in order to supplement the said 3,20016 piezas. Consequently, at the despatch of the galleon there would be nothing else to do except to distribute the said piezas and issue the permits for its lading—collecting 10,000 pesos for the royal duties, at the rate of two per cent, for this purpose rating the 3,200 piezas at 128 pesos and 1 tomin, and the half-chests at 300 pesos and pay at Acapulco thirteen per cent, regulating the 3,200 piezas at 256 pesos and 2 tomìns, and the 300 half-chests at 600 pesos each. This would result in the royal duties at both ports amounting to 140,000 pesos, and in return would be brought back, for the account of the permission, a million pesos; and thus would be avoided sworn declarations, and other dubious measures to which the previous regulations were subjected.

75. The Audiencia of Manila in a letter of November 9, 1722, taking into consideration another which they had written on August 6, 1713, in which they set forth the losses which that commerce had suffered—in [the wreck of] their galleons, the unsuccessful fairs of Acapulco, and the excessive pecuniary extortions that they had suffered in Acapulco on account of the royal duties and in other ways—to the end that new measures might be taken by his Majesty for the rigorous reëstablishment of the commerce of those islands, describe (influenced by the urgent representations made by the city and by previous information obtained by each auditor) the affliction which has been caused by the new decree of October 27, 1720. They declared that they judged necessary for the maintenance of these islands and the propagation of the holy gospel, not only the permission for the silk and the stuffs prohibited by the cited despatch, but also the increase of the permission from 300,000 to 500,000 pesos. The Audiencia affirmed that the Spaniards could not exist without this commerce, because the culture of the fields was in the hands of the natives and the management of the guilds [gremios] in those of the Sangleys and their mestizos; that the salaries and pay with which the military officers, soldiers, and civil officials were recompensed did not reach half the annual expense of their families, in

consideration of which it was commanded to include then the distribution of the lading of the galleons; and that, while the permitted amount was 300,000 pesos, and the number of citizens so great, the investment of each one, even if all were alike in wealth and services, did not amount to 400 pesos, the profit on which was not enough for the proper support of a man who was not actually poor, and on this account they could not increase their wealth. When the Europeans see that it is useless to transport goods to those regions where there is not, outside of commerce, any motive which would induce them to remain, or which would bring other new traders, those who consider the matter have reason to fear that in a few years the capitals of those who live there will be consumed, and that others will refuse to enter into the same experience; then Philipinas will be left to the Indians and Sangleys, the gospel ministers without the guards of Spaniards for their protection, the military posts without garrisons, the natives without any control, and everything on the blink of a deplorable ruin.

76. That with the commodities which were allowed by the said royal decree, the lading of the annual galleon could not reach the gross amount of the 300,000 pesos of the commission. From this it resulted that that amount was diminished and the traders exposed to evident loss in Nueva España, on account of the abundance of those very articles of merchandise; and that would result in cutting off the proceeds of the many and large charitable funds, founded on the merchandise risked in those galleons, for the support of clergymen, hospitals, convents, divine worship, dowries to orphan girls, and many other alms—which, even though they were no more than those which were administered by the brotherhood of La Misericordia, and by the tertiary Order of St. Francis, were of the greatest importance, and their failure a most notable affliction to all the islands.

77. That by the exclusion of the stuffs and silks, which were the principal articles of commerce of the islands with China, all that commerce [i.e., with Nueva España] would come to an end, since all the rest was of so little value that it could not, without the substantial aid of the silks, allow any profit. From this would result another great difficulty in the propagation of the holy gospel, that if the Chinese do not come to the trade they will lose the opportunity for conversion which so many have attained, attracted by familiar intercourse with the Spaniards, with the occasion of this commerce, and there would be great difficulty in introducing the gospel ministers into those dominions; and these are motives which have always engaged the chief attention of his Majesty, to judge by the laws. The Audiencia concluded by expressing the opinion that the prohibition of the silks should

be removed, and an increase be granted in the permission to 500,000 pesos, with the number of piezas which the city was proposing—this regulation being made in proportion to the number of citizens, in order that the islands might maintain themselves, and thus obviate the serious inconveniences that were experienced; and, as for the duties which the city proposed, this question was referred to the decision of the Council.

78. The fiscal of that Audiencia, Don Pedro Bedoya,17 in a letter of November 15, in the same year, 1722, in consequence of the duplicate copy which he received of the royal decree of October 27, 1720, states on his part—after repeating his previous opinion regarding its execution, as given to the city of Manila, the action taken by the governor, the recourse by the city to the Audiencia, and the report made by that body—what his opinion is, in fulfilment of his obligation, in regard to the memorial of the city and the merchants; it is brought under four heads, which are:

I

The necessary dependence which the maintenance of these islands has on the commerce, in order that the Spaniards may maintain themselves in them; and the benefit from the charitable funds, in which are annually expended 75,000 pesos—which sum proceeds from the trading of the 150,000 pesos which are carried in the annual galleon on account of the said charitable funds.

II

That if the prohibition of the stuffs and other commodities from China remains, their former control of the trade therein will be disturbed, and the royal decrees issued for this purpose (some of which are compiled18) will be subverted—such as those which command that the commodities which they convey shall be bought from the Sangleys; and that if this [Chinese] commerce is prohibited that of Nueva España becomes unprofitable, as the bulky commodities do not fill up the amount of the permitted trade, and it will not be possible to pay the cost of traffic in them without those from China.

III

That for the maintenance of these islands, the support of the Spaniards, and the success of the charitable funds, it is necessary that the amount permitted be increased to 500,000 pesos and a million of returns, with the inclusion of the fabrics from China.

IV

The regulation of the lading, in order to avoid infractions of the law [is necessary]; as also that the dubious and burdensome obligation of making sworn declarations be laid aside, and that the quality and number of the commodities which are transported must appear in the registers.

79. [These points made by the fiscal are discussed at length by him in a report addressed to the king, dated November 15, 1722. Among other things, he states that the merchants prefer one galleon of 800 or 900 tons burden to two of 500 tons each, as being less expensive (on account of requiring fewer officers and men), safer (as carrying larger cannon) and less exposed to danger from either enemies or storms, than the two smaller vessels; that the industry and love of gain displayed by the Chinese who reside in the islands have secured to them the control of all the crafts and useful arts, and of the commerce of the islands save that with Nueva España, which is therefore the only resource of the Spanish citizens; that the current rate of income19 is but five per cent in the islands, while that commerce brings in fifty per cent; that most of the rural estates [haciendas] are possessed by the religious orders; that houses constitute property of little value, on account of the frequent fires and earthquakes; and that consequently the charitable foundations [obras pias] have been necessarily based on the Acapulco trade. It is also declared that the annual situado from Mexico amounts to no more than 50,000 or 60,000 pesos, while the annual budget of the government expenses amounts to 500,000 pesos, which the royal treasury of the islands must pay from the proceeds of the duties on merchandise. The request of the Manila citizens for a permission to send 500,000 pesos' worth, in 3,500 piezas, is very moderate; as the trade has been conducted, the 300,000 pesos' worth has made 4,798 piezas, for the last five years—which is evidence of the infractions of law which have been committed in that commerce. Moreover, the proposition of the city that the duties belonging to the crown be levied on the number of the piezas, will be likely to prevent many of the frauds which are now practiced in this direction. The fiscal opposes the request of the city that the seamen be allowed an increase of the small amount already allowed them, free from duties, for investment on their own account, declaring that it will but increase the illegal trade already prevalent, and that the proposition to allow them 40,000 pesos' worth of trade (with twice that amount in returns for the merchandise) would allow the seamen a greater investment than even the citizens, since the former average only 115 men to each galleon. He advises that the officers of the ships be permitted to have a share in the lading of the ship, in place of their present wages; and that one large galleon be occupied in the trade to Acapulco, rather than two small ones. He reminds the king of the opening afforded by the trade between Manila and China for the conversion of the Chinese and the entrance of the gospel into that heathen empire.]

80. [The treasury officials at Manila also write, seconding the proposal to despatch one large galleon; and they add that the royal exchequer of the islands will be ruined if the decree of 1720 is enforced, "for the commerce would cease, and consequently the royal duties which it was producing."]

81. The archbishop of Manila, the dean and cabildo of that church, and the provincial of the Society [of Jesus], in their letters of November 6, 7, and 8 of the same year, support the entreaty of the city; they deprecate the ruin (both spiritual and temporal) of the islands, and express the same opinion as that of the Audiencia and the fiscal, as will be seen by their letters, which follow below.

82. The provincials of St. Dominic, St. Francis, and St. Augustine (both calced and discalced), in their memorials of the same year expatiate on the necessity and advantage of changing the aforesaid decree of 1720, and granting likewise to the islands the increase of the permitted trade which they solicit; and they reproduce in detail what the other prelates and ministers say.

83. [The letter of the archbishop (Fray Francisco de la Cuesta) states that he has been urged to write it by the city and merchants of Manila, and the bureau of the Misericordia; and he begins, very naturally, by arguing that the religious interests of the Philippines and of China depend upon the maintenance of the commerce of the islands. He refers to the opposition made to it by the merchants of Andalusia, which he thinks has no good foundation, since their trade with the other European nations drains from España more money than does that of Filipinas from Nueva España—this last being their ground of complaint against the Manila trade; but even if the Sangleys and other heathen carry away silver from Manila, "they have not harmed the [Spanish] crown, and are friendly to the [Christian] religion; while it is certain that the European nations, even if they are not all opposed to religion, at least have been at various times hostile to the crown, and that the amount annually transported by the said nations to Great China and other heathen kingdoms exceeds four millions [of pesos].... And although the argument [of the Andalusians]—that the fabrics from China cause injury, at the expense of those which are transported from Cadiz—would have some weight if all the fabrics in which the Andalusians trade were manufactured in España, since they are not made there the above argument has very little value." The Spaniards in Filipinas regret that so grievous burdens and restrictions are laid upon them through the influence of the Andalusians, and especially that the result of these must be very detrimental to the charitable funds which so greatly depend upon the Acapulco trade. Two-thirds of these, or 100,000 pesos, belong to the Misericordia alone,

whose educational, religious, and charitable labors are so important to the public welfare and the maintenance of the Spanish colony in Filipinas; the remaining 50,000 pesos belong to other institutions. The archbishop therefore urges the king to accede to the requests of the Manila merchants.]

84. [The dean and cabildo of the Manila cathedral also support the merchants; they fear lest the income of the church will suffer from the impaired condition to which the decree of 1720 threatens to bring the Filipinas colony. They adduce similar arguments to those contained in the preceding letters, all taking for granted that the prohibition of Chinese silks means the ruin of the Acapulco trade. Incidentally this letter states the following facts of interest: "The poverty of the soldiers is such that they always go about as mendicants and in need; for as they receive no more pay than that of two pesos and a fanega of rice—which is given every month to the soldiers, but to the convicts who serve [forzados] in the troops only the rations—if they could not find refuge in the aid given by the citizens, the alms from the charitable funds, and the broken food at the convent doors, and in what the more industrious can earn by doing errands, they would certainly perish." The prebends of the cathedral find their salaries—which range from 500 to 200 pesos yearly, besides the dean's 600—pitiably small and inadequate, and they must even resort to the charitable funds and to the gifts of friends to eke out their incomes. The same difficulties beset the parish ministers; but worst of all is the condition of the poor clerics who receive no pay, who have no income save occasional offerings for masses and the alms of benevolent persons.]

85. [The provincial of the Jesuits, Father Joseph Fernandez, seconds the appeal of the merchants.20 He states that since 1709 the fortunes of the wealthy citizens are nearly all ruined—by calamities, unsuccessful sales at Acapulco, the failure of the galleons to make the voyage, poor crops in Filipinas, or the quarrels of the governors and auditors—and those who formerly made contributions to the religious orders now need and ask for help from them. "This city of Manila (and in it all the islands) is reduced to eight or ten private persons who are able with their own wealth alone to make up the 300,000 pesos which your Majesty allows for their commerce; and the number of its citizens who, as Spaniards, can call themselves such is very nearly 882—although it is true that there are millions of converted natives, and those who are not converted are innumerable. All these citizens depend for their preservation on the three or four piezas which are yearly allotted to [each of] them, according to their merits, in your Majesty's galleon; and as most of them have not the means of their own to fill this space they have to give it up, or sell it to those who are richer; or they must ask for money from the charitable funds of the Misericordia, the tertiary

Order [of St. Francis], or the religious, in order to fill their space on the ship. As they cannot ship therein anything except the coarse cloths and other goods which your Majesty names in your new regulations, the product of which is hardly enough to pay the expenses on them—duties, freight-charges, and carriers' fees—the poorer citizens will see themselves forced to seek some other way [to make a living]. That means the desertion of these islands for India, and consequently a great diminution in the number of your Majesty's vassals; and the islands will be exposed to the invasions of the Dutch and other enemies of your royal crown and of the natives. No few of these invasions have been experienced in recent years, and at this time we are being raided by the Mindanaos, the Joloans, and the Burneyans. And I can assure your Majesty that in the space of less than twelve years I have seen this stage21 of the citizens of Manila changed five times. For, as it is composed of some who come from Europe (and they count for many), and of others who come from Nueva España, on account of the difference of the climate from that in which they were born they do not remain long; both classes, seeing the little comfort that they can find here, and how small incentive there is from riches (which is that which most influences those who do not possess enormous estates), either die in a short time, worn out with the misery of this country; or they leave the islands, to look for a more comfortable residence. Thus it comes to pass that only we religious and other ecclesiastics remain, with some persons who belong to the richer class (who are few), and these are Europeans, whom affection for their native land is always drawing away. If this [which I have mentioned above] happens (which may God not permit), all these millions of Christian natives will be left abandoned, and exposed to [the danger of] returning to their heathen condition; and of being possessed by the Dutch, or the Chinese, or any other nation that may find a profit in them." The argument that the prohibition of the trade in Chinese silks will check the drain of silver from Nueva España is refuted by the provincial; he says, "For we who are near China, Batabia, the Coromandel Coast, and other ports of India, know with certainty that the ships and pataches that come to them from Europa to trade in them carry hardly any money for their traffic except the silver, with the stamp and seal of your Majesty, from Perù or from Mexico; and as those vessels have directed their route from Europa by way of Cape Verde, Buena Esperanza [i.e., Good Hope], Cape Comorin, and Sincapura, it must be supposed that they do not obtain the said silver anywhere else than from the commerce in Europa. Your Majesty could, in the course of several years, prevent the silver that comes from Mexico to these islands from passing over to China, to the Coast, or to Batabia, by commanding your governors and other officials at Manila to make strenuous efforts that in the islands the natives, mestizos, creoles, and various other castes who live in them and are naturalized as subjects, be compelled to weave the cloth goods which are manufactured in other regions; and these people are no less skilful for the mechanical and even the liberal arts than are those of other nations. As for the fabrics of cotton, these people are able to weave them, for their own consumption, more durable and of better quality than the cloths which come from China and the Coast; and as for the silk goods, the hose which these natives weave are those which bring the highest price at Acapulco. The colors for dyeing the goods are furnished by the country itself; for there will be shipped from here to the empire of China during this year more than thirty champan-loads of sibucao, or campeche, a wood from which the Chinese obtain carmine for their dyes; and the other colors they obtain from trees and roots which also are found in these mountains in abundance. As for the cinnamon, it grows very abundantly in the island of Mindanao, where your Majesty has the fort and garrison of Samboangan, with some missions that are administered by priests of my order, and by other religious from the discalced of St. Augustine. It would be of no little advantage to be able to cultivate the cinnamon, as the Dutch do; for the silver which that nation would be obliged to carry for that product would remain among the vassals of your Majesty, and thus there would be an end to that difficulty (which the merchants of Sevilla certainly exaggerate) of your Majesty forbidding the shipment of the goods which your royal decree specifies, which are those that have some value, in order to be able to pay the cost on the more bulky goods. Who will have courage to weave them, or hunt for them, when he knows that he must lose on them? In these islands abundance of gold is collected in various placers, in which work the slow and patient disposition of the natives is occupied; but as their minds are so careless and ignorant they content themselves with washing out only the exact amount of their tribute, which is five reals for each person. But if your Majesty would give your royal directions to your governors and ministers, in the course of time it would be possible to secure the production of this gold in abundance; and if it were sent to Nueva España, and exchanged for the silver necessary for the maintenance of these your wretched vassals, the result would be that the latter product would always remain in the dominions of your Majesty. In these islands, also, some pearls are secured by diving, and in these seas some amber is gathered. In the mountains there is no lack of numerous civet-cats; and the civet, if measures were taken for its production, might be no small source of wealth to your vassals, and consequently furnish huge amounts to your loyal treasury." Father Fernandez mentions that Felipe IV "spent in twenty years 170,000 ducados solely in sending religious to preach the gospel in Philipinas;" and that the monopoly on the buyo industry had produced in one year 11,000 pesos to the royal treasury, and that on wine 18,000 pesos; (but these amounts apparently refer to the price paid for a three years' contract, rather than to the annual income of the crown from these sources).22]

86. All the papers and reports which have been mentioned in this "Period vii" having been received in the Council, and the deputies from Philipinas, Don Francisco Diaz Romero and Don Antonio de Echandía—who deposited their credentials and letters in the office of the secretary—having presented themselves in it, they set forth their claims and stated, in a printed memorial (which they handed in on June 14, 1723) the injuries which the islands were receiving from the practice of the decree of October 27, 1720. They entreated that its execution be suspended, and orders given that the commerce be continued with the yearly galleon in the same manner, so far as the lading was concerned, as was in use at the time when the aforesaid despatch was received there [at Manila]. The memorial, in eight leaves, is as follows:

87. [This memorial by the city and merchants of Manila presents in detail the amount of their annual commerce in the various kinds of merchandise that are permitted in the decree. The gold exported from Filipinas to Nueva España amounts to less than 12,000 pesos, and is sent not as bullion or coin, but in the form of the slender chains [bejuquillos] wrought by the Malay natives for personal adornment; for in no other form could it compete with the abundance of gold mined in Mexico. The Chinese porcelain is shipped in small quantity, being mainly an article of luxury, like the gold ornaments; moreover, it is bulky and fragile. As for spices, Manila complains that the market for these in Nueva España is already appropriated by the merchants of España who send spices in the trading-fleets to Vera Cruz; in the fleet (of seventeen vessels) commanded by Don Fernando Chacón was carried the enormous amount of 170,737 libras of cinnamon, and more than 70,986 of pepper and cloves, besides various bags and chests of all these kinds of spice the weight of which was not noted. The only products of the islands which have commercial value in Nueva España are wax, lampotes, Ilocos blankets, and cordage; and the value of all that is exported of these, even counting with them the previously mentioned gold chains, does not go beyond 30,000 pesos. The linen goods have hitherto been shipped from Manila to Acapulco only to fill in empty spaces in the allotments of lading, and have amounted to hardly 60,000 pesos, on which very little profit was obtained. If the main part of the galleon's cargo has to be composed of these linens, the Acapulco market will be overstocked with them, and the prices there will be so low that Manila cannot afford to send another cargo of this sort. Moreover, as these goods are procured from the foreign factories at Batavia, Madrasta, Patàn, Punticheri, and Vengala, as soon as the traders at those posts understand that the Manila galleons must carry most of their lading in goods to be procured at those factories they

will advance their prices enormously, and the galleon will be compelled to sail in ballast, and then only to procure the situado. The floss and raw silk which is the only form of that product permitted to Manila is so bulky a commodity, and the consumption of it in Nueva España is so small, that it too has been shipped only to fill up space; moreover, "for several years it has been increasing in cost, on account of the great amount of it which the Dutch, English, and French obtain from China for the fabrics which are manufactured in Europe." The deputies, to substantiate their statements, refer to the official reports of the viceroys of Nueva España, and offer to bring forward evidence in their favor from various persons at Madrid who have resided in Filipinas. They claim that the Manila trade in silken fabrics has not harmed the merchants of España, since the silk which is produced in that country is hardly sufficient to supply the home demand, and it is necessary to bring to it foreign silks—exporting to Nueva España some goods which have little demand in España; but even these do not occupy one hundred and twenty-five toneladas of space. The greater part of the silk goods woven in España are silks and velvets, and if the value of these has fallen, it is not the importation of Chinese goods which has caused this, but the change in the style of magistrates' robes,23 in which those goods are used, and the small amount of them that is used in the military service. "Just as in these kingdoms [of España] most of the persons of rank are clothed in no other fabrics than those which come from foreign countries on account of either their better quality or their luster—so the same thing occurs in Nueva España, where they follow in everything the customs of Europa; and for this reason most of the silken fabrics which are carried thither in the trading-fleets are from the kingdoms of Inglaterra and Francia, and the provinces of Holanda—as silver and gold tissues, brocades and laces of the same sort; hose, and other stuffs, the sale of which does not injure that of the Chinese silks, on account of the greater value placed upon the former. Therefore, as the silken fabrics which the aforesaid shippers carry [to Nueva España] are not all from the mills of España, but these Spanish silks are in very small quantity and of the sort which are rejected here, it is evident that the injury is not to the commerce of Andalucia, but to the foreign nations. For, since all the gold and silver which comes [to España] is carried in trading-fleets and galleons—except what is obtained for wines, brandies, oil, and other products—the slender profits which the traders of Philipinas gain from the sale of the Chinese fabrics will also be given up for their benefit by the foreigners on account of the abundance of the products from their own mills which they will ship to Cadiz, in order that these may be carried to the Indias." The argument is repeated, that most of the profits in the Acapulco trade must go to European foreigners, if it is restricted to the few and unimportant products of the islands, and thus the enemies of España are strengthened; while if the Chinese trade is allowed those profits fall into the hands of people who cannot and will not injure the Spanish power. The enforcement of the decree will injure not only the citizens of Manila, but the revenues of the crown, which amount annually to an average of 228,557 pesos, besides the duties produced by the Acapulco trade, which amount to 250,000 pesos more. The treasury will have no means to buy the rice of the Indians, their only valuable product; the Sangleys will have no occasion to trade at Manila, which will lose the amount of their licenses (more than 23,000 pesos), besides the import duties and alcabalas which they pay there, which amount to more than 37,000 pesos; and the situado sent to both the Philippines and Marianas must be taken from the Mexican treasury directly, which will be too heavy a burden for it. The king is reminded of the poverty of the Philippines in all natural resources save rice, and their dependence on the Acapulco traffic for money, clothing, and all other needs save that of food. The recent building of two small galleons has caused the treasury a great amount of expense, quite disproportionate to that of the one large vessel which hitherto had been used for the Acapulco trade—to say nothing of the extra expense caused by the duplication of crews, officers, and soldiers which is thus rendered necessary. The smaller ships are less able to resist either storms or pirates, and the few experienced seamen in the islands must be divided between them, when they should be massed in one vessel. Again is mentioned the dependence of the missions, and the conversion of the heathen, upon the Acapulco trade; the Indian villages that are more or less christianized now number 457, with 111,683 families, who are in danger of relapsing into heathenism, or being converted to Mahometanism, if the missions cannot be kept up.]

88. The Council, on June 14, 1723, agreed that this memorial should go to the fiscal with all those that came before, with the letters of the Audiencia, officials, and prelates which had been laid before the Council on the twelfth of the same month.

89. The consulate of Cadiz, by a memorial presented in the Council on the twenty-first of the same month and year-being informed of the petition from Manila requesting that changes be made in the decree issued on October 27, 1720—asked the Council to order that the argument recently brought forward by Manila in regard to this be communicated to them; this having been referred to the fiscal, he was of opinion that the aforesaid document should be communicated to the consulate, as had been done in the year 1720 by order of his Majesty; and the Council agreed to this by a decree of July 12, 1723.

90–92. [On September 4 following, a conference was held by the representatives of the commerce of Sevilla, to consider the question of the Philippine commerce in Chinese silks and the royal decree forbidding that trade; a copy of the memorial sent from Manila, and other documents bearing thereon, were submitted to that body by the consulate of Cadiz, who had already taken action thereon, and now asked for the support and coöperation of the Sevilla merchants. In a formal resolution by the latter, they express their entire concurrence with the views of Cadiz, and request the king to enforce the decree of 1720. They make light of the statement regarding the great amount of spices carried to Nueva España by Chacón's fleet, and intimate the probability that the remonstrance by Manila is really instigated by the traders of Nueva España, who, on account of the enormous profits which they make by sending money to the Philippines for investment, must be most affected by the proposed restrictions on the Manila commerce. Sevilla answers the argument of Manila that only one hundred and twenty-live toneladas of Spanish silks are sent to Nueva España, by declaring that even that small amount will soon be reduced to nothing unless the king strictly prohibit the introduction by the Filipinas ships into Nueva España of fabrics woven of silk and gold or silver; also that the silk-mills of España will be ruined and abandoned, and consequently the cities of that country will be inundated with poor people and criminals. On the day before this conference, a similar one was held by the consulate of Cadiz and representatives from the merchants of that city, who made a vigorous remonstrance against the injuries caused to Spanish commerce and industry by the Manila-Acapulco trade, and especially by the frauds and the infractions of law therein, on which they expatiated in the above conference. In the report drawn up by them they mention several of these. For instance, the merchants of the City of Mexico sent large sums of money to Acapulco for preparing the Manila galleon for its voyage; "and in the three months during which the ship was detained at that port it unloaded an enormous cargo, held its fair, and returned laden with silver, without wintering in that kingdom, on account of the easy and prompt disposal of all that it carried. This cargo was usually 10,000 or 12,000 bales, half of silken fabrics and half of linen goods, [lencería], the proceeds from which reached four millions of pesos; and all this in pesos, eight-real and four-real pieces, since in exchange for the said goods they did not desire or carry any produce, nor even doubloons, nor bars of silver, for all must be new pesos and of Mexican coinage, these being the coins which are current in Turquìa, to which country they were going, since the greater part of the said goods come thence." Reliable witnesses have told of mule-trains entering Mexico laden with Chinese stuffs, which must amount to almost the value of the goods carried by the eighteen vessels in the trading-fleet which that year came from Spain under Don Manuel de Velasco; and the market of the latter was ruined by the former. "Although the silk fabrics which the ships bring from Philipinas have not the quality or durability of those from España, and the linen goods are all of cotton, and do not last half as long as do those from France, yet as the former are sold cheap, and have a good surface, and are showy, while they last the commerce of España is checked and suspended." The merchants of Mexico send so much money to Acapulco that not enough is left to send the trading-fleets back to Spain, which are compelled to winter at Vera Cruz in order to obtain the proceeds of their cargoes and equip the vessels for the return voyage. "So sweeping and irreparable is the great injury which these goods from China, or from the Turks (which is the more certain), cause to the most important cities of España that when the said ship was not allowed to carry those goods Sevilla had more than 12,000 looms for the manufacture of silks of every kind; and with these, even without other stuffs, so great a number of people were employed on them, and so great was the opulence of that city and of all its domain, as is made evident by the great services which on all occasions Sevilla rendered to his Majesty, with sumptuous buildings—churches, hospitals, government buildings, and private houses. But without greater casualty than that of the importations in the ships from China, that city found itself in a straitened and miserable condition, not two hundred looms being left in it, on account of there being no consumption for its fabrics; and the great mass of poor people, who then supported themselves by their labor, are now miserably perishing. No less proof is afforded by what is occurring in Granada; for there more than 12,000 looms were employed only on taffetas (both double and plain), satins, plushes, and all kinds of silk-weaving; and more than 50,000 persons, men and women, were engaged in the industry and labor of making silk goods. For this reason, the amount of silk worked up each year was more than 180,000 libras, from which proceeded considerable profits to the royal exchequer, for the duty on each libra amounted to thirteen reals and three cuartillos; but, with the one but sufficient reason of the importations of Chinese goods, [that industry] has so fallen away that the amount of silk sold in that city at each gathering of silk does not reach 40,000 libras, and the number of looms operated, on coarse stuffs, is less than 2,000—a similar condition to those of Sevilla.... The same troubles are suffered by Cordova, Jaen, Ezija, Priego, and Alcalà la Real, with many other places which in both the Andalucias were growing and being maintained by the said manufactures. It is not less worthy of attention that the silk-growers of the aforesaid kingdoms of Sevilla, Granada, Cordova, and Murcia are, for lack of sale for the silk that they produce, giving up the cultivation of the mulberry-trees, and abandoning their farms and the places where they dwell." Cadiz cites the action of Conde de Monclova, viceroy of Peru, who prohibited the shipment of Chinese goods from Acapulco to South America, making them contraband and confiscable, recognizing "their poor quality and lack of durability, and the great detriment which this trade caused to the merchants [of Peru], who go down to Portovelo to hold the fair [at the arrival] of the galleons, which has been the greatest in the world;" and urges the king to enforce strictly the decree of 1720. Such action would greatly benefit the realms of Spain, and would not cause injury to the Philippines, because none of the said Chinese stuffs are made in the islands; "and the only ones who could grieve over it are the Turk, and other princes of Assia, Mahometans, and enemies of our holy Catholic faith." As for the complaint of Manila that the propagation of that faith depends on the silk trade, Cadiz refuses to believe this, and refers the king to a document in Manila which refutes that notion. This is *"a memorial or report made by a minister of that Audiencia, N. Calderòn, in which is inserted another, written by Father Fray Victorio Ricci,24 of the Order of Preachers, who was for many years a missionary in the empire of China, and afterward in the Philipinas Islands; it was sent by the Supreme Inquisition to its commissary in the islands, in order that he might send to his Majesty information on the points therein.... In these papers it will be clearly evident that the progress and propagation of the faith is not diminished by depriving the islands or the kingdoms adjacent to them of the commerce prohibited to them, or by the restriction which his Majesty has laid on it;"* the above prohibition, therefore, is not the cause of the ruin of the citizens of Filipinas.]

93–94. [These replies by the merchants of Andalusia call forth another memorial from the Manila deputies, which occupies fourteen printed sheets. They repeat their former arguments, enforcing them by reference to the despatches from the Audiencia of Manila, the archbishop, and the various religious bodies there, and still more to the letters previously addressed to the king by the viceroys of Nueva España; and they adduce various instances from the history of the Manila-Acapulco trade to the same effect. They also undertake to refute the charges made by the merchants of Sevilla and Cadiz, and claim that the latter have misrepresented certain facts. We note here some points made by the Manila envoys, as giving new information on the matter at issue. They say that the maintenance of Filipinas, including the missions and military posts, costs the Spanish crown annually 515,568 pesos, for which sum the royal treasury of Mexico should be responsible, according to the laws of the Indias; but it sends thither only 40,000 pesos in money and some 60,000 in goods, and even this remittance comes from the duties which the Manila galleon pays at Acapulco. But in 1637 and for some years later, the situado sent to the islands amounted to more than 325,000 pesos in money, and enough goods to make up the 500,000 pesos. This, however, was largely the result of the failure of the Manila merchants to ship goods to Mexico, a proceeding caused by the undue harshness and severity of the royal visitor Pedro de Quiroga;25 but it led to the abolition (by royal decree of September 3, 1639) of the restriction on the kinds of goods permitted to Manila, only limiting the amount of their investments. It is strange that Manila has pursued this commerce for one hundred and forty years without any protest from Andalusia until now; the decadence of the latter is due rather to lack of economy in the use of their wealth than to the competition of Filipinas; and Andalusia has always encountered trouble, since the persons interested in the greater part of the lading of the galleons and fleets have been and are foreigners—French, English, and Dutch. Andalusia claims that the galleon unlades at Acapulco more than 12,000 piezas, half of them containing silk goods; but the certificates of the royal officials show that in the ten years from 1710 to 1720 the total number of piezas (in ten galleons) was 36,895, including therein the 4,299 half-chests in which the silk goods were shipped—making the average lading of each galleon only 3,660 piezas. The detention of Velasco's fleet was not due to the arrival of the Manila galleon, but to other causes. The fleet of 1698, in charge of General Mascarùa, was sent lightly laden, and in 1699 Velasco's fleet followed it, but encountered the other at Vera Cruz; the presence of the two large fleets at one time, and the ravages of yellow fever [bomito negro, i.e., "black vomit"] at that port, rendered it impossible to sell the goods to advantage, to transport them to Mexico, or to equip the vessels for the return voyage. When Velasco could set out for Spain, he received news of the death of Carlos II, and the danger of war between Spain and other powers, which made the merchants unwilling to risk their property on the seas at that time. Finally the Spanish fleet was escorted to Spain by a French squadron of warships, but on reaching Vigo was attacked by an English and Dutch fleet, which inflicted considerable loss on the Spaniards. Moreover, the trading-fleets sent from Spain to Nueva España are nearly twice as large in the last few years as they used to be, which overstocks the colonial markets with goods. Manila claims that the decadence of the silk industry in Andalusia is due to the pest which ravaged that province (with especial mortality in Sevilla) in the middle of the past century; and that part of the remaining population had emigrated to Murcia and Valencia, where they had cultivated mulberry-trees and built up the manufacture of silk goods. Another reason assigned by some writers for the decrease of prosperity in Andalusia was the imposition, at that time, of heavy war-taxes. As early as 1666, the city and the merchants of Sevilla had represented to the crown "their lamentable condition, and the ruin of their looms, caused by the imposition of the millones26 and the concourse of foreigners to Cadiz to introduce their own merchandise." This led to a resolution by the royal Council that the decree of January 25, 1661, should be enforced, which provided that the custom-house and collection of duties for the Indias should be withdrawn from Cadiz, and that the galleons and fleets should take on their lading in the river of Sevilla and the port of San Lucar. As for the stuffs from foreign countries which, it is alleged, are brought to España and crowd out the manufactures of that country, these are only the fabrics which the more industrious French, English, and Dutch make with the raw material, both wool and silk, which España exports. In 1696 Sevilla complained to the king of the injury which it was experiencing from the importation of foreign goods, but did not mention the Chinese stuffs among these. "In Madrid and Valencia the manufacturers are at present complaining that the price of silk has risen very high, not because the crop [that is raised in España] is not an abundant one, so much as on account of the so great export, not only from that kingdom but from other regions, to foreign countries, that which the French alone have bought this year amounting to more than 300,000 doubloons; and if asked about this, any dealer in these goods or any official will answer with entire candor, without blaming the commerce of Manila." The foreigners bring back these silk goods to España, in order to supply with them not only that country but the Indias, through the fleets and galleons; "and this is what the consulate [of Cadiz] is defending, in order that these goods may, by not introducing into Mexico those from China, be sold [there] with a higher reputation." The highest authorities all concur in the statement that the Spanish silks sent to Nueva España do not amount to one hundred and twenty-five toneladas. The statement that the Manila galleon carries from that country 4,000,000 pesos is unwarranted; the only possible ground for it is that in 1717 the viceroy allowed the galleon to carry to Manila 2,000,000 pesos, because for three years past no money had been sent to the islands—on account of poor sales at Acapulco, a galleon forced back to the islands by storms, etc.—on condition that the king's ten per cent be paid on that amount. In other years the amount of money illegally shipped has been very small. Cadiz has alleged that money has been scarce there for some years; but Manila declares that from December, 1720 to July, 1723 over 40,000,000 pesos worth of gold and silver, in coin and bullion, has been landed at Cadiz, without including the value of the other products of the Indias. Cadiz asserts that the money obtained from Nueva España goes to the Turks, the enemies of the Catholic faith; but the Spanish merchants are continually furnishing money to other enemies of the faith, the English and Dutch. Moreover, the commodities which the Manila galleon carries are not obtained from the Turks, but (through the European factories) from Indostan, Tunquin, Lao, China, Japon, and the Philippine Islands; while Manila is not even permitted to trade with Arabia and Persia, whose products are carried to the ports of the Levant, and at those fairs the traders from all the European nations buy those goods, with money which has come from the Indias. Manila declares that the trading-fleets carry to Vera Cruz no Spanish products save wines, brandies, oil, raisins, and almonds, and the previously-mentioned small amount of silk goods; all else in their cargoes is of foreign make. The spices which the decree of 1720 allows to the islands will not suffice to pay the expenses of the voyage, especially when Manila must compete with the trading-fleets from Spain in the shipment of these products. The collection of royal duties on goods is regulated by "cubic palmos in accordance with the measurement of the bales [frangotes] and piezas which are shipped." As for the memorial by Calderòn, Manila asserts that it does not bear on the present question; that auditor, in the time of Governor Curuzalaegui (in which occurred an uprising of the Sangleys), sent a letter to the king remonstrating against the liberty given to the Chinese, and advising that they be not allowed to have intercourse with the Indian natives, or even to live in the Parián. This tolerance had been extended to them for the sake of attracting them to the Christian faith, but Calderòn regarded it as no longer necessary, since they had, even then, a number of Christian missionaries in their own country. In his letter, he cited Father Ricci in support of some of his statements. While the Spanish silks sent to Nueva España amount to only one hundred and twenty-five toneladas, those of foreign make sent thither from Spanish ports are more than a thousand toneladas. The French, English, and Dutch trade at Canton, where the main part of their commerce is in raw silk.]

95–96. [The above memorial was referred by the Council to the fiscal, on October 6, 1723; and on December 22 following, a printed answer to both of those by Manila was placed before the Council by the consulate and merchants of Cadiz. They remind the king that when Filipinas was first discovered the ships brought back to España abundance of gold, pearl, amber, civet, wax, and fabrics of Ilocos; and for some time afterward these and many other valuable products were exported from Manila, which became the emporium of both Eastern and Western India. In those early times, when so much zeal and energy for the conversion of the heathen was displayed, it was not necessary to the missions to depend upon the trade in Chinese silks; but, for the sake of benefiting the natives of the islands, and to check the drain of silver to foreign nations, the Spanish government (by decrees of 1589 and 1596) authorized the barter and exchange of the products of Filipinas for those of China, under the system called pancada. But Manila has distorted this into the assumption that the Chinese trade was intended for the maintenance of the Spanish colony in Filipinas, and that it was to be without restriction, save in its amount—although, as a fact, the trade in silk fabrics of China was not introduced until many years later. The system of distributing the commerce among the citizens of Manila replaced the earlier pancada, and led to such abuses that Felipe III attempted to check them by a severe decree (1620); and later enactments placed the Acapulco commerce on such footing that it flourished greatly, to the mutual advantage of Filipinas and Nueva España, and to the enrichment of Manila and its citizens. That commerce benefited the poor citizen as well as the rich; but the trade in silks is only for the benefit of the wealthy merchant and the rich consumer, as they are articles of luxury. The earlier commerce of Manila also supported and stimulated the consumption of Spanish silks in Nueva España and Peru, and the silk industry flourished in the mother-country; but the later introduction of Chinese silks into the American colonies, and the frauds and excess connected with this trade, have ruined the silk industry on both sides of the Atlantic, and even impaired the prosperity of Manila. Cadiz claims that the merchants of Mexico have committed many frauds, and transgressed the ordinances, and prevented the execution of these, in regard to the Manila trade, and do so with the collusion and aid of the officials: for instance, the galleon "Nuestra Señora del Rosario" arrived at Acapulco on January 11, 1699, and the Manila citizens attempted to compound the duties on the cargo for 100,000 pesos; but the royal fiscal opposed this, showing that the ship had brought 6,754 piezas of lading, without counting a considerable quantity of pepper and other goods outside of the registration. It was also found that although the law restricted the entire cargo to the value of 250,000 pesos, and its ownership to the citizens of Manila, this vessel contained goods to the amount of 233,966 pesos which belonged to the citizens of Puebla alone, and it was estimated that it must contain at least a million pesos' worth of goods belonging to merchants in the City of Mexico. The Mexican government compelled the payment on these goods of duties amounting to 50,000 pesos more, and would have investigated the whole matter, to ascertain the exact amount of the illegal shipments; but the commercial interests of Mexico exerted such influence against this that the Audiencia desisted from the undertaking. Again Cadiz accuses the importation of Chinese silks into Nueva España of having ruined the silk industry in España; although those goods are so thin and poor that they are worn out even before the Manila galleon leaves Acapulco, they are so cheap and showy that they undersell the better goods from España even competing with the latter in Vera Cruz, where the Chinese goods are purchased by the traders of Habana, Puerto Rico, Cartagena, and other Spanish colonies; and all this is overlooked by the Spanish officials in high places, because they profit by this illegal traffic. If the king will prohibit the importation of silk woven with silver and gold, and "check the hand which Mexico moves at the command of Manila," the silk industry will be revived in España, its people will be kept from idleness and poverty, and foreign countries will no longer drain its resources. Cadiz desires Manila to content itself with the spice-trade, which is a staple and profitable line of commerce, and which

Manila can carry on more cheaply and promptly than Spanish merchants can; the spices sent from España on Chacón's fleet were needed to supply the scarcity of them at that time, as the Manila trade had been interrupted temporarily; but if the latter be regular, such shipment from España could not occur again. From the year 1690, the indult ran from 50,000 to 74,000 pesos, on the basis of the 250,000 pesos allowed to the Manila trade; but it is evident that the duties ought now to amount to above 500,000 pesos, on the enormous quantities of Chinese silks that the galleon of 1,000 toneladas carries.]

97–105. [This memorial, with like protests from the cities of Toledo, Ezija, and Murcia, was sent to the fiscal, who on March 16, 1724, handed in his opinion on the question at issue—that is, whether the decree of 1720 should be changed or enforced. He lays down three propositions: First, that the trade in Chinese stuffs should not be prohibited to the citizens of Filipinas, since it is necessary to their maintenance, those islands having no profitable mines or commercial products; moreover, the introduction and propagation of the Catholic faith therein is an obligation of justice as well as of religious zeal, and was so recognized by Felipe II, when he refused to abandon Filipinas; and to fulfil this obligation the Spanish colony there should be sustained. For this purpose the trade with Nueva España had been granted to Manila, to such extent as should be necessary for its preservation, that is, to the amount of 250,000 pesos, and 500,000 in returns; and in the permission given to Manila to trade with China there had been, and should be, no restriction as to the woven silks of that country. Second, this trade ought, nevertheless, to be strictly confined to the amount of their permission, and all frauds to be prevented; for the complaints of Spanish producers and merchants had been caused by the frauds and abuses in the Manila trade, rather than by the mere fact of its including Chinese goods; the fiscal even suggests that they have an official representative at Acapulco to aid in the unlading and inspection of the Manila galleon, and report thereon to the viceroy, which would aid in preventing frauds and enable the Spanish merchants to discuss the question more intelligently. Third, that in case the trade in Chinese silks be prohibited to Manila, that in spices should be absolutely prohibited to the Spanish merchants and given exclusively to those of Filipinas; while the American trade in silks should be free to the Spaniards.]

106–111. [The Council considered this question on April 6, and decided that the decree of 1720 should be changed; they recommended that the Filipinas trade be continued as before the decree, and employing but one large galleon; that the decree of 1702 should be enforced, save that the goods should be valued not by actual inspection of the bales but by invoices presented by the shippers, with their sworn statements that the goods were their own; nor should any indult, payment of double duties, or other form of composition be tolerated; and that the royal officials at Manila, Cavite, Acapulco, and Mexico should be held responsible for the fulfilment of these regulations, under severe penalties. This proceeding was approved by the king, who issued despatches in accordance therewith (June 17, 1724) to the viceroy of Nueva España and other officials concerned therein; and on August 8 the merchants of Cadiz were invited to nominate a deputy to watch the Acapulco commerce.]

PERIOD VIII

Relates the plan presented by the deputies of Philipinas for regulating the commerce of that country, in the year 1724; and its results, up to that of 1730.

112–113. [On September 28, 1724, the deputies from Philipinas presented to the Council another printed memorial, in which they proposed a plan for preventing the abuses of the Manila-Acapulco trade. This document contains ninety-four paragraphs; it enumerates the provisions of the decree of 1720, the objections made thereto at Manila, the difficulties of navigation on the Pacific, and the reasons why one large galleon is better for that commerce than two small ones; describes the frauds and injustice practiced in the lading of the galleon, for which the responsibility rests mainly on the governors of the islands, who use their great power for their own personal advantage, regardless of the rights of the citizens; and opposes the requirements that each shipper must swear that the goods he sends are his own, that no one to whom space is allotted may sell or transfer it to another person, that the valuations of goods must be made by samples, and some other restrictions which seriously embarrass the citizens who have but little wealth to invest. It is represented that the seamen are allowed to carry each 30 pesos' worth of goods as a private investment, in order to encourage Spaniards to enter the marine service; but this ought to be increased to 300 pesos (the allowance made to the men on the fleets that go to the Indias), for more Spaniards are needed on the Acapulco trade-route—hardly one-third of the men on a galleon being of Spanish birth, the rest being Indians and on the rivera of Cavite. The citizens of Manila ought to be allowed to carry back all the produce of their shipments, since but few of the products of Nueva España are adapted to their needs in the altogether different climate and other conditions of the islands. They also ask that they be allowed to compound the payment of dues at 100,000 pesos each voyage, or less pro rata if the amount of goods shipped fall below the 300,000 pesos allowed for the trade. The transgressions of law connected with the Acapulco commerce have been mainly committed by high officials, but have not been so great, or so injurious to Spanish trade, as Sevilla and Cadiz represent; the deputies assert that "these abuses cannot be checked, or most of them even ascertained, so long as the terms of the concession are in pesos," and that it ought to prescribe a definite number of piezas, of specified measures and weight. They therefore propose a new ordinance for regulating the traffic, which embodies the above suggestions and requests, with some additional points. They ask for a permission of 4,000 piezas, of which 500 shall be half-chests filled with silks and very fine cotton goods, "which do not admit the use of the press;" the size and weight of the piezas is fully described. They ask permission to ship pepper and storax besides the amount of the permission, without restriction of quantity. The galleon for carrying these goods should be of dimensions here specified—the keel sixty codos [or cubits] long, the breadth of the vessel twenty codos, and the inside depth of the hold ten codos—and its crew should contain 250 men, besides the officers. The governor should not be allowed to act on the committee for distributing the allotments of lading-space; in his place is proposed the archbishop, the other members to represent the Audiencia, the municipality, and the merchants. The amount of merchandise which may be sent by the governor and all other royal officials ought to be limited to one hundred piezas, and this should go outside of the permitted amount. A share in the lading is asked for the ecclesiastical cabildo of Manila, on account of their poverty and their high dignity and character; also for the officers on the galleons, and for the widows of merchants and military officers. An allotment of space should be made transferable; and permission should be given to send some packages of goods intended as gifts to friends, affidavit being made that these are not intended for sale. The governor and officials of the port of Acapulco should not be allowed to exercise any authority or pressure over the Manila traders, beyond the proper inspection of the vessels and lading and the collection of duties; and the traders should be allowed to sell their goods as they please, either in or out of the fair there, or transport them to Mexico, if they prefer. They should not be expected to pay alcabala on the first sale at Acapulco, or any extraordinary imposts. The memorial specifies the provisions to be made for the lading and inspection of goods at both Manila and Acapulco, the functions of certain officials, the penalties for transgression of the regulations, and the customs duties to be paid on each kind of goods; and offers certain payments to be made by the Manila merchants, which will add much to the royal revenues. It states the present number of "citizens and traders" in Manila as 868.]

114–121. [The above document was handed to the fiscal, who advised the Council not to make the concessions therein asked, as they would destroy the entire system on which that commerce had thus far been conducted, and abrogate the provisions of the decree but recently granted for the benefit of Manila, which gave that city sufficient advantage. On January 12, 1725, the Council requested one of the ministers, Don Antonio de la Pedrosa, to examine the scheme proposed by Manila, and render an opinion thereon. He was willing to grant a number of the concessions requested, but would insist that the total of the permitted trade be restricted to 300,000 pesos, and the returns to 600,000 pesos, as before; and he proposed even harsher penalties for the transgression of the laws governing the trade. The Manila deputies, on learning of the opinions of the aforesaid royal officials, desisted from their efforts to obtain further concessions from the Council, but appealed to the king, who sent to the Council a decree (dated July 22, 1726) permitting the scheme of Manila to be tested (although with some restrictions), for two years.]

122–127. [The deputies of Manila were not satisfied that this concession should be limited to a term of two years, and again petitioned the king, asking that the trial be made for two or three five-year terms, on account of the many difficulties which that commerce must encounter. The king consented (October 21, 1726) to extend the term to five years, and a despatch of September 15 prescribes the conditions and regulations under which the trial of the new plan should be made—for a term of two years, extended to five by another decree of October 31. The annual galleon shall carry no more than 4,000 piezas, 500 of these being half-chests [medios caxones] containing the silken fabrics and the finer ones of cotton; the rest shall be half-bales [medios fardillos] bags [churlas] of cinnamon, cases of porcelain, and cakes of wax. The size or weight respectively of these packages is prescribed: the half-chests and half-bales shall be each 1¼ vara long, ⅔ vara wide, and ⅓ vara deep,27 an allowance of two dedos on each measure being made for the outside cover or packing of the half-chest and for the compression used on the half-bale. The bag of cinnamon shall weigh 150 libras gross (that is, including all packing and covers), but at Acapulco it may be allowed four or five libras more of weight, the difference between the weight of Manila and that of Nueva España. The case [balsa] of porcelain must be one vara high and 2¼ varas in circumference at the mouth, no allowance being made. The cakes of wax must weigh twelve arrobas at Manila, four or five libras being allowed at Acapulco for the difference in standards of weight. Besides the 4,000 piezas, unlimited pepper and storax may be shipped; and Chinese cabinets and screens [biombos] may go in larger boxes than the regulation size, provided that the capacity of these be figured in terms of piezas. Passengers on the galleons are allowed each two chests containing their personal property, without any articles of merchandise. The dimensions and crew of the galleon shall be as stated by the Manila deputies. The committee for allotting lading-space shall be as suggested by them, save that the governor shall be included therein. Space is allowed to the extent of 100 piezas to the governor and other royal officials for their personal shipments, but these must come out of the 4,000 piezas. A limited amount of space is allotted to the ecclesiastical cabildo and to the officers on the galleons; also to the widows of traders and military officers. Allotments of space may be transferred to other persons who are approved by the committee. Due provision is made for the valuation, registration, and lading of goods at Manila, and the inspection and sale at Acapulco; for the allowance of small quantities of merchandise to the Spanish seamen and artillerists; for the shipment of the returns from the investments, whether in money or goods; and for penalties against transgressors. The Manila merchants are to pay alcabala on any sales outside of Acapulco; 25,000 pesos annually on each galleon which shall arrive at Acapulco (afterward changed to 20,000 pesos a year during the five years' term), as a contribution to the royal service; duties of five per cent at Acapulco "for the embarkation of the entire product from the aforesaid 4,000 piezas, and the pepper and storax, which is the same that the traders of España pay at Cadiz;" and the following specific duties: for each half-chest, 45 pesos; each half-bale, 30 pesos; each bag of cinnamon, 25 pesos; each cake of wax, 18 pesos; each case of porcelain, 12 pesos; each chest of cabinets or screens, 18 pesos for each of the piezas to which the chest is equivalent; and each arroba of pepper or storax, 12 silver reals.]

(To be concluded.)

1 In this document we resume the history of the commerce between the Philippines and Nueva España which is presented in the Extracto historial (Madrid, 1736), the first two "periods" of which appeared in VOL. XXX of this series (q.v., pp. 23–101). The great length of this work compels us to condense and abridge most of it here; but "Periods" ii–vi are presented in full (save for the text of some long decrees), as being of earlier date, and covering a longer space of time, while they are comparatively brief in statement. In thus condensing this work, it has been our aim to retain all matter of vital interest and real value, eliminating only "vain repetitions" and matters of trifling importance. The first memorials presented by Manila and Cadiz respectively

set forth various facts connected with the Manila-Acapulco trade, on which are based their main arguments, each endeavoring to justify its own side of the controversy and its demands from the Spanish government; the succeeding memorials largely repeat these statements and arguments, in new combinations, with wearisome iteration—kaleidoscopic effects produced by the same old bits of glass—which it seems useless to reproduce in our translation. But we have carefully preserved all new facts, dates, and arguments adduced, and whatever will throw additional light on that commerce, or on the social and economic conditions of Spain, the mother-country, at that period, since these must naturally affect those of her colonies. Wherever possible, we have used the exact wording of the text, and have made full citations from it which are indicated by quotation-marks; and the numbers of sections are everywhere retained, thus facilitating easy reference to the original work. The Extracto, thus made accessible to English and American readers, and all that is really important in it presented in compact form and accurate translation, is a valuable addition to the history of commerce, as well as to that of colonial development and administration. Not are its psychological aspects less interesting and valuable, although perhaps not so obvious at first glance; it shows the demoralizing effects on the Spanish people of their conquests in the New World and of the flood of wealth poured into Spain in consequence of these, and the results of too paternal a mode of government in her colonies—in both cases destructive to ambition, industry, personal initiative, patriotism, and even common honesty. (Cf. notes in our VOL. XXX, pp. 71, 77.)

2 Expediente: "the collection of all the papers belonging to a subject in a transaction," here evidently referring to the documents pertaining to the Manila trade, which as Abreu says (see VOL. XXX, p. 24), were placed in his hands by the Council of the Indias (of which he himself was a member) for use in compiling the Extracto.

3 Consulado: equivalent to the American phrase "board of trade."

4 See section 35, post.

5 The phrase regulacion de derechos apparently means, in reality, a (special) rule for the payment of duties; that is, if the Manila merchants would pay the 100,000 pesos which they had offered as an "adjustment" according to the special rule for the collection of those duties—a rule going above the duties as prescribed by law—they should be permitted to do so, and should be excused for the penalties which had accumulated, or at least for the back dues remaining unpaid during the time when the "indult" bad been conceded to them of compounding the duties at 74,000 pesos only. The stress seems to be laid upon the fact that they must not be permitted to consider their payment as an "indult," but us an arrangement, and one that was based on a somewhat higher rate than had previously been granted to them. Even though it may be considered as a sovereign favor to them, objection is made to having it specifically stated as an "indult."

The usage of the word *indulto* in this connection will become more clear if it is remembered that it means a special favor in one form or another, a grace of the sovereign, a special exemption from rule or penalty. Barcia and others define *indulto* as an impost levied on the cargoes of the galleons from the Indias; but it seems doubtful if this be strictly correct, as no impost by that name can be found in *Leyes de Indias* or *Ordenanzas de Bilbao*, even in connection with *averías* and *almojarifazgos*. I take it to mean, rather, the exemption from the duties on ships' cargoes which would, under other provisions of law, be owed. There is one interesting instance of the use of *indulto* to signify exemption, in *Teatro de la legislación universal de España é Indias* (Madrid, 1790–97; 28 vols.), ii, p. 341, under the head, "Administration of averías," where it is provided by Carlos II that "the proceeds of certain *indultos* for gold, silver, and merchandise unregistered shall be applied to the fund from averías, in order that it may result to the benefit of those who shall not have transgressed the laws of registration; and notification shall first be given to the Council." This seems to confirm my belief that the *indulto* was not properly a tax, but the favor of an exemption, in cases, from the tax; or of exemption (in this case, it would appear) from the penalty to fall upon him who had evaded the tax by concealment; it was, then, by derivation a composition of the tax. But the king here provided that it should not be paid into his coffers, but be applied to the fund from averías, thus swelling the fund from which all shippers benefited, and to which they were supposed to contribute to make the trade possible; see the chapter on "Averías," in *Leyes de Indias*. The foregoing statements suggest a reason why the royal authority was opposed, in this Manila trade controversy, to having the composition of the duties, and of the penalties which the merchants had incurred by past violations of the rules, regarded or considered as an "indult," and not as a "regulation" or rule specifying a lump sum to be paid as duties. This indult might (by this and other laws) have had to go into other funds; though I know of no fund for averías in the Manila trade, yet the Spanish mere desire for uniformity of legislation and practice might explain this strenuous objection to considering this regulation as an indult or grace of the sovereign (in the special sense that had been established for this sort of favor) in the galleon trade with the West Indies.—James A. LeRoy (now [1906] U.S. consul at Durango, Mexico).

6 The Duke de Alburquerque took possession of his office as viceroy of Nueva España on November 27, 1702; his term of office lasted a little more than eight years. Little of importance occurred therein except several raids by pirates (among whom was Captain William Dampier) in Mexican waters. Alburquerque was succeeded (January 15, 1711) by Fernando de Alancastre, Duke de Linares, who was an able, vigorous and benevolent ruler, and spent or bequeathed the greater part of his fortune for the benefit of the poor—whose number and sufferings were enormous at this time, through unusual calamities of floods and earthquakes, famine and pestilence. Linares's term of office expired on August 15, 1716, and he died in June of the next year; he was succeeded by Baltasar de Zúñiga, Marqués de Valero. (Bancroft, Hist. Mexico, iii, pp. 278–290.)

7 Spanish, harrieros, "muleteers;" for goods and silver were transported across Mexico by pack-trains of mules.

8 That is, the present attempt by Linares to inquire into and settle past irregularities; for it gives those who are suspected an opportunity to compromise the affair.

9 That is, not only because money can (speaking generally) easily open the way for a settlement in such case, but because, in this specific matter, it is a fair supposition that large speculations cannot be carried on with small capital— and indeed most of these Mexican transgressors are too poor to pay the penalties incurred by their past infractions, if these were strictly adjudged against them.

10 Barracan is a woolen fabric impenetrable to water, about half a vara wide, of which rain-cloaks and other articles are made; picote is a coarse, rough fabric made from goat's hair (Dominguez).

11 At fol. 40 verso of the Extracto, elefantes are defined as "linen goods of that country [i.e., Filipinas], having no durability, and but little valued in that kingdom [i.e., Mexico]."

12 It is apparently a lapsus calami by which the consulate of Cadiz is mentioned in nos. 61–64, and that of Sevilla in nos. 45–50, here cited in the text; but the commerce of both cities was included under the former consulate.

13 Linens (Spanish, lienzos and lencería) have always been one of the chief products of China, especially around Canton; and the term "Canton grass linen" is often used to define the particular kind of linen most commonly produced there, which very closely resembles the linen produced from flax. The European languages have always defined these Chinese textiles as "linen." The term "elephant" must here refer to the mark or brand of a certain kind of linen goods; the Chinese are greater devotees of the "trademark" idea than perhaps any other people. The mark of a kind of goods to which they are accustomed is known today as the "chop," and it is exceedingly difficult to induce them to try a new "chop" if the old one has established itself.

"Cambayas" are cotton cloths from Cambaya. "Chitas" (more generally spelled "chites") mean India calicoes, and sometimes chintzes. The Filipinos knew how to weave in colors, although not to figure goods (as they do not yet); and the Spaniards would be apt to designate by the words lienzos and lienzos pintados (perhaps also by elefantes) the Philippine fabrics woven from hemp and banana fibers, which have somewhat that texture, and which have stripes of red, blue, and other colors run through them more often by far than they are left plain. Strictly speaking, these are neither linens nor cottons; but they have the feeling of linen rather than of cotton. The goods thus designated probably included not only those of Philippine manufacture, but those made in India and other Eastern countries and traded in at Manila. Sayasaya was the Spanish name for a kind of Chinese silk; and I would conjecture that pitiflores meant some kind of Chinese brocade.—James A. LeRoy.

The term "Canton grass linen" mentioned above apparently means the fabrics made from the so-called "China grass" (see VOL. XXII, p. 278). Note the statement in sec. 92, *post*, that the *lencería* sent to Acapulco "are all of cotton," evidently being made in imitation of the real linen goods; cf. the statement in Casa-Fuerte's letter, in VOL. XLV, sec. 164. The name "chimones" in the text suggests, especially in view of its context, the Japanese garment called "kimono," so generally adopted in America for negligé wear.—Eds.

14 In the text, mantas de hilazos, evidently misprinted for Hilocos. On fol. 61 a similar list has mantas de Ilocos.

15 i.e., of the vessel and carge, in case of attack by enemies— whom the seamen would resist more valiantly if they also had property of their own to defend.

16 In all, making 3,500 piezas, as in sec. 79, post; the same explanation is given on fol. 110 verso of the Extracto.

17 A marginal note in the text adds to this name "y Ossorio."

18 Spanish recopiladas, apparently meaning that these decrees have been included in the official Recopilación de leyes de Indias.

19 "The censos yield only five per cent." Censo refers to annuities in some form or other, and especially to "quit-rent;" it also sometimes means "interest," which is a derivative and special meaning; in a general sense, it may be rendered "income." —James A. LeRoy.

Dominguez (Diccionario nacional) enumerates several different kinds of censo (which he defines as "a contract by which one person sells and another buys the right to receive a certain annual pension"); the statements in our text relative to the status of houses and lands in and near Manila would indicate the probability that the censos there mentioned were what Dominguez calls consignativos, "in which a certain amount is received for which must be given in return an annual pension, giving security for the said sum or capital with rent-producing property or real estate." He instances as a censo reservativo the arrangement made by Joseph with the Egyptians (Genesis, ch. xlvii), by which, after all the land in that country had become the property of the crown, the people received back their fields on condition of their paying to the king the fifth part of their produce, which constituted an annual pension or quit-rent (censo). The same word may also mean "census" and "tax-register;" Dominguez states that when the Spaniards conquered America they found the tax-register established in Mexico and Peru. —Eds.

20 A marginal note at the beginning of each of these letters states its authorship; but that on the Jesuit provincial's letter adds, "with very well-grounded arguments" (muy fundamentalmente).

21 Spanish, theatro; that is, the personnel of the Spanish body of citizens.

22 Cf. the prices paid somewhat later for the wine monopoly, in the first document of VOL. XLVI.

23 Spanish, trage de golilla. The golilla was "a certain ornament made of pasteboard faced with taffeta or other black fabric, which surrounded the neck, over which was placed a pleating of gauze or other white stuff, which was starched. At present this decoration is used only by the togated officials and others attached to the courts of justice." (Dominguez.)

24 For notices of this missionary, see VOL. XXXVI, pp. 218, 219. Calderon's memorial is more fully described post, near the end of sec. 94 of the Extracto.

25 See account of Quiroga's proceedings in VOL. XXX, pp. 50–52, 85–88, 91, 105.

26 Millones: "an excise or duty levied in Spain on wine, vinegar, oil, meat, soap, and tallow candles, to defray the expenses of the army" (Velázquez).

27 These dimensions are equivalent in English or U.S. measure to 41¾ inches long, 22¼ wide, and 11⅛ deep; and the allowance of two dedos, to 1⅓ inch.

BIBLIOGRAPHICAL DATA

The documents contained in this volume are obtained from the following sources:

1. *Jesuit missions.* — From Murillo Velarde's *Historia de Philipinas* (Manila, 1749); from a copy in possession of Edward E. Ayer.

2. *Condition of the islands, 1701.* — From Ventura del Arco MSS. (Ayer library), v, pp. 201–230.

3. *Events of 1701–15.* — From Concepción's *Historia de Philipinas,* viii, pp. 299–391; from a copy in possession of the Editors.

4. *Government of Bustamante.* — The first part is from Concepción, ut supra, ix, pp. 183–424; the letters of Otazo and Cuesta are from Ventura del Arco MSS., iv, pp. 249–295.

5. *Letter from Santistevan.* — From a MS., probably the original, in possession of Edward E. Ayer.

6. *Commerce of the Philippines.* — From the *Extracto historial* (Madrid, 1736) of Antonio Alvarez de Abreu; from a copy in possession of Edward E. Ayer.